Michael Coffman has made an enormous contribution by exposing the underpinnings of the radical environmental movement and its devastating attack on individuals and our great Nation. All those who are constantly exposed to the aggressive and deceptive tactics of the 'eco-saviors' —members of the media, legislators, landowners and the general public—will be enlightened by Coffman's exposé of their real agenda and pagan beliefs.

> Peggy Ann Reigle, Chairman
> *The Fairness to Land Owners Committee*
> with more than 12,000 abused
> 'mom and pop' members in 45 states

Saviors of the Earth is must reading for companies and individuals who donate to environmental organizations believing that by doing so they are helping themselves and the environment. Dr. Coffman has done outstanding work exposing the philosophies driving national environmental leadership. He clearly shows that these earth saviors will never compromise until they totally transform and possibly destroy our economy through regulation and litigation to conform with their earth-based ideology.

> U. S. Senator Stephen Symms, Retired
> President, Freedom Alliance

D0354633

SAVIORS
OF THE
EARTH?

SAVIORS
OF THE
EARTH?

MICHAEL S.
COFFMAN

NORTHFIELD PUBLISHING
CHICAGO

This book is dedicated to those Americans who, through long hours and love of the land and sea, labor to provide all Americans and the world with food, homes, and other products derived from our rich and largely renewable natural resource base. It is especially dedicated to people such as Peggy Reigle, Bob Voight, David Howard, Ann Corcoran, Leon Favareau, Marilyn Hayman, and hundreds of other Americans from every walk of life who have selflessly picked up the noble task passed on by our forefathers to keep the flame of freedom bright in America. These are America's real environmentalists and stewards of our land and water.

I also dedicate this book to my wife, Suz, for her tireless effort in supporting and assisting me in the writing of this book. And finally, I commit this book to my children, Tamera, John, and Geraldine, to my grandchildren, Audrey and Nyssa, and to all the children of America—that the American Dream may be passed on to them untarnished and intact. God bless America.

CONTENTS

PREFACE

There comes a time in many people's lives when events demand that they step out of their normal routine and take action that can change their lives forever. That time came for me in 1991 when it became apparent that there was an agenda behind the environmental movement that was far from being in the best interests of America, or even the environment itself. I have always considered myself to be an environmentalist. I have dedicated my teaching and research career to studying ecosystems to find better ways to use and manage our natural resources while improving their protection. Some managers found my recommendations for changes in management to be too conservative, whereas others believed they were not conservative enough. Among my colleagues I was somewhere in the middle, and that's about where I wanted to be. I have always believed that a balance between protecting the environment and human use is possible. Although scientists should always strive for ways to "do it better," the improvement in how our resources have been managed and protected over the past forty years is amazing. America has nothing to be ashamed of.

During the last half of the 1980s and early 1990s I was chairman of the Forest Health Task Group of the National Council of the Paper Industry for Air and Stream Improvement. It is the mission of this research organization to define environmental problems so that the paper industry can both protect the environment and provide essential products all Americans depend on in their everyday lives. It surprises most people that such an organization has been in existence since the 1940s, resulting in huge gains in energy conservation and chemical recycling—not because of government regulations, but because it made good sense to do so.

Like farmers and other users of America's vast natural resources, much of industry willingly makes such improvements because improvements represent the future and make good economic sense. Without the soil, farmers could not grow crops. Without healthy forests, paper companies could not make paper. Protecting these resources is their future. The accusations that these organizations and companies knowingly destroy ecosystems and resources because of greed borders on the absurd, considering such greed would put them out of business within a few short years.

The question has historically been one of finding better ways to manage and use our resources while protecting them. Improved understanding of our ecosystems and advanced technology have permitted resource managers to do an increasingly better job at meeting both objectives in a cost-effective manner. Until the mid 1970s the environmental community provided legitimate and needed input into finding the balance between use and protection. Starting in the 1970s, however, the environmental equation began to shift from "wise use" of our resources to one of "no use." Even more serious, the demands for "no use" policies began to be justified by pseudoscience grounded in emotion rather than in true science.

The shift to emotion became clear during the acid rain debates in the 1980s. Arguments between environmental leadership and industry were no longer over different interpretations of the same scientific data; rather, environmental leadership had taken a quantum leap into speculation and emotion, where true science was ignored. The Forest Health Program in which I was involved spent more than $1 million annually researching issues such as acid rain. Along with the federal Acid Rain Precipitation Assessment Program, this research found that although the acid rain problem was potentially serious, it was a manageable problem. Environmental leadership made it into a catastrophe. At first I considered such emotionalism mere political hardball. If America wanted to ignore nearly $600 million in research that showed acid rain not to be the catastrophe once believed and wanted to spend up to $40 billion per year on a minor problem, so be it. But after winning the most successful effort to date, environmental leaders continued to proclaim that the Clean Air Act was a failure and that acid rain was still destroying America. It soon became obvious they truly believed this in spite of the overwhelming evidence to the contrary. Why? If these leaders really wanted to find solutions to environmental problems, as they claimed, why were they still asserting that acid rain was a catastrophe? It didn't make sense.

By 1990, theories about global warming and ozone depletion became the catastrophes of the decade. Although I was gun-shy after the acid rain hysteria of the 1980s, global warming and ozone depletion were scientifically plausible. If there was solid evidence that what the theories proposed was actually happening, we needed to find it. I, along with others, recommended to the paper industry that research be done. Combining forces with federal efforts, a massive effort was begun to define the extent of the problem and possible consequences. This book discusses some of that research. As a result, by 1991 I became convinced that, as in the case of acid rain, there was little evidence for either the global warming or ozone depletion "catastrophes."

In spite of increasing evidence against any environmental catastrophe, environmental leadership continues to proclaim with absolute certainty that an apocalypse is imminent. Why? Certainly part of the reason could be greed—catastrophes are mandatory if people are going to contribute to environmental organizations —but greed didn't explain all of it. In July 1992 I decided that if solutions were going to be found, I had to determine the whys of this contradictory phenomenon.

What I found changed my life forever—causing me to leave a comfortable job to expose the duplicity behind the agenda of environmental leadership. For what I found was a view of reality contrary to the principles upon which America was founded and has flourished—a view of reality that is affecting every man, woman, and child in America in an increasingly negative manner; a belief system that could prohibit us and future Americans from ever attaining the American Dream. Unbelievable sums of money are being diverted into meaningless laws and regulations that these self-proclaimed saviors of the earth hold sacred. Hundreds of thousands of jobs have been either lost or never created, causing vast dislocation and suffering for Americans. Americans are going to prison because of trivial violations of environmental laws and regulations, receiving longer prison sentences than murderers.

Ironically, I found that this agenda is supported by only a very small minority of environmentalists. But it is funded by billions of dollars and carries tremendous political clout. It is threatening the economic and social fabric of America. Yet, in spite of the implications of what I discovered, this book is not about some grand conspiracy but about the hypocritical power and politics of an agenda and belief system rapidly becoming the law of the land —a belief system that is being forced on America by a powerful minority using the politics of fear and guilt. Much of my research has been investigating what these leaders have penned; the excerpts included here describe their agenda in their own words. Legitimate concerns of the majority of environmentalists and Americans are being used by these "earth saviors" to create what they call an environmentally pure society—destroying lives and families in the process. If Americans (including the majority of environmentalists) understood the implications of this agenda, they would reject it. Rather than protecting and saving the environment, the earth saviors will ultimately destroy it.

Leaving my job to break new ground was not an easy decision. I have never thought of myself as one who would take up such a cause, and I find it uncomfortable. I also knew that when I moved away from "perceived truth," my motives would be questioned and many would think that I had become an extremist myself. But as this book details, the majority of scientists and a growing number of concerned citizens are realizing the duplicity of environmental leadership and the seriousness of the environmental agenda. These scientists and citizens, like me, are alarmed about the economic and social consequences of this environmental agenda.

The problem we all face is overcoming the perception of many Americans that these so-called apocalypses are proven scientific fact—especially in the face of the shrill attacks launched against anyone who takes an opposing view. The attacks leveled against President Bush when he did not want to attend the 1992 Earth Summit in Brazil merely provides a case in point. Yet, as this book details, in spite of these personal attacks, tens of thousands of Americans are waking up and taking a stand against this deceit even as they continue to be concerned about legitimate environmental issues. It is my hope that this book will provide the needed information to wake up millions more to the questionable methods and philosophies disguised by the call to "save the earth" and galvanize them to action.

Modern industrial civilization . . . is colliding violently with our planet's ecological system. . . . The ferocity of its assault of the Earth is breathtaking . . .

> Vice President Albert Gore
> *Earth in the Balance*, 269

Green politics demands a whole new ethic in which violent, plundering humankind abandons its destructive ways, recognizes its dependence on Planet Earth, and starts living on a more equal footing with the rest of nature. The danger lies not only with the odd maverick polluting factory, industry, or technology, but in the fundamental nature of our economic systems.

> Jonathon Porritt and David Winner
> *Friends of the Earth*
> Quoted in *Reason Magazine*, August 1991

1

THE COST OF ENVIRONMENTALISM

DEVASTATION

Tears streaming from her eyes, Bonnie Ellen drove the long, lonely two hours back to her home. She had just watched her husband, forty-seven-year-old William Ellen, being taken into custody to spend the next six months in a federal prison. A host of questions tumbled through her mind. How was she going to pay the bills after the enormous legal costs had drained their finances dry? How was she going to respond when inevitably asked by their two children, ages two and four, "Why can't Daddy come home?" How was she going to take care of all the injured animals that were brought to their Wild Care treatment center? How, in the bizarre world of environmental regulation and green mandates, could her husband be going to prison as a convicted criminal for the heinous crime of wetlands destruction—while in the very process of creating wetlands? How could this happen in America?

The Ellens' gripping tragedy is but one of many in a rapidly escalating legacy of human devastation wrought by an avalanche of senseless environmental regulations. Sadly, the anguish and misfortune suffered by the Ellens is likely but the first in a growing number of shattered families during the 1990s. What happened to Bill Ellen could happen to any American, not necessarily because of the same offense, but rather because environmental irrationality is rapidly becoming a central organizing principle of our great nation.

Ellen's story began in 1987 when he was hired by Paul Tudor Jones II, a Wall Street trader, to create a 103-acre wildlife sanctuary within a 3,200-acre hunting and conservation preserve in Maryland. Ten wildlife ponds were to be created and adjacent wetlands vegetation enhanced to provide habitat for all forms of wildlife, especially ducks, geese, and other migratory waterfowl. Bill and Bonnie Ellen loved wildlife. So much so, that in 1986 they had started a federal and state licensed nonprofit wildlife restoration organization called Wild Care. According to Peggy Reigle, founder of the Fairness to Landowners Committee (a national private property rights organization in Cambridge, Maryland), "Ellen had rehabilitated and returned nearly 2,000 ducks, geese, loons, egrets, herons, squirrels, song birds, deer and other creatures to the wild."[1]

From the very start of the sanctuary project, Ellen made sure he worked closely with the Maryland Department of Natural Resources (DNR) in clearing the land and building the ponds. "My responsibility was to make certain that the plan was feasible from both the regulatory and cost perspective," he said, and to "avoid sensitive environmental areas such as wetlands." A tidal wetlands regulator for the Virginia Marine Resources Commission in the early 1970s, and a marine and environmental consultant for twenty years in Virginia and Maryland, Ellen was qualified. To ensure there were no misunderstandings in the work on terrestrial wetlands, Bill invited personnel from the U.S. Army Corps of Engineers (Corps), U.S. Department of Agriculture Soil Conservation Service (SCS), and two dozen scientists, as well as the Maryland DNR to visit the site and provide advice—which they did.

This team approach seemed to work well. In February 1988 Bill was told during what he thought to be a routine visit by Corps personnel who were advising him that some dirt from road construction and other activities was accidentally spilling onto what they perceived to be wetlands. They gave Bill a form letter that discussed compliance requirements to avoid a "cease and desist order." Ellen noted what was required to comply, and, taking the advice of the Corps, purchased $120,000 worth of special equipment. Even though these federal wetlands were so dry that summer that the swirling dust had to be sprayed with water to avoid risk to equipment and operators, Ellen followed the Corps instructions. Alex Dolgos, a Corps official, approved of the changes in June 1988. But Dolgos would later testify that Bill violated the agreement.[2]

On February 15, 1989, the Corps issued a cease and desist order on the project. Bill did not receive it for almost a week because it was sent to Jones rather than to Ellen. On the morning of March 3, an on-site inspection by Dolgos and Jim Brewer, a wetlands expert with the SCS, was undertaken. Dolgos reaffirmed his opinion that there were areas where wetlands were being incidentally filled, and he ordered Ellen to stop work. Ellen was informed that before he could resume construction, he would have to hire a wetlands consultant to perform a complete wetlands delineation of the area, and the maps had to be approved by the Corps. Ellen told the Corps officer that he would have the wetlands construction site mapped (which he did that weekend), and he would shut down all work except that on a three-acre administrative management complex site, which had already been delineated by Brewer as an uplands a month before. Without further comment, the Corps enforcer left.

Believing with all reasonableness that he was doing no wrong, and without a clue of the bizarre events he was unleashing, Ellen permitted two loads of clean dirt to be dumped on the administrative site. Perhaps intuition told him that he should assume nothing about wetlands classification, and all work on the complex site was stopped as well—two hours after the Corps enforcer left. But it was already too late. The decision to permit the two loads of dirt to be dumped, Bill was later to find out, put him well on his way to being a nefarious environmental criminal.

Apparently the Corps would permit no insubordination in their quest of saving wetlands, and they launched a criminal investigation that would put "Ellen on trial nine months later in federal court facing the Justice Department on six counts of knowing violations of the Clean Water Act."[3] One of these was later dropped. Ellen was accused of "filling" five wetlands totaling some 86 acres within the 3,200-acre project. Three of these counts were for mistakes that had occurred a full year before and which were corrected when Ellen bought the specialized equipment. The last two were for the two loads of dirt, which just happened to be dumped on top of a tabletop-sized "micro" wetlands Brewer had missed in his initial delineation work.[4]

In light of such a focus on the minutia, one has to question whether the Corps and EPA were more interested in protecting

the environment or in making a regulatory scapegoat out of Bill
Ellen. Alex Dolgos, who brought the charges, later made clear that
the purpose was the latter in a statement on the MacNeil/Lehrer
NewsHour: "It's a matter of a person flaunting the Federal Government. Forget the wetlands."[5] What mattered to Dolgos was unchallenged federal control of private land, not the protection of the
environment. This same bureaucratic arrogance and disregard for
real environmental concerns was also reflected in a new definition
of wetlands—a definition that would send Bill Ellen to prison.

What Ellen did not know at the time was that the Corps, Environmental Protection Agency, Soil Conservation Service, and
Fish and Wildlife Service had been quietly meeting for some time
to revise the definition of a wetland. Environmental leaders had
applied tremendous pressure on these agencies to broaden the definition to double the land area the federal government exercised
jurisdiction over. How was this done? The old definition, written
in 1987, defined wetlands as:

Those areas that are inundated or saturated
by surface or ground water at a frequency
and duration sufficient to support, and that
under normal circumstances do support,
a prevalence of vegetation typically adapted
for life in saturated soil conditions.

Although somewhat vague, there was little question that the
site had to be wet to qualify. Not so with the new definition. The
new definition was so all-encompassing that almost anything could
qualify as a wetland so long as two of three criteria were met: (1)
the soil was classified as being "hydric,"* (2) the water table
reached within eighteen inches of the surface for as little as seven
days during the growing season, or (3) hydrophilic (water loving/
tolerant) vegetation was present.[6] There are some 7,000 plants
that qualify as being hydrophilic, plants such as impatiens, poison
ivy, and loblolly pine—all commonly found in the eastern and
southeastern United States. Man-made agricultural ditches, pine
forests, and 40 percent of drought-stricken California also qualified under this new definition.[7]

---

* Soils having characteristics of being saturated with water for long periods.

With the new definition, a wetland no longer had to be wet, or even damp, to qualify as wetland. In fact, it didn't even have to be a hydric soil as long as there was "evidence" of water sometime in the past. Without so much as a public hearing, this definition went into effect in March 1989, effectively more than doubling the acreage of defined wetland in the United States. At the same time, that single bureaucratic redefinition caused much of Maryland to instantly become a wetland, including most of the project site over which Ellen was supervisor. Dorchester County, in which the project was located, went from 84 thousand acres of wetlands to 259 thousand acres![8]

It was by the *new* definition that Bill Ellen was to be tried as a criminal—even though he had never even heard of it before because of the secrecy in which it was implemented. In fact, it didn't even go into effect until March 20, 1989, one year *after* three of the violations took place! That didn't matter though. An appellate court later ruled that this was legal because the regulation itself hadn't changed, only the interpretation of it.

As bizarre as these events were, however, it was during the four-week trial that Ellen really entered the twilight zone. Before the cease and desist order was given, Ellen had created 45 acres of wetlands.[9] But in testimony paid for by our tax dollars, one of the EPA's top wetlands scientists, Charles Rhodes, stated that the wetland creation was a degradation of the environment. Why? "Because ducks and geese would defecate in the ponds."[10] Seemingly perplexed, U.S. Judge Smalkin asked, "Are you saying that there is pollution from ducks, from having waterfowl on a pond, that pollutes the water?"[11] The answer was affirmative—ducks and geese are great polluters, and creating wetland ponds for their use is tantamount to wetlands destruction, and a violation of the Clean Water Act. This, in spite of hundreds of naturally occurring fresh and saltwater ponds in the area. These natural ponds also have high concentrations of ducks and geese. But for some unexplained reason, ducks and geese don't pollute these "natural" ponds, according to Rhodes's testimony. The Corps solution to this pollution was to blast a 400-yard channel from the ponds Ellen created to the Chesapeake Bay to permit these "pollutants" to tidally flush out into the bay.

After thorough sampling, it turned out that the land upon which Ellen was working was not a hydric soil after all. Not to be dissuaded, however, Rhodes "claimed the temporary presence of water as well as blackened tree leaves found on the site indicated wetlands."[12] When Ellen testified that the expert he had hired could not find blackened leaves, Rhodes argued "they weren't able to find blackened leaves because earthworms tend to eat these leaves." Yet, if that were the case, how did the federal enforcers find them? We have only their word on it.

Although the site upon which he dumped the two loads of dirt had never seen a drop of surface water, Bill Ellen had technically "filled a wetlands," and he was found guilty by an urban jury in Baltimore.[13] Jane F. Barrett, Assistant U.S. Attorney who helped prosecute Ellen, claimed "it was a *premeditated* environmental crime" (italics added). Further justifying her position regarding this crime, Barrett continues, "These are not wholly victimless crimes. Everyone suffers from water and air pollution. People should go to jail for these crimes." For two loads of dirt?

The prosecution asked for a prison term of 27 to 33 months. The average time a convicted individual actually spends in prison or jail for assault is only 6.4 days; for robbery, 23 days; for rape, 60 days; and for murder, 18 months![14] The judge apparently saw through the smoke, however, and gave him the minimum possible term under federal law—six months imprisonment, plus an additional four months of home detention, and one year of supervised release. Judge Smalkin added:

There is a fine line between wetlands avoidance and wetlands incursion (i.e., between conduct that requires no permit at all and conduct that requires a permit), which depends upon the understanding and application of complex scientific and biological criteria that are very difficult even for experts in the field to agree upon. *The fact that a government employee says a permit is required does not necessarily make it so.*"[15] (Italics added)

Breckinridge Wilcox, the prosecuting attorney, declared after the sentencing, "Today's sentencing of William Ellen should send a clear message that environmental criminals will, in fact go to jail."[16] And indeed they are—in increasing numbers each year.

The implications resulting from Ellen's case, and others like it, are far-reaching. These laws are so ambiguous that they can, and are, being construed to mean anything an enforcer wants.

They represent the perfect weapon to intimidate or imprison any-one an overzealous regulator, motivated environmental leader, or disgruntled neighbor wants out of the way for whatever reason. Violations are literally being committed by tens of millions of un-knowing Americans each year.

What most Americans don't realize is that almost every one of us could innocently find ourselves in the same quagmire. If Bill Ellen, who was versed in environmental regulation, and who tried to work in every way with the regulators, could run afoul of these obscure regulations, what hope does the typical American land, home, or business owner have? The truth is, very little. Most Americans have no idea how high the water table gets on their land, or whether the soil is hydric, or if the weeds and brush on their property are hydrophilic. Most don't even know what the terms mean. With this type of mentality, it's no wonder that more and more hapless Americans are falling victim to a burgeoning war chest of impossible-to-comply-with environmental regulations.

THE ENVIRONMENTAL AGENDA

The Bill Ellen tragedy is but one of a growing legacy of human suffering and affliction—a legacy born of a hidden agenda that ap-pears to be driving the alarmist rhetoric emanating from national and some state environmental leaders. These leaders believe man-kind is not only destroying ecosystems, but also planet Earth. In order to save the earth, they believe, the social and economic structure of America and the Western world must be totally trans-formed.

The magnitude of the transformation these leaders demand is staggering. They are not talking about just change, or even a big change. They are demanding *total* transformation—a transforma-tion equivalent in magnitude to what occurred in the collapse of the USSR in the early 1990s. Environmental writer Thomas Berry captures the enormity of this transformation in the Sierra Club book *The Dream of the Earth*: "We must be clear concerning the order of magnitude of the changes that are needed. We are not concerned here with some minor adaptations, but with the most serious transformation of human-earth relations that has taken place at least since the classical civilizations were founded."

For good or bad, this environmental agenda will affect every person in America for generations to come.

THE ALBERT GORE FACTOR

This agenda received a tremendous boost with the election of President Bill Clinton and Vice President Albert Gore in 1992. Much has been written by columnists and others about the extremist positions and solutions Mr. Gore has taken in his book *Earth in the Balance*. But few Americans really understand how those positions and solutions will affect them. Gore is leading the Clinton administration's environmental policy. Gore states that the environment must be the central organizing principle of civilization. He demands that every law, regulation, treaty, tactic, strategy, and plan must be used to save the earth. Rhetoric and minor policy changes, Gore decrees, are merely forms of appeasement to avoid the gut-wrenching transformation that all Americans are expected to undergo.[17]

At the front line of this epic battle, Gore claims, are new brave fighters standing in the breach, ready to go to war against the industrial juggernaut:

Standing bravely against this new juggernaut, a new kind of resistance fighter has appeared: . . . They fight against the odds, with little hope of prevailing in the larger war but with a surprising record of success in skirmishes that slow the onslaught and sometimes save the particular corner of the ecological system they have been moved to defend.[18] *The agendas of the environmental movement and the democracy movement must become intertwined.*[19] (Italics added)

Polls reveal that most Americans agree with Vice President Gore. Environmental leaders and activists are seen as the poor underdogs sacrificing their lives for the greater good of all Americans. Supposedly underfunded and outgunned by the giant multinational corporations, environmental leaders are truly modern-day heroes. Few Americans realize, however, that these leaders often draw six-figure salaries and have an annual war chest of many billions of dollars to lavish on their three-front war: lobbying, litigation, and education.[20] They often outspend the so-called multinational corporations by 10:1; yet most Americans believe just the opposite.

Vice President Gore says he believes the new "central organizing principle" of government can only be accomplished by increasing the power and involvement of environmental leadership—the very ones who have a solid history of forcing this agenda on America through ever-constricting laws, regulations, and litigation.

How is this done? First, by pressuring Congress to pass extremely restrictive laws. Regulating agencies are then threatened with lawsuits if they don't enforce regulations in the way these leaders demand. Finally, these "poor" environmental leaders spend hundreds of millions of dollars to drastically change the intent of the original law through the courts until it doesn't even resemble the law passed by Congress. Section 404 of the Clean Water Act under which Bill Ellen was prosecuted and sent to prison is but one of many examples. In the 1960s there were about 25,000 pages of new regulations in the federal register each year. Today there are more than 80,000 pages annually. We are being strangled by regulations, and our economy is suffering as a result.

AN ABUSE OF POWER?

The Clean Water Act of 1972 has done a tremendous amount of good in cleaning up our rivers and waterways, many of which at the time were little more than open sewers. Within Section 404 was language that permitted the Corps to exercise regulatory responsibility for the "discharge of dredge or fill material into navigable waters of the United States." The intent of Section 404 was to keep toxic waste from being discharged into major waterways and municipal water supplies and to control indiscriminate dredging and filling of navigable rivers. Nowhere does this law even mention the word "wetlands." Little did the lawmakers know that environmental leaders and the Corps would eventually expand this definition—without any further legislative action—to include land that never saw a drop of surface water and that is often miles from the nearest stream or river.

Like the Endangered Species Act and many environmental laws enacted since it was passed, the environmental lobby saw in the Clean Water Act a made-to-order opportunity to expand its land-use agenda into the lives of most Americans. In a constitutionally questionable decision of *Natural Resources Defense*

Council v. Callaway in 1975, a district judge expanded the government's "navigable waters" jurisdiction to "isolated wetlands" that were miles from the nearest stream, let alone navigable waters. The test that was devised to permit them to do this? As long as migratory waterfowl "might" land in the wetlands, there is a jurisdictional connection between the navigable waterway and the isolated wetland. Understandably, this has sarcastically been labeled *the glancing goose test.*

In lawsuit after lawsuit, liberal courts, with the assistance of well-funded environmental groups and bureaucrats, have expanded the interpretation of the "navigable waterways" provision so that it eventually included dry land that could be many miles from the nearest flowing water. The toxic requirement had also been circumvented. A 1983 case, *Avoyelles Sportsmen's League v. Marsh*, found that merely moving clean soil from one spot to another on the same wetlands thereafter qualified as a "toxic discharge" under the Act. And the strictest interpretations of these ever-constricting regulations are being enforced by those who are being popularly called "the green police" or "eco-gestapo" by their ill-fated victims. Some 274 million acres—including farms, ranches, industrial sites, even entire cities—would be officially "waters of the United States" under the new wetlands definition.[21]

Bernard N. Goode, former chief of the wetlands regulatory office of the Corps, is greatly saddened by what has happened: "It was not the original intent of Congress to enact a wetlands protection statute, but a water quality act."[22] Through their paranoiac assault on the language of the Clean Water Act, environmental leaders have successfully created a "new" regulation Congress never intended.

Ellen's story is not an exaggeration or an isolated incident. Following a series of hearings on "The Effects of Wetlands Protection Regulations on Small Business," John LaFalce (D-NY, House Small Business Chairman) and a dozen colleagues signed a letter to then President Bush "to alert [him] to the regulatory travesty currently masquerading as federal wetlands policy. . . . This uncertainty surrounding this regulatory nightmare is causing severe economic dislocation, if not potential devastation." As the backlash and outrage grew, hundreds of thousands of Americans demanded that Congress address this issue. But with the upcoming 1992 election, Congress sidestepped the controversy by referring the issue to the National Academy of Sciences, with a recommendation to be reported back to Congress in six months. Two years later, action has yet to be taken by the National Academy.

Such is the legacy of the "new freedom fighters" exalted by Vice President Gore. And holding true to his beliefs, Gore has made sure that these same environmental leaders were appointed to key leadership positions within our government.

THE GREEN MACHINE

Carol Browner, a past key environmental adviser for Senator Gore and past head of the Florida Department of Environmental Regulation, is now the head of the Environmental Protection Agency. Browner did the background work on Gore's book *Earth in the Balance.*

George Frampton, past president of the Wilderness Society, was nominated as Assistant of Interior for Fish and Wildlife and Parks under Bruce Babbitt, who himself was formerly the Chairman of the League of Conservation Voters (LCV). The LCV is a political action umbrella group for big national environmental organizations. Babbitt proclaimed in his introduction to the LCV's 1991 Environmental Scorecard (of Congressional votes): "We must identify our enemies and drive them into oblivion."[23]

Alice Rivlin (Chairman of the Board of the Wilderness Society) and Jim Baca (board member for the Wilderness Society) were appointed Deputy Director of the Office of Management and Budget and Bureau of Land Management respectively. Babbitt appointed Brooks Yeager of the National Audubon Society for his chief of staff. Kathleen McGinty, Vice President Gore's top environmental adviser in the Senate, was appointed to head the Council on Environmental Quality. Bonnie Cohen of the National Trust of Historic Preservation was appointed Assistant Secretary for Policy, Management, and Budget, and mining industry foe John Leshy was appointed Solicitor.

Babbitt and Frampton are not the only players appointed to key administration positions who sport extreme environmental viewpoints. Many other former environmental leaders from the National Audubon Society, the Wilderness Society, and other national environmental organizations have also been appointed to positions within the Clinton/Gore administration. It is true that environmental leaders should not be excluded from holding administrative positions within the government any more than conservatives during Republican administrations, but one has to question the president's claim that he wants to have balance in controversial environmental issues when so many key positions in the administration are held by those holding preservationist views. This green machine brings with it an agenda that could mean big trouble for every family in America for a long time to come.

George Frampton, for instance, has publicly stated his desire to take 26 million acres of northern forestland in the northeast away from landowners and turn it into a vast wilderness area for the benefit of nature, at the expense of hundreds of thousands of jobs. Frampton oversees National Parks and the Fish and Wildlife Service, both of which are highly controversial agencies in the environmental debates. It is perhaps not accidental that Frampton's nomination as assistant to Babbitt was postponed for nearly two months because he started issuing orders before he was even confirmed by the Senate.

The National Park System is accused by hapless landowners of strong-arm land condemnation tactics under the guise of a "willing buyer, willing seller" smokescreen. A survey of 1,110 so-called "willing sellers" to the Park Service in 1992 found that *none* were really willing to sell. According to the sellers, the pressure varied, but the message from the Park Service was crystal clear: sell your land or go to court.[24] The Park Service has also been found by the Inspector General to have a sweetheart arrangement with the Nature Conservancy and the Trust for Public Land. The Conservancy and Trust apparently buys land at bargain prices and then sells it to the Park Service for inflated prices. Former Secretary Manuel Lujan had proposed new policies to correct the problem, but Secretary Babbitt torpedoed them right after Clinton's inauguration in January 1993. Clinton himself abolished the Council on Competitiveness, a highly effective group that had previously provided critical advice for the president on ways to make American business more competitive in the global market. Does this mean that American competitiveness is of secondary importance to environmental concerns for the president?

The Fish and Wildlife Service enforces the extremely controversial Endangered Species Act, which victims accuse is a hammer to take land without compensation. Rightly or wrongly it has already put tens of thousands of people out of work and out into the streets. Both Clinton and Frampton are committed to making the Endangered Species Act even stronger and expand its use. The first step is to double the current number of species listed and to accelerate review of hundreds (thousands?) more. Nobody denies the need for an endangered species law, but the way it is currently written would guarantee the spread of spotted owl controversies to suburbia. All Americans could suddenly find themselves embroiled in owl-like controversies throughout the country. The implications are staggering, yet most Americans are unaware of them.

Take, for instance, the March 5, 1993, decision by the Fish and Wildlife Service to list the Delta smelt as a threatened species. This fish occurs only in the Suisun Bay and the Sacramento–San Joaquin estuary near California's San Francisco Bay. It is threatened, according to the Fish and Wildlife Service, by large diversions of the river's fresh water for agricultural and urban use. This provides a double-whammy effect that could deny critical water both to the water-starved suburbs around the San Francisco Bay and to farmers producing food for all Americans.

If acid rain, global warming, ozone depletion, and ecosystem destruction threaten our very survival, then we would all agree that strong action must be taken to stop them. If our society must be transformed to save the earth, then maybe we should give environmental leaders and Vice President Gore our support. But a growing majority of well-known scientists and leaders say environmental leaders are wrong. Why are their voices being ignored? Who's right? Furthermore, Vice President Gore asserts that we must reestablish our spiritual connectedness to the natural world if we are to have any hope of saving it. What does he mean?

Are we destroying the earth and her ecosystems? Will more regulations solve our problems? Are environmental leaders true modern-day saviors? And, most important, what does all of this mean to the typical citizen who just wants to protect our environment, live in peace, and maintain or improve the quality of life that is the hallmark of living in America? This book will explore claims of environmental catastrophes, their inaccuracies, and the so-called spiritual reasons that these leaders believe we must totally transform America's social and economic structure to save Earth. The truth will shock most Americans.

A *hypothesis is always more believable than the truth, for it has been tailored to resemble our ideas of truth, whereas the truth is just its own clumsy self. Ergo, never discover the truth when a hypothesis will do.*

> Niccolo Machiavelli
> *The Prince* (1513)

S*ome individuals are absolutely convinced from their very limited reading that we are headed for disaster via global warming. Strangely, no amount of evidence seems to shake this crowd. They appear to have a religious attachment to the issue. . . . They are not going to accept anything but the threat of disaster. . . . Any suggestion that some greenhouse effects will be beneficial is absolutely forbidden. They care about their [own version of the] environment more than they care about science.*

> Dr. Robert Balling
> Director of Climatology, University of Arizona,
> in *The Heated Debate*, 150

2

ECOLOGICAL REALITIES OF ENVIRONMENTALISM

ENVIRONMENTAL CATASTROPHES

Ed Bradley, with an apple covered by a skull and crossbones prominently displayed behind him, prepared to make the jolting revelation destined to bring economic devastation to dozens of apple growers. With a somber face and voice, he reported to "60 Minutes" listeners across America that Alar,* "the most potent cancer-causing agent in our food supply," had been sprayed on apples that were fed to our children at school. Over the next several days, parents went into a panic.

For two weeks in 1989 America was gripped in a growing state of hysteria. In an incredibly orchestrated media manipulation effort by the NRDC (National Resources Defense Council) in February 1989, the nation was shocked by horror stories about chemical death in our kids' classrooms. Without checking the scientific facts about the NRDC's claims, "60 Minutes" aired the story. On cue, day after day, new revelations came out in different newspapers and other media sources around the country.

At the time, no one knew that the NRDC was coordinating the "releases." Days later, actress Meryl Streep, who knows abso-

* Alar is a growth substance applied mainly to apple trees.

lutely nothing about Alar, provided the final catalyst in creating mass hysteria by forming "Mothers and Others for Pesticide Limits." In graphic detail only possible on network "Evening News," she asserted that "science" had shown that Alar could cause cancer, and Alar-treated apples were being fed to schoolchildren.[1]

Even after the assurances of dozens of highly reputable scientists that the allegations were untrue, people accepted the Bradley/Streep version of "the facts." Hundreds of apple growers faced economic disaster—some even went bankrupt—over distorted allegations passed along, without question, by journalists and an actress—allegations that were later shown to be totally groundless.[2]

In April 1989, at the height of the Alar scare, fourteen scientific societies, representing more than 100,000 professional food scientists, toxicologists, and nutritionists, issued a joint report which said the primary hazard present in our food supply comes from bacteria and naturally occurring toxins—not man-made pesticides. It was ignored. Most people are still unaware of this report, nor do they know that the entire episode was the result of a brilliantly executed plan orchestrated by the NRDC. The plan succeeded, but at the cost of destroyed lives and families.[3]

The misrepresentation of the scientific facts about Alar were so blatant that the apple growers have filed a class-action libel suit against both the NRDC and "60 Minutes." The suit charges that the NRDC and "60 Minutes" knowingly misrepresented the facts in a manner that would cause harm to the farmers in order to falsely discredit Alar. The case is still pending, but both the NRDC and "60 Minutes" have asked to settle out of court. The farmers have refused.

TACTICS AND STRATEGIES

Andrew Dobson, in his in-depth studies of the environmental movement in Europe and America, explains that environmental leaders use fear tactics because that strikes terror into the hearts of people: "What could be better, from the point of view of advertising an idea, than to be able to claim *that failure to embrace it might result in a global catastrophe that would **leave no one untouched**"* (italics and bold italics added).[4]

Throughout environmental literature runs the conviction that only a radical transformation of our society—from our economic structure to our religious beliefs—will be sufficient to save the earth. Dobson maintains there is an underlying belief among environmental leadership that the radical changes required in society are so far-reaching that *nothing short of an environmental catastrophe* could precipitate a willingness to change.[5]

Dobson also claims that some environmentalists believe the delivery of the message of impending catastrophe will, in itself, be sufficient to generate social change. But it also seems possible that the constant message of impending disaster is being used to precondition the populace so that when a perceived disaster occurs (fabricated or real), it will be accepted as truth. If that is the strategy, it seems to be working.

Albert Gore, for instance, claims in *Earth in the Balance* that the destruction of the earth is approaching holocaust proportions, requiring passage of new laws and treaties and the total transformation of our society to avoid total ecological collapse.[6] Throughout his book, Gore repeats almost every environmental horror story and catastrophe paraded by environmental leadership. In spite of the glaring inconsistencies and distortions in claims made by environmental leaders, Gore takes their assertions at face value, without questioning the larger agenda behind the statements.

But Gore is not alone. The majority of Americans believe these stories. Two polls taken in 1990—one by the Democratic research firm Marttila & Kiley, the other by the Republican firm Market Strategies, Inc.—found that a whopping 68 percent of Americans implicitly believe that the threats to the environment are as serious as political activists claim! This drops to a dismal 15 percent of the American public who trust what government scientists say about our environmental problems, and a mere 6 percent who trust those scientists seen as representing industry. The American people, however, do not have the resources Al Gore has to find the truth.

Most only know what they are told. When the people of any free nation begin to base economic and social policy on fantasy, the nation will not survive long. It is therefore imperative that a better understanding be gained of the science behind "environmental catastrophes." A classic example of how Americans were duped through fear is the use of pseudoscience to "prove" that the use of chemicals in agriculture and forestry is destroying the earth. Alar is not the only chemical example. Dozens of chemicals used in agriculture and forestry are under attack.

THE USE OF CHEMICALS

As you walk down the food aisle in a local supermarket, you might see a can of spaghetti sauce that proclaims "all natural ingredients, contains no chemicals." The thought immediately comes to mind, "That is a safe, nutritious product." You decide to buy it. At the check-out counter a smart aleck clerk holds up your can containing "no chemicals" and proceeds to deflate your ego. "What propaganda," he says. "Contains no chemicals, huh? You'd think people would be smart enough to know that everything is a chemical! And 'natural' doesn't mean best. I just learned in my chemistry class that 'natural foods' are a greater source of poisons and carcinogens than man-made chemicals." This scenario is not as silly as it may seem. We have been taught for more than thirty years to feel terror at the mention of the word "chemical."

The long string of ecological chemical catastrophes was unleashed on America in 1962 with Rachel Carson's attack on DDT in her book *The Silent Spring*. Carson maintained that pesticides initiate a "chain of evil" that constitutes "the most alarming of all man's assaults upon the environment." Reckless claims made by Carson and others that DDT killed birds and could cause many extinctions of species led the list of horrors. Accusations that it would cause cancer in humans were made. It was even alleged that DDT would remain indefinitely in the soil and water and would kill all the algae and plankton in the ocean, thereby eliminating the source of food for marine life and oxygen for terrestrial life. Carson's book led to speculation that DDT was responsible for the thinning of eggshells of hawks, ospreys, falcons, and eagles. The resulting fragile eggshells of these birds of prey supposedly caused the death of chicks—a belief that is still accepted today.[7]

Prior to the publication of Carson's book, the U.S. Public Health Service had proclaimed that DDT was the most important substance ever developed. Its "total value to mankind is inestimable" through protection from infectious diseases and insect pest degradation of food production and storage.[8] DDT was used to control typhus, malaria, yellow fever, sleeping sickness, plague, and encephalitis. All of these diseases are insect borne, and all were epidemic in the United States at various times in the past. The use of DDT saved literally millions of lives around the world each year.[9]

However, DDT's success led to overuse, causing a buildup in the environment. During the chaos resulting from Carson's book, DDT was found in small amounts in birds, animals, and even people. Although the overwhelming evidence showed the product to be safe, a reduction in its use was certainly called for. But the detection of DDT in the environment elevated the controversy to hysterical levels, and rather than restrict its use, EPA administrator William Ruckelshaus banned DDT in 1972. Later Ruckelshaus admitted that "decisions by the government involving the use of toxic substances are political."[10] Today, millions of people around the world are once again dying from insect-borne diseases that were nearly controlled by DDT.

None of the wild claims against DDT was ever substantiated. Bird populations that were supposedly being affected, including those of hawks and falcons, were actually increasing during this time, according to Audubon Society counts. Eagle populations were declining, but it has been since demonstrated that thinning of eggshells predates DDT. Apparently, there are many natural causes of egg thinning. Later tests showed no direct effect of DDT on these birds or their eggshells.

Paul Ehrlich, an environmental guru at the time, charged that DDT in seawater would kill all phytoplankton, threatening earth's oxygen supply. But it was later shown that 93 percent of DDT introduced into water degrades in thirty-eight days. Finally, even to be a minimum threat of causing cancer, DDT would have to be ingested at 100,000 times the maximum rate found in the environment.[11] It's incredible that Ehrlich and others like him continue to make insupportable predictions of catastrophe that *consistently* prove wrong, yet they are faithfully quoted by the press.

The list goes on and on. "The technique," says Dixy Lee Ray, former governor of Washington and chairman of the Atomic Energy Commission, "of making unsubstantiated charges, endlessly repeated, has been also used successfully against asbestos, PCBs, dioxin and, of course, Alar."[12]

THE CREATION OF PSEUDOSCIENCE

Perhaps the most important outcome of Carson's book and the ban on DDT by Ruckelshaus was that it gave credibility to *pseudoscience,* where mere theory and observations become scientific fact. In the quest to fulfill hidden political agendas, it is now legitimate to use pseudoscience to create emotion and hysteria and focus political pressure to disparage genuine scientific evidence. As in the case of the Alar scare, pseudoscience relies on distorted information based in alarmism. Such alarmism is designed to scare Americans into taking radical action—action, one can only suppose, that will lead to the fulfillment of a larger political agenda.

This, of course, does not mean there are no problems or that chemicals should be used indiscriminately. Environmental accusations are usually based on some truth. Harmful chemicals have been found in groundwater aquifers. However, most of these are found in incredibly small amounts that pose absolutely no health risk. The EPA was so convinced this was a major problem that it launched a $12 million, three-year study, the National Pesticide Survey, looking for 126 different pesticides and some of their breakdown products in rural and urban drinking water wells. The results? *No detectable level* was found in 110 of the 126 pesticides tested! That is great news because it means that herbicides, insecticides, and fungicides properly applied on farms, forests, and golf courses are generally not finding their way to the aquifers. Instead they are being absorbed and held in place by soil particles, where they are degraded by natural processes into harmless compounds.

Only six pesticides or degradates were found in quantities higher than the Health Advisory Level, and then only in *a very few wells*. A breakdown product of Dacthal (a broadleaf weed killer used primarily on lawns), was the most commonly detected pesticide. If anyone is guilty of chemically polluting aquifers, it is typical American homeowners who apply chemicals to get rid of dandelions in their lawns. But don't get too concerned. Even in this case, the Dacthal breakdown product was nearly always detected at only about 0.1 percent of the level of health concern! Yet, the fact they are detectable at all (sometimes in parts-per-trillion) provides live ammunition for environmental horror stories of the "real" dangers of cancer to people and animals.

Nonetheless, there are serious problems. Even though the majority of chemicals found in groundwater put no one at risk, some have been found in concentrations that do pose a risk to society. Once these risks are confirmed by true science, alternative chemicals or conservation practices should be, and are, being used.

The realization of this as a persistent and growing problem has opened an entirely new area of research and technological development. This research hopes to develop products that are environmentally safe. One example might be to develop products that are unable to reach the water table because they are tied up in the soil until they break down into harmless by-products. But these products take an average of ten years and $10 million to receive EPA approval for labeling.[13]

Americans should remember that the vast majority of the more serious hazards and toxins are found *naturally* in the environment and in our food. Research has shown that we typically eat an estimated "10,000 times more of nature's pesticides than of man-made ones."[14] "Natural" is not always safest! Dr. Bruce Ames, the University of California, Berkeley, scientist who developed the procedures used today to test for carcinogens, notes that 99.99 percent of the pesticides we consume occur naturally in plants. In fact Ames asserts there are more "known carcinogens" in one cup of coffee than in the pesticide residue on all the food one person could comfortably eat in a year.[15]

Environmental double-talk is not restricted to chemicals. Scientists seriously question whether other "catastrophes" are as serious as environmental leaders claim.

ACID RAIN

Many people can remember photos of the ghostly death of entire forests in Europe and the eastern United States. Bearing a silent testimony to the insensitivity of man, these forests were supposedly killed by that deadly chemical soup, acid rain. People still envision acid-scorched leaves, dissolving buildings, and tumor-ridden fish when they think of acid rain. People find it hard to believe that acid rain is not the disaster environmental leaders have made it out to be. Like the DDT "catastrophe," however, pseudoscience, hysteria, and emotion prevailed over science.

It is not that science showed acid rain doesn't cause damage; it does. Rather, the issue is the gross distortion of what science showed to be a "manageable problem." After nearly ten years and nearly $600 million of high quality research done within the National Acid Precipitation Assessment Program (NAPAP), science revealed acid rain caused only marginal damage to some lakes and streams in the Northeast and was not causing widespread death of our forests.[16] The damage to forests was limited to very high mountains, which occupy less than .01 percent of all of our eastern forests.[17] Joseph Barnard points out:

> Intensive [research] has not supported initial concerns that North American forests are suffering widespread damage caused by acidic deposition. Most forests are apparently healthy. Known

> forest health problems are in most cases attribut-
> able to natural stresses and/or past land manage-
> ment practices. With the possible and notable
> exception of high-elevation red spruce in the north-
> ern Appalachians, acidic deposition has not been
> shown to be a significant factor contributing to cur-
> rent forest health problems in North America. [18]

This does not mean it would never be a problem. There is some evidence that over a long period of time, acid rain could negatively affect some soil types. But no evidence shows it to be an immediate disaster.

It was also demonstrated that damage by acid rain to buildings, agricultural crops, or humans was negligible to none. Most damage to lakes was probably done by the 1930s, according to Lawrence Kulp, former Director of Research for NAPAP. In fact, Kulp claims that if "current conditions of acid deposition remain constant, we can expect little change in these lakes over the next half century."[19]

Does this sound like a crisis? Although science arguably shows that legislation was justified, it also *clearly revealed that acid rain was not the crisis first believed.* There was time to approach the problem rationally. Yet, the NAPAP research results were almost totally ignored when modifications to the Clean Air Act were made in 1990. Many analyses have shown that billions of *our* dollars could have been saved if the act properly considered the results of this massive scientific investigation. Despite the unnecessary high cost, environmental leaders said that the act did not go far enough! Instead, a very expensive bill was passed in an atmosphere bordering on hysteria. Worse, because of the short time schedules set by the new act, old technology (smokestack precipitators and disposal in landfills) must be used rather than newer clean coal technology. This will cause environmental problems in the future.

According to Kulp, had the legislation been written to solve the problem with the new clean coal technology, the same results would have been realized at little to no additional cost.[20] But that would have meant waiting another five to ten years, and such a compromise was untenable to environmental leadership. Instead, the hysteria they created will cost Americans up to *$400 billion* over the next ten years, depending on whose estimates you believe. Tragically, it will be spent on something that is only marginally better than much less expensive alternatives.

GLOBAL WARMING

Visions of melting icecaps and flooded coastal cities, killer heat waves and droughts, and forest death and fires of holocaust proportions are but a few things that come to mind when the subject of global warming is mentioned. On June 23, 1988, NASA scientist James E. Hansen, head of the Goddard Institute for Space Studies, testified that he was "99 percent" sure that the greenhouse effect was causing global warming. At the heart of the global climate change controversy is carbon dioxide emissions. Carbon dioxide is one of many greenhouse gases that trap the sun's energy in the earth's atmosphere; it is alleged to be the worst offender. According to environmental leadership, we must stop these emissions no matter what the cost. Failure to do so means the catastrophic destruction of the earth. On the other hand, carbon dioxide emissions are also at the heart of America's economy, indeed, that of the entire Western world! To implement these extreme controls would cost not only trillions of dollars, but civilization as we know it. It may be a cost we'll have to bear if these predictions are true. But are they? Our very civilization may depend on the answer.

Some environmental leaders and politicians would have you believe that almost all scientists agree global warming is occurring. Vice President Albert Gore asserts that 98 percent of all atmospheric scientists agree that catastrophic greenhouse warming has begun.[21] That is simply not true. A February 1992 Gallup poll of climatologists and atmospheric physicists yielded the conclusion that only *17 percent* of these scientists believed there was scientific evidence for greenhouse-caused global warming.[22] That means *83 percent* believed there was no evidence for greenhouse warming. Further, nearly 60 percent believed there was no evidence for *any* type of warming, though two-thirds thought that global warming was "possible."[23] The most disappointing statistic of all emerging from this poll is that the media cite only 2 percent of these scientists—those with the worst predictions.[24]

These statistics are almost the reverse of the declarations made by environmentalists and some politicians—including Vice President Gore. Simply stated, the American people are being misled. Perhaps the vice president has also been misled, or perhaps he somehow reversed the numbers. But, whatever the reason, the misrepresentation of scientific opinion appears to be an exact repetition of the "misinformation" campaign that provoked the DDT, Alar, acid rain, and wetlands hysteria.

THE HEATED DEBATE

There is some truth in the claims made by scientists and environmental leaders. The warmest global temperatures did occur in the 1980s as environmentalists have claimed. What they don't tell us is that 90 percent of the warming during the past 100 years had already occurred by 1940.[25] In fact, the entire 100-year increase in temperature can be explained by a five-year increase that took place between between 1917 and 1921.[26] But the increase was so benign that nobody noticed it for sixty-six years. Although the biggest temperature increases occurred during the first half of the twentieth century, the big increases in carbon dioxide and other greenhouse gases did not occur until *after* 1950![27]

How could most of the warming occur *before* greenhouse gas emissions begin to accelerate? In fact, global temperatures plummeted during the 1960s and early 1970s, engendering cries that the next *ice age* was upon us by many of the same scientists now crying global warming! Why did global temperatures plunge during the 1960s when greenhouse gas emissions were most rapidly accelerating? Indeed, the Greenland ice sheet is still growing, and the ocean surface is cooling.[28] Somehow, these truths are omitted from the catastrophe predictions issued by environmental leaders.

Global temperatures did appear to increase suddenly in the latter 1970s and to reach all-time highs in the 1980s. But these temperatures were taken at ground level weather stations. Satellite data, which measure the temperature near the total earth's surface far more accurately than weather stations, do not support these ground measurements. Patrick Michaels, associate professor of environmental sciences at the University of Virginia and past president of the American Association of State Climatologists, observed: "Northern Hemisphere satellite data, like those for the Southern Hemisphere, show no warming since the platforms were launched in 1979. Moreover, the very warm years of the 1980s, which are so evident in the land-based record, simply do not appear in the satellite readings."[29] Extensive tree ring analyses show the same result—no warming in the past twenty-five years.

Another interesting contradiction involves the climate models that have been used by environmentalists for their forecasts. It would only be logical that if they were accurate, they should be able to predict our current climate based on what has happened over the past 100 years. They fail the test miserably. Early (mid-1980s) climate models predict that the 40 percent increase in greenhouse gases since the turn of the century should have been accompanied by a temperature increase of more than 2°C.[30] But that hasn't happened. The increase in global temperature, at worst, has only been 0.45°C.[31]

Even more damaging to the global warming theory is the existence of substantial evidence that the majority of the 0.45°C increase can be explained from a variety of natural or non-greenhouse causes.[32] It is not that these climate models were developed by incompetent scientists. Rather, the dynamics of our climate are far too complex to be modeled with our current understanding of climate behavior. Yet, some scientists and environmental leaders put more weight on unproven models than on actual data. In fact, these doomsayers claim that "the [observed] data don't matter."[33] Instead, they assert that some unknown "random" variable has kept the temperature from reflecting the real warming![34] That's about like saying "newly developed" solar models show the sun really comes up in the west, and we shouldn't pay any attention to what we actually see every morning. Some unknown factor is making it appear that the sun comes up in the east! Perhaps these apocalyptic naysayers can convince themselves with this circular reasoning, but few Americans will buy it—that is, if they were ever told the truth.

A flavor of the scientific uncertainty of this issue is provided by NOAA (National Oceanic and Atmospheric Administration) scientist Thomas Karl and others. They reported in December 1991 that an analysis of nearly 750 weather stations in the U.S., China, and the Soviet Union over a forty-year period showed *little or no increase in mean maximum temperature.*[35] Rather, Karl's analyses reveal a small increase in nighttime temperature, and an actual *reduction* in the seasonal extremes in hot or cold temperatures in the Northern Hemisphere. In other words, temperatures have become more *favorable* the past forty years!

From this, Karl concludes that either the equations in the climate models predicting the day/night cycle are incorrect, or "the observed warming in a considerable portion of the Northern Hemisphere landmass is significantly affected by factors unrelated to [the] greenhouse effect."[36] Karl proposes that this day/night shift in temperature may be caused by increased cloudiness or increased aerosol (chlorofluorocarbons [CFCs], sulfate/nitrate haze), or it may be the result of natural fluctuations.

Indeed, increased "aerosol loadings" may very well be far more important than greenhouse gases. Volcanoes, which emit huge volumes of dust and sulfates, play a large role each year. Robert Balling, Director of the Office of Climatology at the University of Arizona, provides strong evidence that "over 20% of the variation in the global temperatures can be explained by the [amount of] dust in the stratosphere." Balling concludes that when the amount of dust is considered, "one-third of the global temperature trend of the past 100 years disappears!"[37] It is fascinating that 1992 was one of the coldest years in the past 100 years. Why? The eruption of Mt. Pinatubo in the Philippines in 1991.[38] Once again nature demonstrates that her natural forces dwarf anything that man can do—good or bad.

The other form of aerosol loading, sulfates, naturally comes from ocean plankton and from volcanoes as dimethyl sulfides and various sulfates. In turn, plankton populations can explode if the ocean warms or if carbon dioxide increases.[39] Sulfates also come from the burning of fossil fuel—the very stuff from which acid rain is created. Sulfates have an interesting property of attracting moisture—they provide a platform for water vapor to condense upon and therefore help in cloud formation. Clouds formed from sulfates rather than dust are also brighter than those formed from dust. They reflect about 9 percent more sunlight (and therefore heat energy), providing an even greater cooling effect than other clouds.

The background sulfate aerosol today is about three times that of 100 years ago. This equates to the amount of sulfate added to the atmosphere from one very large volcano. But are there more clouds today? Yes—about 2 percent in all regions of the United States, according to James Angell in a 1990 article in the *Journal of Climate*.[40] Roughly a 4-percent increase in global cloudiness will neutralize the temperature effects of a doubling of carbon dioxide. To date, there has been an effective carbon dioxide increase of 40 percent, with a corresponding increase in clouds of 2 percent. Should we be amazed there is no measurable increase in global temperature? Furthermore, more clouds should mean more rain. Is there evidence for more rainfall? Again, the answer is yes—the 1970s and 1980s were the wettest in U.S., European, and Soviet (now Russian) history.[41] North Africa has experienced lower rainfall, but that is a predictable outcome of increased cloudiness because of global circulation patterns.[42] Whereas the equatorial air masses rise and drop more rain due to the increased cloudiness, those same air masses become even drier as they descend over traditional deserts such as in North Africa.

Clouds trap heat during the night and reflect solar radiation during the day. Increased cloudiness should therefore result in warmer nights and cooler days. It should have surprised no one when Thomas Karl found exactly that relationship. Additionally, nights are longer in the winter than in the summer, so the night-time warming should be more pronounced in the winter than summer. Climatologist Patrick Michaels has partitioned Karl's data into winter and summer months and found that to be the case. Winter days in the Northern Hemisphere are now 0.6°C warmer, whereas summer days are 0.4°C *cooler* when Karl's data is extrapolated to a 100-year basis. Conversely, winter nighttime temperatures are 1.8°C warmer, whereas summer nighttime temperatures are only 0.4°C warmer.[43]

Do you notice something about these trends? They describe a pattern of cooler summers, warmer winters, and longer growing seasons. Our climate is actually getting better. Better for humans, better for wildlife, and better for crops. Crops are especially bene-fited if you consider that most crops grow better and produce more with increasing carbon dioxide! Rather than being a disaster, increasing carbon dioxide has a greater chance of being a major boon to life on earth!

If this is not convincing, a recent article in *Discovery Magazine* provides some sobering food for thought. While analyzing ice core data, scientists have recently discovered evidence that graph-ically reveals the resiliency of the earth. Richard Alley of Penn State University, and Kendrick Taylor of the Desert Research Institute in Nevada have found that the North Atlantic region heated up by a whopping 12° in *three years or less* following the last "ice age" some 11,000 years ago![44] This is five to six *times* the increase forecast by the doomsayers to occur in 50 years due to the global warming catastrophe! Yet the earth is alive and flourishing.

The climate we enjoy today is a result of that phenomenon. In fact, the so-called *climate optimum* was reached some 1,500, 5,000, and 8,000 years ago, when temperatures were a full 1°C higher than today.[45] Although we cannot be negligent in what we do to our environment, it appears unlikely that ecologic catastro-phes are imminent, even if the atmosphere does warm a bit.

CONCERN VERSUS PANIC

Although Karl, Balling, Singer, Michaels, and other climatologists do not deny there could be a greenhouse effect, it is not happening the way scientists previously thought. It is a far more complex problem than first believed. And, so far, the overpowering scientific evidence refutes it. If the greenhouse effect is manifested in the form of increased nighttime temperatures instead of increased daytime temperatures, it is unlikely to have the dire consequences predicted by radical environmentalists on either terrestrial ecosystems or the polar icecaps. Interestingly, that is the same type of conclusion reached in the acid rain research—yet simplistic, very expensive solutions were legislated.

Karl and his team conclude their article by saying such day/night variations "must be better understood *before we can confidently project the climate or climate impacts on future society and ecosystems*" (italics added).

Given that statement by one of the most eminent atmospheric scientists in the world, and the nearly overwhelming evidence that global warming is not happening, should we charge off—as some environmentalists demand—and enact legislation costing Americans up to $3.6 *trillion*? Merely stabilizing carbon dioxide emissions in the U.S. would cost our economy $95 billion in the first year alone, with higher costs later, according to a study by Charles River Associates.[46]

Wilbur Steger of CONSAD Research Corporation of Pittsburgh, an economic think tank, warned in 1992 that "at least six hundred thousand workers in America's most basic industries will lose their jobs if a carbon tax or other policies are enacted to reduce carbon dioxide emissions. . . . It would produce annual losses in Gross National Product of 1.7 percent through the year 2020 and put the U.S. economy into a deep-freeze."[47]

Blind attempts to cure one environmental problem have a record of producing tragic secondary consequences. Robert Crandall of the Brookings Institution and John Graham of the Harvard School of Public Health have reported one such negative consequence. The reduction of automobile size and strength to meet tighter fuel standards (also demanded by environmental leadership) has caused between 2,000 and 4,000 additional highway deaths each year.[48] Can we expect more of these types of solutions in the future?

The United Nations Environmental Programme, Worldwatch Institute, World Resources Institute, Environmental Protection Agency, Sierra Club, and others argue that the cost in human tragedy is a cost well incurred if there is even a remote chance that global warming will occur with all its forecast catastrophes. But they are still not telling Americans the whole truth.

Dr. Balling, using the extreme recommendations from the "Policymakers Summary" of the Intergovernmental Panel on Climate Change, found that even these severe policies had little effect at reducing warming. Balling reports that the net reduction in warming would be only 0.2°C![49] The bottom line according to Balling?

The public, and presumably many decision makers, appear to believe that various policies can *stop* global warming. In reality, the policies seem to have remarkably little effect on the warming, despite efforts made to maximize, or even inflate, the climate impact of these policies.[50]

But Dr. Balling also notes that the apocalyptics seem to have a religious attachment to this issue that will not be shaken no matter how much evidence is presented. He says that he is dumbfounded that their version of the environment is more important than science and truth.[51] These earth saviors are likely to continue to promote unworkable, horrendously expensive solutions to problems—even before the existence of those problems has been verified by science.

This does not mean we should not be concerned, or that no action should be taken. More research is needed—perhaps even well-thought-out legislation. For the foreseeable future, however, there is little question that this debate belongs in the scientific arena, not in the policy arena. Whatever action is eventually taken should be done with correct information, based on the best science available, not on supposition, pseudoscience, and emotion that is irresponsibly favored by most environmental organizations and some politicians! Albert Gore, for instance, calls for a worldwide "carbon tax" on fossil fuels that is estimated to cost more than $200 billion annually![52]

Aside from these kinds of drastic measures, environmentalists do offer good, low-cost suggestions that are sound advice even if global warming does not occur. Creating new forests by planting trees; using residue from tree and farm crop harvesting as fuel for energy, where possible, instead of coal; recycling; planting trees on south sides of buildings to reduce air conditioning costs; and other measures are no-lose suggestions as long as they can pay their way. Levying a small carbon dioxide emissions tax may eventually be necessary, but it should be designed so that the income goes to finding viable alternative fuels, never as a means of forcing a reduction in emissions.

THE DANGERS OF EMOTIONAL HYPE

These issues are extremely complex—too complex for simple solutions based on emotional hype. Yet, that is exactly what we are hearing from environmental leaders and a small minority of scientists. We came dangerously close to signing extremely costly treaties at the 1992 Earth Summit at Rio de Janeiro.

During the Earth Summit we were barraged with the "fact" that global warming was proven by science. At best that image was a gross distortion of reality. At worst, it was a lie. What few realized was that the so-called fact was based upon a falsified summary of a scientific report on global warming published in 1990.

This summary, produced by the Intergovernmental Panel on Climate Change (IPCC), was the centerpiece of the global warming call-to-action at the Earth Summit. The primary report, the *Scientific Assessment of Climate Change*, was the result of a meeting of nearly 200 climatologists, scientists, bureaucrats, and administrators from around the world. It basically outlined the uncertainties noted above. But when the IPCC produced the document of this meeting, the uncertainties outlined by the scientists were minimized by the one to three carefully chosen people who wrote each chapter. The uncertainties disappeared entirely in the executive summary.[53] Instead of uncertainty, the summary concluded that the greenhouse effect "poses a *significant* environmental threat"[54] (italics added). According to Christopher Folland, assistant to Sir John Houghton of the United Kingdom Meteorological Office who wrote the summary, the summary would have had no value to policymakers if it were punctuated by repeated cautions and "on the other hand" statements.[55] Since its release, the summary has been presented to political leaders and the public as an "authoritative statement of the international scientific community." But it was a fraud.

Enraged, forty-eight American scientists who contributed to the original report formed the Science and Environmental Policy Project (S&EPP). Led by Fred Singer, Atmospheric Physicist and Director, Science and Environmental Policy at the University of Virginia, the S&EPP challenged the "unsupported assumption that catastrophic global warming follows from the burning of fossil fuels and requires immediate action."[56] In a separate action, an additional 46 prominent scientists and intellectuals in the United States, including 27 Nobel Prize winners, joined 218 scientists in other countries and presented what is called the Heidelberg Appeal to the Heads of States Attending the Earth Summit. This appeal states that the global warming theory, ozone depletion theory, and other "catastrophes" paraded before the world are based on "pseudo-science, irrational preconceptions, and non-relevant data."[57]

Tragically, any scientist who disagrees with the apocalypse machine is ignored. The worst offender in this stacking of the deck is Vice President Gore. As senator, his hearings on global warming were loaded about 10:1 with theorists proclaiming that global warming was real, whereas, in the real scientific community, the ratio of apocalyptic naysayers is almost the opposite. He has even avoided inviting testimony from those in his hearings who would disagree with him.[58] Worse, "if a scientist states publicly that global warming may not be occurring . . . he can expect a personal attack [from Gore], signed by the senator and delivered by him to a nationally prominent newspaper."[59]

Newsweek's Gregg Easterbrook relates in the July 6, 1992, issue of the *New Republic* that "Gore and the distinguished biologist Paul Ehrlich have ventured into dangerous territory by suggesting that journalists quietly self-censor environmental evidence that is not alarming, because such reports, in Gore's words, 'undermine the effort to build a solid basis of public support for the difficult actions we must soon take.'" So much for truth, integrity, and freedom of speech. After all, what's a few trillion dollars to a career politician—even if the policy is based in unsubstantiated theory when the overwhelming facts say otherwise? After all, the American citizens will pay for it.

OZONE

In spite of the abundance of hot air emanating from the Earth Summit, the year of 1992 would prove to be the coolest in many decades. Not to be outdone by the freeze that nature put on global warming fear tactics, environmental leaders appear to have switched to ozone depletion as the next "can't-wait-for-science" catastrophe. The ozone depletion theory claims that CFCs eventually drift into the stratosphere where they are broken by solar energy into highly reactive chlorine atoms. These reactive chlorine atoms then destroy ozone found in the stratosphere.

CFCs (chlorofluorocarbons) are used in refrigerators, air conditioners, aerosol spray cans, and fire extinguishers (as halons), and they have many other uses. These substances are extremely inert, and, in every measurable way, the most effective, safest, and cheapest chemicals available to us for these purposes. But, as will be discussed later, the ozone depletion theory has put their use in jeopardy.

Ozone *naturally* varies by as much as 50 percent each year.[60] It is thickest during the hemispheric winter months when it is more than two times thicker at the poles than at the equator. There is also a strong correlation with the eleven-year cycle of sunspot activity. Typically there are about 3 to 5 percent higher ozone levels when sunspot activity is high than when it is low.[61] Two record *maximum* peaks of ozone have been caused by sunspot activity since the 1950s—one in 1968, and one in 1978. Minimum levels were recorded in 1962 and 1985 when sunspot activity was low.[62]

Ozone, in turn, absorbs damaging ultraviolet (UVC and UVB) radiation from the sun. Ultraviolet light is essential to life. It is vital for young children to be exposed to ultraviolet light to prevent the childhood disease rickets. Ultraviolet exposure catalyzes a chemical reaction in the skin that is essential to the production of vitamin D, which is required for the growth of strong bones. Lack of vitamin D may also be implicated in the onset of adult osteomalacia (osteoporosis) in which the bones of older people, primarily women, become brittle. In the U.S., there are 1.2 million bone fractures annually among the elderly, and 20 million Americans are afflicted with osteomalacia.[63] It is likely that more UV exposure would have helped them.

In spite of its benefits, ultraviolet radiation can also be nasty stuff. At high doses it has the ability to destroy living tissue. UV can even cause a breakdown of certain leafy plant tissues if levels are high enough. In fact, UV is so efficient at this that it is used to kill bacteria in highly sensitive labs where decontamination is essential. UV is what causes sunburn on humans and can cause carcinoma skin cancer on some people. Fortunately, the much more serious skin cancer, melanoma, does not seem to be related to UVC radiation.[64] Studies done in Australia indicate that indoor workers are more susceptible to melanoma than outdoor workers.[65] It may be that UVA, which is not absorbed by ozone, is implicated in causing melanoma, but this link has not been definitely established.[66]

So it is ultraviolet light, not ozone, that is the real concern. Anything that would cause an increase in the amount of ultraviolet radiation reaching the earth's surface would be an "environmental catastrophe" in the making. And ozone depletion is the perfect vehicle. What gets lost in the ozone depletion debates is that there is actually less ultraviolet radiation reaching the earth's surface today than twenty years ago! Also, the amount of ultraviolet radiation actually reaching the earth's surface naturally declines by 1 percent for every six miles one moves closer to the equator. Ultraviolet radiation decreases by 5,000 percent from the north or south poles to the equator.[67] Such minor details apparently don't bother apocalyptics pushing the ozone depletion scare stories, however. Instead, they have shifted America's attention to their *theory* that ozone is being depleted by CFCs.

HOLES, EMOTIONALISM, AND UNWORKABLE SOLUTIONS

The first detection of an ozone hole at a pole was in 1956–58, when it was thinner than anytime since—including the past few years.[68] As in the case of the global warming issue, the first (and worst) measurements of these holes occurred *before* the triggers proposed by the environmentalists (in this case, CFCs) became a significant factor! Ozone *holes* never actually form; the ozone layer merely thins during the time of maximum levels—in late winter and early spring (for each hemisphere), and mostly at the polar regions. The little ozone thinning that occurs at our temperate latitudes is most likely caused by the same sulfate aerosols discussed above involved in global warming and acid rain.[69] It is hard to imagine that there are many sunbathers or crops growing during this early springtime period of thinning. It is even more interesting that ozone is *naturally* thinnest during each hemispheric summer. In other words, the ozone within the so-called holes in late winter is still actually thicker than the normal thickness during the hemispheric summer! Again, such minor details apparently do not deter some scientists and environmental leaders bent on saving the earth from mankind.

In March 1988, NASA's Ozone Trends Panel made the bold proclamation that the ozone layer had been depleted by as much as 2 to 3 percent! Putting this into perspective, a 2 percent reduction is equivalent to the *natural* decline in the ozone thickness from Boston to Washington, D.C., or between Portland, Oregon, and Sacramento, California! If a 2 to 3 percent reduction is important, then those Americans who live in the South are already in big trouble! Somehow these qualifiers were overlooked, and the press release sent shock waves throughout the world. Calls were made to ban CFCs. In 1990 an international agreement called the Montreal Protocol was revised and signed by the United States and other nations to totally ban CFCs worldwide by the year 2000. Richard Benedick, Deputy Assistant Secretary of State for Environment was the U.S. negotiator in the treaty. Benedick's comments about the treaty are revealing:

The most extraordinary aspect of the treaty was its imposition of short-term economic costs to protect human health and the environment against unproved future dangers . . . dangers that rested on scientific theories, rather than on firm data. At the time of the negotiations and signing, no measurable evidence of damage existed. . . . By their action, the signatory countries sounded the death knell for an important part of the international chemical industry, with implications for billions of dollars in investment and hundreds of thousands of jobs in related sectors. [70]

There still is no evidence to support the drastic actions called for by the Montreal Protocol. Yet it is now law, and the cost in human tragedy resulting from this treaty is likely to be beyond the comprehension of most Americans.

Interestingly, the Ozone Trends Panel is supposed to give impartial judgments on ozone depletion. But it is hard to see how this can be done when the panel was composed of the scientists who authored the ozone-depletion theory in the first place! This is like putting the fox in charge of the henhouse and then putting the same fox in charge of investigating the disappearance of the hens! With this in mind, it should surprise no one that the report upon which these catastrophic predictions were made was never released to other scientists for peer review until December 1990—nearly three years later, and after CFCs were banned![71] In all respects, CFCs were banned without any opportunity for unbiased review by outside experts.[72]

But the absurdities don't end there. The panel once again issued dire warnings on October 22, 1991. The ozone layer, they claimed, was depleted by as much as 8 percent! And this time the depletion extended into the summer months.[73] EPA Director William Reilly immediately declared that this would translate into an additional 275,000 skin cancers.[74] Pandemonium resulted, and new calls for CFC reductions were demanded.

What nobody ever mentions is that the 300-page report documenting these "new findings" on ozone depletion was somehow "lost." Once again, the report can't be found to be verified by other scientists.[75] How can any drastic policy decision, such as the total banning of CFCs by the year 2000, be based on what can only be described as garbage science?

THE COST

Banning CFCs is *extremely* serious. There simply are no cost-effective replacements for CFCs. All replacements are ten to thirty times more expensive than CFCs, and some are toxic, flammable, and corrosive. The CFC's replacement of choice, R-134a (called Suva by DuPont), is still a potential ozone depleter, though less so than Freon. As such it is also scheduled to be phased out by the year 2000. It is far more expensive than Freon, is far less efficient in cooling, and cannot be substituted for Freon in existing equipment. That means that equipment will have to be *replaced* when the existing Freon within them needs recharging.

There are nearly one *billion* freezers, refrigerators, and air conditioners in the U.S. that would have to be scrapped! Replacing just the refrigerant would cost between $10 and $30 billion, up from $1 billion in 1988. But the demand for refrigerants is expected to increase by fivefold through 2000, escalating the cost to $50 to $150 billion. The refrigeration industry privately believes the real cost of banning CFCs will be in the range of $500 billion to $1 *trillion* by the year 2000.[76] If so, that works out to be about $5,000 to $10,000 per American family for replacing not only their own refrigerators and air conditioners, but also paying for the higher costs in refrigerated food. But that's only the beginning. R-134a is extremely corrosive. Engineers expect compressors on refrigerators and air conditioners to only last about three years. The ban will cost Americans hundreds of billions, perhaps trillions, of dollars for a much inferior product.

The cost of losing CFCs will be measured in human tragedy as well. We are warned that air conditioners will not be able to keep homes, hospitals, and offices cool during days in which temperatures exceed 90°F. The same problem is true for refrigerators, but at least they have better insulation to lessen the impact. The problems associated with food spoilage, heat stress on the elderly and ill, and other secondary effects can only be estimated, but they are potentially staggering—especially in climates where summer temperatures regularly exceed 100° or 110°. Robert Watson, head of the Ozone Trends Panel and a strong proponent of banning CFCs, has admitted that "probably more people would die from food poisoning as a consequence of inadequate refrigeration than would die from depleting ozone."[77]

Watson's prediction may turn out to be the understatement of the century. Due to the severe impact of losing CFCs on the refrigerated food transportation and storage industry, some estimates suggest that 20 to 40 million people will die yearly worldwide from hunger, starvation, and food-borne diseases.[78] Even if these estimates prove to be high, America appears to be bent on taking a giant step into the twilight zone—at a horrible cost in human tragedy.

SELECTIVE SCIENCE

All this is without any credible evidence that ozone depletion is occurring or that CFCs even reach the ozone. There is strong evidence that the vast majority of CFCs meet their demise not in the stratosphere as claimed by the apocalyptics, but in the soil under our feet!

The ozone depletion theory hypothesizes that Freon has a life of 100 years. Even though it is four to eight times heavier than air, some of it somehow makes its way into the stratosphere where it then destroys the ozone. But back in 1988, two Australian scientists, Aslam Khalil and R. A. Rasmussen, were doing some gas exchange studies on termites in the soil for which they used Freon to calibrate the exchange process, since it was supposedly inert and would not interact in the process. They ran into some problems—big problems. The Freon kept disappearing. Eventually they found the soil microbes were using the Freon as a food source! Freon was being decomposed in a matter of a few days or weeks, not one hundred years![79]

This finding presents some serious problems to the ozone apocalyptics. It doesn't take a Ph.D. to figure out that if CFCs are four to eight times heavier than air, the majority of these gases that escape their containers will ultimately meet their demise in the soil by ferocious soil microorganisms. How has this new information been treated? It has been ignored.

Ironically, the amount of chlorine from CFCs estimated to make its way to the stratosphere pales in significance compared to the implications of how much chlorine is produced *naturally.* Seawater, volcanoes, fuelwood burning, and ocean biotic life naturally produce about 650 million tons of chlorine annually. In comparison, the amount of chlorine produced in CFCs is 750,000 tons, of which only 7,500 tons are estimated to reach the stratosphere by the breakup of CFCs![80] In other words, nature produces about 8,000 times more chlorine annually than man does with CFCs. And that assumes that none of it is consumed by soil microorganisms.

The catastrophe theorists claim that *none* of the naturally produced chlorine gets into the stratosphere. Indeed most of the chlorine directly from seawater is in the form of salt which generally rises but a few dozen feet, then drops back to the sea. But some salt can be carried to high elevations where it can ionize. Even if the amount of chlorine in salt is completely discounted, there are huge sources of chlorine produced in gaseous forms— naturally. About 36 million tons of chlorine gas are emitted from volcanoes, and 5 million tons of methyl chlorine and other chlorine gases are emitted from algae, kelp, and plankton each year. Those who claim that natural chlorine can't get to the stratosphere ignore research that demonstrates that large thunderstorms, the jet stream, and significant volcanic eruptions provide mechanisms to propel this naturally produced chlorine into the stratosphere.[81]

For instance, on December 14, 1989, the *ash* resulting from the eruption of Mt. Redoubt in Alaska caused the loss of all four engines of a 747 jet aircraft, flying at 25,000 feet—well within the ozone belt at that latitude. Fortunately, the pilot was able to restart the engines before the plane crashed. The substance that clogged the jet engines was solid ash! Chlorine, bromine, and fluorine gases emitted by volcanoes (all greenhouse gases) are pushed even higher. It is estimated that Mt. Redoubt put more than a million tons of chlorine into the atmosphere.[82]

It has always been a curiosity that an ozone "hole" forms each year at the South Pole, but not at the North Pole. Since there are more CFCs emitted in the Northern than Southern Hemisphere, this just doesn't make sense. What Americans are never told, however, is that a mere seven miles from McMurdo Sound—where the ozone measurements are taken—there exists a volcano called Mt. Erebus. Mt. Erebus began an active cycle of eruptions in 1972 that has been continuous to this day. Volcanologist William Rose published in *Nature* magazine that Mt. Erebus ejects more than 1,000 tons of chlorine *each day* into the atmosphere, or more than 350,000 tons each year. Compare this to the *annual* global release of 7,500 tons of chlorine from CFCs, which allegedly make their way to the stratosphere. Again, not all of Mt. Erebus's vented chlorine makes it into the stratosphere. But the polar jet stream, at a maximum altitude of only 13,000 feet at that latitude, could pick up quite a bit of this gas and deposit it within the polar ozone layer. Mt. Erebus is but one example of hundreds that discount the ozone depletion theory.

In summary, ozone depletion theorists still have major hurdles to overcome, each of which deflate any catastrophe implications. First, ultraviolet radiation reaching the earth's surface is at an all-time low, partly due to increased haze and cloud formation.[83] Second, CFCs are likely decomposed in weeks rather than one hundred years, providing minimum opportunity for these heavier-than-air molecules to reach the stratosphere to destroy ozone. Third, ozone thinning (hole formation) occurs only in the polar regions. In those middle latitudes in which 99.9 percent of all life occurs, the little ozone depletion that may be occurring is most likely caused by sulfates, not CFCs. Fourth, all ozone depletion occurs in the hemispheric winter, when few people are sunbathing, and few crops are growing—indeed, little if any growth is occurring. Fifth, and most important, at worst CFCs and other man-caused ozone depleters will reduce the ozone layer by only about 10 percent. There is a natural annual variation of 50 percent. The real killer, ultraviolet radiation, increases by 5,000 percent from the equator to the poles.

Admittedly, not all the evidence is in on the ozone depletion theory. Once again, however, the overwhelming evidence is that Americans are being hand fed grossly distorted and misleading information. At best this issue belongs in the realm of scientific debate and not in policy debate. One thing is now certain; these distortions are going to cost us dearly.

How can scientists in good conscience ignore contradictory evidence when the stakes are so high? Melvyn Shapiro, an atmospheric scientist at NOAA has made the sobering comment that

---

. . . this is about money. If there were no dollars attached to this game, you'd see it played in a very different way. It would be played on intellect and integrity. When you say that the ozone threat is a scam, you're not only attacking people's scientific integrity, you're going after their pocketbook, as well. It's money, purely money.[84]

Although there are likely other reasons discussed later in this book, this is a sad indictment. Fortunately, this extreme is confined to just a small percentage of scientists. But they hold positions of influence—and apparently want to keep it that way at any cost to the rest of humanity. There is a real danger that when Americans realize they have been deceived, they will lose faith in all scientists and disregard important information that is based on good science. More and more scientists are disowning their colleagues who prostitute themselves in such a manner, but they too are ignored by the media.

As with global warming, Vice President Gore has no tolerance for those who disagree with his theory of ozone depletion. No sooner had Gore assumed the office of vice president, than he started to dispose of those who disagreed with him. The Department of Energy's director of research, William Happer, Jr., raised the scientific evidence that ultraviolet radiation had actually been *decreasing* when it should have been increasing, according to the ozone depletion theory. If that was the case, reasoned Happer, then we have nothing to worry about and can eliminate the ban on CFCs. Gore's reaction? Not only was Happer axed, but the UV radiation network of sensors showing the decline in UV radiation was deactivated as well.[85] In the words of a top Democratic staffer, Mr. Happer is "philosophically out of tune" with the new administration.[86] The perfect solution: get rid of any data and people that refute what the vice president "knows" to be true. Don't forget, Vice President Gore, as the saying goes, is "only a heartbeat away from the presidency."

MT. PINATUBO AND OZONE MYTHS

On February 3, 1992, NASA sent a third shock wave around the world by announcing that record high levels of chlorine monoxide were found in the stratosphere at the *North* Pole. It was widely speculated that the formation of a huge ozone hole was imminent—perhaps extending as far south as then President Bush's vacation home in Kennebunkport, Maine! For weeks headlines linked the "vanishing ozone" to CFCs and other ozone-eating man-made chemicals. Horror stories played to the fears of all citizens as the *Washington Post* portrayed how "ultraviolet radiation would leak through the diminishing ozone layer" and "could cause 1.6 million additional cases of cataracts and 300,000 additional skin cancers a year worldwide" by the turn of the century.[87] Of course, as in previous apocalyptic press releases, there was no evidence to support these proclamations.

What these NASA scientists failed to mention, however, was that record levels of these and other compounds were *expected* to be found at the North Pole—not because of man-made ozone-eating chemicals, but because of three very large volcanic eruptions the preceding two years. The first was Mt. Unzen in Japan on November 17, 1990, followed by the eruption of Mt. Pinatubo in the Philippines in June 1991, which in turn was followed by a major eruption of Mt. Hudson in August 1991. Mt. Pinatubo was the largest eruption in the past 100 years. It is estimated that these eruptions emitted more than 20 million tons of chlorine, much of which was vaulted directly into the stratosphere.

Seizing the moment, then Senator Gore made appearances on national television and submitted a bill to the Senate on February 6, 1992, calling for a ban on CFCs by 1995. Capitulating, President Bush mandated the ban on February 11. With lightning speed, using deceit and grandstanding beyond anything imaginable, the environmentalists saw to it that an extremely important chemical was lost to humanity—without one shred of solid scientific evidence that it was doing any harm. If there was *any* credible evidence that CFCs and other chemicals could cause the devastation that was ascribed to them, the cost could be worth it. Americans won't know what they lost until it starts to hit them in the last half of the 1990s. Meanwhile, environmental leaders have carved another notch in what is rapidly becoming their anti-human gun. Incidentally, the ozone hole at the North Pole never did develop.

Looming ever larger is the question, "Why do environmental leaders, some scientists, and Vice President Gore see environmental holocaust around every corner?" What has caused this blindness? Perhaps even more important, what does it mean to America? This can be revealed only by uncovering the historical roots of the environmental movement.

The Western idea of progress cannot be separated from a Judeo-Christian cosmology, indeed would not have existed without the philosophical basis provided by the dominant religion of Western history. Thus, to the recurrent question of whether conservationists are against progress, the answer would seem to be yes—at least to progress as it has normally been defined in the West. Standing as they do outside the Judeo-Christian tradition, conservationists naturally see progress in their own way. In this dual sense, in the striking connection between its religiosity and its skepticism toward the onward march of secular events, conservation implies a vision radically different from the American norm.

For all their conservative aspects, conservationists ultimately are more radical than any Marxists. Dissenting from both the capitalists and the communists, they declare that history is not a line but a circle; that meaning resides less in matter than in spirit, less in striving than in stasis, less in humans than in Nature, less indoors than outdoors.

Stephen Fox
The American Conservation Movement, 373

3

EVOLUTION OF
THE CONSERVATION
MOVEMENT

AMERICA'S NATURAL HERITAGE

The image was both spellbinding and awe-inspiring. Framed within the bounds of Mirror Lake, the reflection of Longs Peak and Pyramid Mountain was enshrined in a mosaic of variegated green spruce, multicolored granite boulders and outcroppings, and the majestic mountains themselves. It was a moment of reverence and appreciation for what God had created.

Whether one is backpacking in the Rocky Mountain National Park (as in the above example), visiting the Grand Canyon, or merely passing through one of America's many forested landscapes, the magnificence of nature inspires reflection and appreciation that is often beyond words. During those moments we briefly leave the ordinary and mundane and are cast into the deepest recesses of our souls. It is difficult to imagine anyone who would not be similarly stirred by such sights.

It is equally difficult to imagine anyone malicious enough to intentionally destroy our natural heritage. What type of person could behold such beauty and then seek to destroy it? Such a person could only be filled with greed or numbed with a depraved desire to bend nature to his will until it is no longer a thing of beauty, but an ugly reflection of man. Certainly Saddam Hussein, by dumping oil in the Persian Gulf and blackening the sky for hundreds of miles after igniting oil wells during the Gulf War in 1991, would fit this caricature. Perhaps the finger of accusation could even be pointed at Exxon when the Valdez supertanker spilled millions of tons of oil into the Alaskan marine ecosystems.[1]

But what about the scarred landscape of America—dissected by roads and freeways, blighted with sprawling cities, and buried in garbage? Are not we each equally to blame? Even the most sensitive environmentalist shares in this blame. Where do we draw the line between villain and saint? More important, what standard should be used to make that determination? Therein lies the heart and soul of modern environmental leadership, and the belief we are destroying the earth. But to understand the present, we must first learn from the past.

THE CYCLE OF HISTORY

America's environmental movement is not a recent phenomenon. Nearly a century ago, as now, the central focus was nature against corporate greed:

Much is said on questions of this kind about 'the greatest good for the greatest number,' but the greatest number is too often found to be number one. It is never the greatest number in the common meaning of the term that make the greatest noise and stir on questions mixed with money.
. . . Complaints are made in the name of poor settlers and miners, while the wealthy corporations are kept carefully hidden in the background.[2]

Although this quote could easily be taken from any environmental leader in the 1990s, it was instead said by John Muir in *Harper's Weekly*—in 1897! Perhaps not much has changed in nearly 100 years.

JOHN MUIR

Although great philosopher/conservationists such as Ralph Waldo Emerson, Henry David Thoreau, and others preceded John

Muir, historian and conservationist Stephen Fox, in his widely acclaimed book *The American Conservation Movement*, identifies Muir as the father of the modern environmental movement.[3]

Three years before his first encounter with Emerson, Muir writes of his experiences in the majestic Sierra Nevada Mountains of California: "I am lost—absorbed—captivated with the divine and unfathomable loveliness and grandeur of Nature. Somehow I feel separated from the mass of mankind, and I do not know whether I can return to the ordinary modes of feeling and thinking or not." With this driving philosophy, John Muir would set into motion the first political battles over respecting the intrinsic value of the things of nature.

Muir was born in April 1838, in the town of Dunbar, some thirty miles east of Edinburgh, Scotland. The third child but first son of Daniel Muir, John held a favored position within the family. His older sisters spoiled their little brother, and John spent his early years in "unbroken idyll." As he grew older, however, John was whipped repeatedly by his father for the slightest act of disobedience or perceived fault. John eventually called his father a "Christian Zealot." Though John read his Bible and grew pious beyond his years, he could never please his father. Brokenhearted, John found solace in the natural world.

When John was eleven years old, Daniel Muir broke ranks with the Presbyterian church. Following in the steps of the Pilgrims, the elder Muir moved his family to America. Eventually settling in Marquette County, Wisconsin, Daniel Muir bought eighty acres of virgin oak and hickory and proceeded to clear the land for farming. To John, the prospect of exploring the "wilderness" that surrounded the farm was worth the hard work of pioneer farming. But in a style characteristic of his self-centered, domineering life, John's father attacked the rich soil on which he farmed until it was worn out and depleted, whereupon he moved to another plot of land and repeated the cycle. The land was so rich and so vast that such practices were common, not only in farming, but also in forestry and other natural resource utilization.[4] His father's blatant disregard for the land would have a lasting effect on John.

Because of the demands on him from the hard farm life, John never received a formal education. His wilderness experiences and farm life were his only teachers during his early teen years. Although unnoticed at the time, the contrast could not have been more marked, and the foundation was laid for what would come later in his life. John "developed within himself a hard, stubborn core beyond the reach of any external situation, a knack for separating his spirit from his physical body."[5]

This stubborn core eventually led to defiance of his father's rigid requirements in his latter teen years. He developed an insatiable appetite for literature of any type, especially poetry, much to the displeasure of his father. When it became too cold to read in the winter he started tinkering with tools to keep warm. With the guidance of books and his own imagination he became a builder and inventor. His rapidly expanding and powerful mind became the wonder of the region, drawing praise from the neighbors and scorn from his father.[6]

Eleven years after arriving in America, John Muir struck out on his own. Making a deal with what was to become the University of Wisconsin at Madison, he enrolled in the university. His enrollment was good for both sides. Muir needed to learn grammar and spelling, and the school needed students. Though a recluse and an eccentric, Muir thrived on academics. He enjoyed geology, but it was botany that held his fascination. By studying the hierarchy of species, genera, and orders, Muir believed he saw how all the world was held together by a single harmonious design. In fact, it was during his time at the university that he had his first exposure to the mystic philosophies of nature and the interconnectedness of all things. Several of the faculty were disciples of Ralph Waldo Emerson, and their teachings had a profound effect on Muir. He became enchanted with "the harmony, the oneness, of all the world's life" these faculty taught him.

These early spiritualizations of nature did not shake John Muir's rigid interpretation of Christianity. Rather, that honor belonged to his father, who was incorrectly incensed that his son could believe that anything of importance could be found outside of the Bible. The two men argued violently, in spite of the fact that even at that time people generally agreed that the Bible and science were quite compatible. In the end, Daniel Muir forced John to make a choice—science or Christianity. Science won.[7]

The Civil War wove a constant thread of tension throughout Muir's university years. Since Muir did not have any particular interest in politics or allegiances, the war was merely an intrusion on his studies. After surviving several conscriptions, Muir finally realized he could not survive the next one, and he fled to Canada. At the age of twenty-five, Muir found himself in the Canadian wilderness, where he honed his botanical and survival skills and lost himself in nature. There he had his first spiritual awakening to nature and began a slow, subtle spiritual conversion.[8] This new spiritual oneness with nature would eventually sustain his political battles and set the template for the modern environmental movement.

THE EARLY CONSERVATION MOVEMENT

Although Yellowstone National Park was created by Congress on March 1, 1872, the Conservation Movement did not really get underway until the late 1880s and 1890s. From the start it was a battle between amateur "defenders of nature" and the "enemies of nature." It was the defenders who took time from their jobs to volunteer time and money for the good fight. As it remains today, the enemies were those professional or economic special interests who joined the struggle *because of* their jobs. Even then it was the white hats versus the black hats, nature versus jobs.[9]

But there are major differences between then and now. Conservation began as a hobby with such unlikely supporters as members of the Boone and Crockett Club. These gentleman sportsmen were rich and powerful and were used to winning their battles playing "political hardball." Having made their mark and money, these men were the epitome of the progressive era of the times. Stephen Fox describes them this way:

[Progressives] were moralistic, evangelical, ethnically nativist if not racist, wealthy, and offended by the corruptions of politics. Antimodern and skeptical of technological progress, [progressivism] invoked a vision of the preindustrial community when people lived closer to the land and the natural rhythms of life.[10]

Of course, in addition to these lofty principles, they also hoped to preserve big game for its own sake—and theirs.

Following his arrival in the Sierras at age thirty, John Muir found he had a genius for translating nature's beauty into the written word. During the 1870s and early 1880s, John wrote numerous articles in *Century Magazine* that sensitized both East Coast readers and Boone and Crockett members to the grandeur and importance of the High Sierra wilderness—especially that of Yosemite Valley. But by the early 1880s, Yosemite Valley began to be destroyed by commercialization. In Muir's growing despair the articles slowed, then stopped altogether by 1884. Robert Johnson, editor for the *Century*, attempted to revive John's literary career, but to no avail.[11]

In the spring of 1889 Johnson visited California to gather material on the state's pioneer settlers. During the trip Johnson managed a meeting with Muir that would change the course of both lives. Muir convinced Johnson to visit Yosemite and witness the destruction for himself. Johnson agreed, and he too was sickened by the commercialism that he saw.

SURROGATE STRAW HORSES

The *Century* was noted for its role in adversarial politics, and it picked up Muir's cause with a vengeance. With a readership of more than 200,000, it "dominated the field of polite magazines."[12] Johnson introduced Muir to key influential people, extending Muir's sphere of influence to critical areas. Johnson was even able to convince Muir to resume his writing, this time expressing his political concerns in "scientific" ways that had meaning to his utilitarian Eastern readers, especially those within the Boone and Crockett Club. This started a pattern of using surrogate straw horses to achieve an alternative goal:

> Muir might point out the alleged benefits of Sierra forests in regulating rainfall and preventing erosion. But what really piqued him was the wanton blasphemy of cutting down a sequoia grove that predated the Christian era. So it went: Audubon society members would cite the useful role of birds in controlling insects, but they most cared about birdsong and the flash of color on the wing.[13]

This tactic of using surrogate issues to achieve altruistic goals is still being practiced today. Although it was effective, this "sleight of hand" would eventually stifle the very goal that Muir and other amateur pioneers really wanted—that of total preservation. By using science as a smokescreen to hide their agenda, Muir and others introduced a utilitarian element into the budding Conservation Movement. Man still had a right to use nature for his own benefit, but he must use it wisely.

It is interesting that Muir never called himself a conservationist, because that referred to "wise use" of the resources. Muir really wanted "no use" and freely referred to the need to protect the environment through "preservation."[14] For more than seventy years, a conservationist was one who applied scientific technology to provide benefits to man while protecting the environment. Sometime during the 1960s the definition for a conservationist came to be synonymous to that of a preservationist. In the process "environmentalism" was born.

For several years, Johnson and others had suggested that Muir start a permanent organization that concerned people could join to help Muir reach his goals. Muir, a recluse at heart, shunned the idea for many years. When he finally relented, invitations were sent out "for the purpose of forming a 'Sierra Club.'" John Muir, the announcement said, "would preside."[15] The Sierra Club was born in 1892, and Muir served as its president until his death in 1914. The Sierra Club proved to be one of Muir's greatest joys in his lifetime.

ALLIES

Concurrent to Muir's struggles for Yosemite in the 1880s, botanist Charles Sprague Sargent, director of the Arnold Arboretum at Harvard, was fighting the same battle on a different front. Sargent became the definitive authority on trees in the United States. A Brahmin of great wealth, Sargent was free to pursue independent interests, and in the 1880s he surveyed American forests for the federal government. Although the forestry division of the Agriculture Department had been created in 1876, it had neither money nor power. Overgrazing and harvest practices that resulted in erosion and the *permanent* loss of forest cover (i.e., deforestation) were not uncommon. The findings of Sargent's survey convinced him that reform was necessary, and he convinced the American Forestry Association to endorse his plan for the protection of federally owned forests.

Although Sargent and Muir had briefly met before, it wasn't until the early 1890s that Johnson brought them together again. This coalescing of objectives suddenly shifted the balance of power toward Muir, Johnson, and Sargent. Conservation historian Stephen Fox perhaps sums it up best:

> Conservation was never more an elitist
> conspiracy than at its birth. Sargent, Muir,
> Johnson, and the Boone and Crockett men were
> leaders without portfolio, often pulling strings
> without taking their case to the public. . . .
> A novel idea caught between public indifference
> and corporate hostility, forest protection was in-
> troduced by a combination of subterfuge and ex-
> ecutive fiat. . . . When the reaction came, it
> spoke of the rhetoric of bypassed democracy.[16]

Hardball politics became the means of environmental reform. One of the better-known "back room" political ideas was the attachment of a last-minute amendment to an important bill that was near vote in Congress during March 1891. The bill passed, and the amendment went all but unnoticed. Written by an attorney within the Boone and Crockett Club, the amendment authorized the president to withdraw federal land from the public domain to create "Forest Reserves." Little did Congress know the power they had given the president. Within two years, President Benjamin Harrison proclaimed fifteen reserves totaling some 13 million acres! Pleased with the magnitude of the set-asides, Muir was aghast that sheep were still permitted to graze on the reserves. So in another back-room deal cut during 1893, Muir and Johnson convinced Secretary of the Interior Smith to ban sheep grazing as well.

THE TURNING POINT

Things were going well for these early preservationists. Under the strong influence of Sargent and others, in 1893 the New York State Constitutional Convention declared the vast Adirondack State Forest "forever wild."[17] At the same time, the *Century* held a symposium on another plan of Sargent's to use Army patrols to defend the reserves from poachers. Although the symposium endorsed the idea, there was a dissenting opinion from an unknown twenty-nine-year-old Yale graduate named Gifford Pinchot. Instead of using the Army, Pinchot advocated the creation of a "forest service" of scientifically trained men. Although unknown at the time, the injection of Pinchot into the conservation equation would forever change the direction of the Preservation Movement.

Also a man of wealth and influence, Pinchot was born a Connecticut Yankee. Following his degree at Yale, Pinchot studied forestry in Europe with a zeal to apply his knowledge: "Trees could not only be protected but *managed* for sustained yields."[18] Pinchot first presented himself an admirer of Muir, probably believing that their interest in science and conservation were parallel. They were not. Although both desired to protect the environment, there was a basic philosophical difference between the two men that would prove to be a huge chasm. Muir saw progress as the vehicle by which nature was being destroyed. He was therefore a preservationist with altruistic views, while Pinchot was a professional conservationist with utilitarian views. Pinchot, for instance, had opposed the "forever wild" clause of the New York Constitutional Convention because it forbade lumbering in the Adirondack forest. Muir had supported it.

Pinchot submitted all public questions to a simple formula: "the greatest good of the greatest number in the long run." Muir vehemently disagreed, maintaining that it was merely a smokescreen to fill corporate coffers. Such a formula, Muir believed, improperly focused on human material gain without any mechanism to quantify the value of a pristine wilderness.[19] In desperation Sargent confided to Muir, "We have got to act promptly and secretly in these matters, or the politicians will overwhelm us."[20]

Formulating a plan, Sargent and Johnson attempted to push a government-sponsored forest commission through Congress in 1894. The commission was billed as an effort to review the importance of forests on water supply. But Congress balked at passing legislation for this purpose. Not to be dissuaded, Sargent and Johnson bypassed normal channels and got the National Academy of Sciences to sponsor the commission. Under such sponsorship, Congress did not have to pass special legislation, but merely appropriate $25,000, which they did. Believing they had things under control, Sargent recklessly invited Gifford Pinchot onto the commission, and the six-man commission finally set out in 1896. Not surprisingly, the Sargent contingent of the commission wanted to keep the reserves as untouched preserves, while Pinchot favored regulated use. The final report favored Army patrols and banned sheep grazing, but did allow for some lumbering and mineral exploration.[21]

Although Pinchot lost the battle, the trip proved to be a watershed event and the first step to his winning the war over the next ten years. Sargent later lamented, "It is badly on my conscience that I started his career."[22]

A political storm had been brewing in the West due to the heavy-handed tactics the executive branch used in setting aside reserves without consideration for the interests of the local people. The storm broke when President Cleveland set aside an additional thirteen new reserves totaling 21.4 million acres just before he left office. Annoyed at being outflanked, the Senate amended a popular bill to withdraw the new reserves. The power play failed, however, when Cleveland said he would veto the entire bill if it included the amendment. The Senate capitulated, and the mess was left to the new administration and Congress.

The battle lines drawn, Muir focused his attack on corporate greed and special interests:

Complaints are made in the name of poor settlers and miners, while the wealthy corporations are kept carefully hidden in the background. . . . The public should not be deceived, every acre of the remaining federal forest land not suitable for farming needed permanent protection. . . . Let right, commendable industry be fostered, but as to these Goths and vandals of the wilderness, who are spreading black death in the fairest woods God ever made, let the government up and at 'em.[23]

Congress would have no part in it, however. Losing patience with unilateral action by the executive branch, it passed the Forest Management Act in 1898, suspending all but two of Cleveland's reserves and reversing the 1894 ruling that had suspended mining and grazing. The act called for the scientific management of all federal forest lands for multiple use, which set the direction for natural resource policy and conservation for the next seventy years. The act particularly emphasized the need for using natural resources to support the economies of local communities. Shortly after passage of the act, Pinchot was appointed head of the forestry division in the Department of Agriculture.

Muir's efforts went downhill from there. The U.S. Forest Service was created in 1905 at the direction of President Theodore Roosevelt, who then appointed Pinchot as its first chief. Roosevelt also transferred the Forest Reserves from the Department of Interior to the Department of Agriculture under Pinchot's control. Since the name *Forest Reserves* carried a preservation connotation, Pinchot immediately changed the name to National Forests, where multiple use would predominate. There were some gains for Muir, however. The boundaries of Yosemite National Park were completed in the early 1900s by President Roosevelt. Muir also helped convince Roosevelt to create fifty-three wildlife reserves, sixteen national monuments, and five new national parks. But this so irritated Congress that in 1907 the president was forbidden to add any additional reserves in six Western states without its legislative approval.

Although Roosevelt remained a consummate conservationist and was sympathetic to Muir's wishes, his viewpoint gradually shifted to a utilitarian use of natural resources. Muir's last stand was against the Hetch Hetchy Dam in Yosemite. The dam would provide much needed water for San Francisco, but it would destroy a beautiful valley within Yosemite National Park. Strangely, Roosevelt distanced himself from the controversy, and Muir's pleas fell on deaf ears. Covering the period between 1905 and 1913, the fight sapped the waning strength of John Muir: "Muir stayed active down to the final votes ('I'll be relieved when it's settled, for it's killing me.')"[24] The bill to build Hetch Hetchy was passed late in 1913, and in December 1914 John Muir caught pneumonia and died.

The striking similarity between the tactics and beliefs of Muir, Johnson, and Sargent and what is happening in the 1990s is not accidental. They all held and were motivated by a belief system that was all but suppressed by a professional and scientific approach to conservation until the 1960s. But the beliefs of Muir and others have once again stormed to the forefront, and they pervade the leadership of the modern environmental movement in the 1990s.

Nearly one hundred years later, the same battle is being fought. Modern environmental leadership is using the political tactics pioneered by Muir, Johnson, and Sargent with one important difference: Nowhere is there evidence that Muir deliberately distorted the truth or made use of terror tactics. Sadly, that is not the case for many environmental leaders of the 1990s. Muir's generation maneuvered behind the scenes in secrecy to accomplish their agenda. Such tactics are merely hardball politics and remain common today.

THE NATURE OF RELIGION

As Muir immersed himself in nature during his flight to the Canadian wilderness, the conviction grew that his previous Christian thinking was fundamentally flawed. That flaw, Muir believed, was the Judeo-Christian belief that man was more important than nature and was therefore free to exploit nature at will. By immersing himself in nature Muir began to "experience" what was taught to him by some of his university professors—the oneness of all things working together in harmony.

Such harmony was in total contrast to what Muir had experienced with the rigid views and actions of his father and others who exploited nature. Stephen Fox puts it this way: "Operating from experience, he derived a theological conclusion without the intercession of the theological process. After him, many other conservationists independently reached the same insight by a similar direct immersion."[25] Experience and emotion formed the basis for their theology.

Rather than seeing harmony in the things God created, the various aspects of nature itself became the creator of harmony. Nature had become god, and man had no greater place in this nature/god than any other aspect of nature. Cedric Wright of the Sierra Club noted in the Sierra Club Bulletin in February 1935:

A tree, a rock, has perfect poise and content. In *its* life, a life enclosing whole solar systems within the atom, there surely is a consciousness utterly beyond our comprehension . . . In the contemplation of this, one begins to doubt whether man is, after all, the highest form of life. (Italics added)

It wasn't that the Bible is wrong, or that Judaism or Christianity forces the belief that man can crush God's creation at will. Instead, Muir's interpretation most likely was based on what he *saw*—the abuses of the land by his domineering father and others who claimed to be Christian (or Jewish). The Judeo-Christian Bible does indeed provide specific conservation practices that would protect God's creation if they were followed. Regardless of the reasons, however, conservation historian Stephen Fox ties these beliefs directly to the mystic Eastern religions:

Conservationists* took the philosophical affirmations that seemed absent from the more familiar Judeo-Christian tradition. They may have still called themselves Christians. But their ideas came from elsewhere. . . . Asian religions in particular attracted conservationists as a sound basis for the nature-faith. Hindu, Zen Buddhist, and Taoist ideas were more contemporary than Grecian myths, more substantial and less exotic than fugitive aboriginal religions, and they had long recorded histories and hundreds of millions of adherents. When [early] conservationists spoke in philosophical terms, they invoked these Asian traditions more often than they mentioned Christianity. The Asian point of view generally treated man as just another animal, no more significant, in some cases actually less privileged, than other animals. Further, Asians retained a cyclical concept of time** and typically greeted Western notions of progress with a tempered skepticism.[26]

In spite of the emphasis on the Eastern religions, Greek and aboriginal mythology still played an important role. Thomas Higginson, in a 1884 meeting of the Appalachian Mountain Club, was reminded of "some weird council of old Greek wood-gods, displaced and belated, not yet quite convinced that Pan was dead, and planning together to save the last remnants of the forests they

---

* Stephen Fox uses the term conservationist in the John Muir style of preservationist.

** The concept of reincarnation dominates mythic religions. In the cyclic belief of reincarnation there is no death, merely transitions from one life form to another, i.e., cosmic dust to rocks, to amoebas, to trees, and eventually to low-station humans to high-station humans. The cycle is not necessarily unidirectional, but it depends on the individual's goodness or badness. If bad, it can be regressive.

loved"[27] Ernest Oberholtzer of the Wilderness Society "immersed himself in Indian cultures, adopting their standards of beauty and tape-recording Ojibway religious myths."[28]

Aldo Leopold searched for a metaphysical explanation of the connectedness of all things in nature. He eventually became a convert to the Russian mystic Peter Ouspensky, who urged, along with transcendentalism, that all things in the universe are infused with spirit.[29] Every particle in the universe, according to Ouspensky, was pulsing with consciousness. This reinforced Leopold's dawning sense of "the indivisibility of the earth."[30] Such animistic beliefs are common to aboriginal religions. According to Stephen Fox, after his Canadian wilderness experience John Muir "had more in common with Indians than with most civilized Christians."[31]

Another cornerstone of the early conservation movement is derived from the middle kingdom of psychic phenomena. These unexplained oddities were called spiritualism in the 1800s and are now called parapsychology. Psychic experiences run through the personal histories of many early conservationists, including Muir. It should not be surprising that modern environmental leaders are increasingly involved in psychic metaphysics.

Most early conservationists were enamored with some form of nature/god beliefs, along with the accompanying mystic/metaphysics/psychic involvements. Aldo Leopold (founder of the Wilderness Society), Ralph Waldo Emerson (philosopher and writer), Henry David Thoreau (naturalist/writer), William Brewster (cofounder of the National Audubon Society), and John Muir are the most widely known. But Goethe, Swenborg, Coleridge, Wordsworth, Blake, White, Dorr, and Novalis all played important roles in shaping early conservation/mystic ideas.[32] Nature photographer Ansel Adams, *New York Times* outdoor writer Joseph Wood Krutch, and philosopher Sigurd Olson are some of the more recent ones. Justice Douglas became enamored with Buddhism. And Charles Lindbergh, the first to fly the Atlantic nonstop, became highly involved in Taoism.[33]

Most of these early conservationists came into their mystic beliefs fairly late in life. These Eastern and Western mystic religions merely provided credibility to what they had already come to believe through experience. Muir was first exposed to Eastern mysticism during his Yosemite years by a book sent to him on Hinduism, and later during a trip to India in 1903. So these formal religious beliefs played more of a reinforcing function than a guiding role.

They also played a silent role. Sometimes, according to Fox, the faith of these early conservationists had "no specific name but merely embodied . . . 'a vast impersonal pantheism—transcending the confused myths and prescriptions that are presumed to clarify ethical and moral conduct.' However deeply felt, a pantheist faith was typically expressed at some risk within the constraints of a Christian society."[34] Surely Muir and others must have felt extreme frustration that they had to fight their battles using scientific arguments rather than what they personally believed to be the truth—their god/nature religious beliefs.

All of this changed in the 1960s with the coming together of several phenomena. David Brower, president of the Sierra Club from 1956 to 1971, brought a more radical approach to environmental activism with his Buddhist beliefs. Growing more extreme by the year, his tactics caused so much tension within the organization that he was forced to leave the Sierra Club, whereupon he eventually created the highly radical Friends of the Earth.[35]

At the same time Rachel Carson, steeped in the Buddhist "reverence of life" philosophies of Albert Schweitzer, published her book *Silent Spring*. It was this book that ushered in environmental activism and hyperbole, with pseudoscience as its cornerstone. But these two phenomena were mere precursors to the main event.

It was the New Age Counterculture Movement exploding into the American scene in the 1960s and 1970s that propelled the fledgling environmental movement to dizzying new heights of god/nature worship, mysticism, and radical antimodernism. This movement is proving to have a far greater impact on America than anything else since the Civil War. It also marks the sharp change in temperament between the mystic beliefs of the early conservationists and those of modern environmental leaders.

Nature is quite obviously the physical totality of God's work. Within it, as part of it . . . we become aware that Nature is, in fact, us. The world is Our Body. . . . Mother Earth is not passive. To align oneself with Her energies is to liberate . . . the Godhead within you, to be lifted into a higher state of being.

Bob Hunter
Cofounder of Greenpeace
Greenpeace Chronicles, 18 (August 1979): 3

The web of relationships is what first impinges on our waking consciousness. . . . Every being has its own interior, its self, its mystery, its [sacred] aspect. . . . To deprive any being of this sacred quality is to disrupt the larger order of the universe. Reverence will be total or it will not be at all. . . . We [have] made our terrifying assault upon the earth with an irrationality that is stunning in enormity.

Thomas Berry
The Dream of the Earth
Sierra Club Books, 134

4

POSTCOUNTERCULTURE
ENVIRONMENTALISM

MYSTIC THINKING

Sitting on folding chairs or sprawled on the ground were repre-sentatives of many of the movers and shakers, the cutting edge, the cream of the American environmental movement. Among those present were current or former key leaders of the Idaho Conservation League, Montana Environmental Information Center, the Wilderness Society, the Wildlife Society, the Nature Conservancy, the National Audubon Society, the C. S. Mott Foun-dation, and other local and national politicians, philanthropists, activists, and foundation officers.[1]

The event that drew this assemblage together that bright, summer Wyoming day in 1983 was the celebration of the tenth anniversary of the Northern Rockies Action Group (NRAG; pro-nounced "En-rag"). NRAG was the heart of the environmental movement in the northern Rockies. It had either created or sup-ported every citizens' action group, and it had been in the midst of every environmental battle fought in the northern Rockies. In short, NRAG was either involved or the action didn't happen.

The speaker who held this group in rapt attention at this Jackson Hole dude ranch was Willis Harman, director of the Cen-ter for the Study of Social Policy at the Stanford Research Institute and cofounder of the Institute of Noetic Sciences. The topic of his discussion that was so enrapturing? Noetic science. Noetic science is concerned with the human mind and consciousness and their role in the continuing evolution of humankind.[2] What does noetic science have to do with environmentalism? A lot, it would appear.

Harman explained that the collapse of the "industrial era" was upon us. It was now necessary to build a "trans-industrial era" by "connecting our social, spiritual, and ecological visions."[3] "Positivistic [i.e., normal] science" was the root of many environmental problems of the day, claimed Harman and others. The solution, indeed the only hope, lay in a unified vision of a sacred reality leading to "a natural fusion of science and religion."[4] We must, Harman asserted, "reinvent the world" in our search for the "esoteric* core" and "recognize our essential connectedness." He referred to the world's spiritual and shamanistic traditions and how these people understand that the powers of the mind are nearly limitless. Shamanism is the religious belief of northern Asia that good and evil spirits pervade the world and can be summoned through inspired priests acting as mediums.

The back cover of every Sierra Club Nature and Natural Philosophy book affirms this belief:

We are just beginning to explore what it means to be a part of the universe that is alive. For most people, the emerging view of nature remains in a realm separate from the emotions and textures of daily experiences. This missing link between scientific breakthroughs and the general consciousness is the focus of the Sierra Club Nature and Natural Philosophy Library.

This potpourri of convoluted ideas and strategies is at the heart of the modern environmental movement in the 1990s. It may seem that it has nothing to do with our environmental problems. But unless this phenomenon is understood, it is impossible

---

* Esoteric means secret. In this case it is the hidden or mystic realities of the interconnectedness and oneness of all things in the universe and the corresponding higher level of consciousness that this oneness contains. In other words, the secret knowledge of the cosmic god.

to understand the rhetoric behind the acid rain, global warming, wetlands, deforestation, ozone, and other so-called environmental catastrophes. An environmental catastrophe, it appears, is in the *mind* of the beholder. A mind that knows nature to be the ultimate truth. Nature defines what is right or wrong, what is real or counterfeit, what is sacred or blasphemous. It is what is sending Bill Ellen and others to prison, putting people out of work, and strangling our economy.

Although mystic thinking was rooted in the beliefs of early conservationists, it was the New Age counterculture that brought it into mainstream America. Arising from the ashes of the sixties counterculture, these ex-hippies have grown up to be today's doctors, lawyers, financial consultants, and most important, environmental leaders. The mystic environmental leaders seem to be found predominantly at the national level, although they can also be found in more radical local organizations as well. They probably represent less than 5 percent of those of us who are concerned about the environment, yet they have had a profound effect on America's environmental policy.

A NEW WORLDVIEW

The New Age counterculture movement exploded into the American scene with a violence and irrationality unprecedented in American history. Protests and riots spotted the landscape almost on a daily basis—especially on college campuses. There was even an occasional bombing of an institution. Parents watched in amazement and bewilderment as many of their children rebelled and rejected the very prosperity these parents had fought so hard to obtain. Antiwar, antinuclear, antiestablishment, antimaterialism, anti-bath, anti–short-hair, anti-everything seemed to be the only consistent thread throughout the movement. The motto Make Love, Not War rang out across the continent as these flower children made known their disgust for their parents' values.

Some confused parents thought all this was just a reaction against the unpopular Vietnam War. Others believed it to be one massive drug trip. It was these things, but it was much, much more. At the heart of the counterculture movement lay the total rejection by the hippies of the mechanistic, materialistic values of their parents—indeed, the entire Western world. These kids wanted nothing to do with their parents' abusive, mechanistic world where nature existed only to serve man.

Instead, those in the counterculture saw the vision of a "New Age." The Age of Aquarius was about to dawn upon mankind. In this new world order, there would be no war, no famine, no hatred. Instead there would be universal love where mankind worked in harmony with himself and nature in a mystic dimension never before experienced in the Western world.

Critic Douglas Groothuis perhaps sums it best in his discussion concerning Theodore Roszak, one of the first counterculture writers:

Analysts such as Theodore Roszak locate the sources of our current distress in the great social transformation of the Scientific and Industrial Revolutions. With the advent of scientific experimentation and quantification . . . the modern West began to desacralize the world.

What was once the theater of mystic splendor and spiritual participation was slowly transformed into a cold mechanism of natural laws and regularities. The spirits were chased from the woods and only the trees remained. The sacred grove became the lumberyard as nature was viewed as mere stuff to be technologically utilized by the newfound powers of humanity come of age.[5]

The key to understanding the hippies of the day was not in drugs or riots but in their newfound religion—a religion, they believed, of incredible power and purpose. Love, peace, and harmony were in their grasp. Drugs were merely a means to access that power. In fact, according to former New Age disciple Tal Brooke, drugs were the main entrance into experiencing the power of the Aquarian Age:

In the mid-1960s I encountered Timothy Leary for the first time in Washington, D.C., in a large church sanctuary overflowing with my contemporaries. . . . His soothing voice soon

drew us in. It was evident that he had found
a key to terrible power and knew that when it
was used the world would not remain the same.

Whether through flower power or mass
ecstasy the world would be transformed, and
nothing that the 'straight society' did could
stop the momentum of the truth they had found
. . . opening a major doorway into the New Age:
'LSD does not produce the transcendent experience; it merely acts as a *chemical key.* It opens
the mind, frees the nervous system of its ordinary patterns and structures, and releases
an enormous amount of awareness-energy.'

Here is the key to the mystery which has
been passed down for over 2500 years; the
consciousness expansion experience, premortem
death and rebirth. The Vedic [Hindu] sages, the
Eleusinian [Greek mysticism] initiates and the
Tantrics [Hindu philosophy] all knew the secret;
in their esoteric writings they whisper the message . . . 'It is possible to . . . become aware of
the treasury of ancient racial knowledge welded
into the nucleus of every cell in the body.'[6]

The New Age counterculture movement was not about drugs
or free love; it was about mystic mind expansion and the belief
that everything is god and god is everything. Called *pantheism*,*
this is the same religion of nature shared by their mystic conservation predecessors—with one big exception. The hippies were
taught a blend of many Eastern religions, called Theosophy; they
learned it at a much younger age than did their predecessors.
Rather than seeing a religion through nature, as did the earlier
conservationists, they saw nature through their religion—and embarked upon a holy war against anyone they believed was destroying god.

In what has become known as the "eco-shot heard 'round the
world," medieval historian Lynn White gave a paper at a meeting

---

Pantheism: *pan* is the Greek word meaning everything, all inclusive; *theos* is
the Greek word for god.

of the American Association for the Advancement of Science the day after Christmas, 1966:

Human ecology is deeply conditioned by beliefs about our nature and destiny—that is, by religion. . . . The victory of Christianity over paganism was the greatest *psychic* revolution in the history of our culture. It has become fashionable today to say that, for better or worse, we live in 'the post-Christian age.'

What did Christianity tell people about their relations with the environment? . . . Especially in its Western form, Christianity is the most anthropocentric [man-centered] religion the world has ever seen. *Christianity, in absolute contrast to ancient paganism* and Asia's religions . . . not only established a dualism of man and nature but also insisted that it is God's will that man exploit nature for his proper ends. . . . By destroying pagan animism,*** Christianity made it possible to *exploit nature in a mood of indifference to the* feelings *of natural objects . . .* Christianity bears a huge burden of guilt.

More science and more technology are *not* going to get us out of the present ecologic crisis until we *find a new religion.* . . . We shall continue to have a worsening ecologic crisis until *we reject the Christian axiom that nature has no reason for existence save to serve man.*[7] (Italics added)

White's paper electrified environmental leadership. Published in *Science* the following March, it issued the battle cry against Christianity and all of modern society. White had given environmental leadership something to blame and the vehicle by which to do it: "The environmental movement now had an epistle for spiri-

---

* Paganism is any belief that worships many gods or where everything is god. Usually, as in this example, god is found in some way in nature.

** Animism is the belief that everything in nature is alive and has a spirit.

tual reform."[8] After their true religious beliefs had been repressed for decades, White's paper gave credibility to what conservationists/environmentalists believed and is undoubtedly the most oft-quoted article in environmental literature. Moreover, this paper is *still* compulsory reading for anyone interested in eco-philosophy or the development of science and technology in America's colleges and universities.[9]

Although the history of Christian stewardship has not always been consistent, White's analysis badly missed the mark. Christian leaders had long been alarmed over the excesses of materialism wherever it was found. Whereas the first few chapters of Genesis do call for man to "subdue" nature, the subduing was to be done within the strict confines of a responsible stewardship that respects God's creation. Such stewardship—where man uses and manages God's creation but also respects what He created—is defined throughout the Old Testament.

White and other environmentalists also missed Zoroastrianism, Confucianism, and the Greek and Roman mythic god beliefs, which were even more man-centered than Christianity. Confucian Chinese had deforested much of their nation. Even today, the Buddhists of Nepal are deforesting the Himalayan Mountains, causing massive erosion. Likewise, deforestation and desertification are occurring in Hindu India.[10] Although this modern environmental degradation is, in part, the result of extreme poverty, it still leaves open the question of why such poverty is a consequence of this belief system if it is so superior to that of Christianity. If poverty is the probable result of such a belief system, then environmental degradation is also a natural consequence. If so, rather than being the answer to saving the earth, these Eastern religions glorified by White and many environmental leaders merely provide another path to its destruction.

Though wrong in his analysis, White was perfect in his timing. Environmentalists with a nature/god belief were ready to believe him with an enthusiasm that revealed their "deep-seated antipathy to Judeo-Christianity. . . . *White had proved that the movement rested on radical religiosity.*"[11] Alston Chase, himself once active in the environmental movement, summarizes White's effect on the environmental movement:

White had set environmentalists a three-fold challenge: to find a religion replacing

> Judeo-Christianity which would resolve the
> question of our place in nature; to find a
> science, replacing the one that had produced
> our destructive technology, which would show
> us how nature could be known; and to construct
> a social agenda replacing the one based on
> unlimited growth, which would change our culture
> before it had destroyed the earth. [12]

Fully energized, having clear goals, and having an enemy in sight, environmental leaders declared war on American culture. The first goal would be to implant their religious beliefs.

THE RELIGION OF ENVIRONMENTALISM

New Age environmentalists do not see human beings as set apart from the rest of creation: "At best [humans are] a part of an interconnected whole and at worst as the temple destroyers who desacralized nature."[13] They can't accept a personal, interacting Judeo-Christian God, because they believe they are god themselves—along with all of nature. Brian Swimme and Thomas Berry explain this in the Winter 1993 *Amicus Journal*, published by the Natural Resources Defense Council. The only solution, they claim, is to replace Christian beliefs with a theology that understands nature as sacred, where the interconnectedness of all things is clearly understood:

> With all our learning and our scientific insight,
> we are somehow failing in the fundamental role
> that we should be fulfilling—enabling the earth and
> the universe entire to reflect on and to celebrate
> themselves, and the deep mysteries they bear
> within them, in a special mode of conscious self-
> awareness. . . . In the curvature of the universe,
> things are bonded together in such a way that
> everything has a shared existence and a common
> destiny. . . . It has been consistently presented in
> mythic form. From earliest times this vast em-
> brace bonding all things together in the magnifi-

cence of the created order has been understood
in the maternal metaphor, the Great Mother.[14]

People can call it what they want, but sooner or later they will see
the truth that all religions lead to the same truth—that god is
found in the interconnected sum total of all things in the cosmos.*
This means the Christian-based social structure of America must
be transformed into one that is based on the new theology:

What began as a scattered revolt against
Western secularism and traditional Christianity
has matured into an elaborate and full-orbed
assault on Western culture. But it is more than
an assault; it is a proposal for conquest.
New Age advocates believe that the failure
of secular humanism** and the rejection
of Christian theism has left us with a crisis:
the megatonnage of nuclear terror threatens to
vaporize us; [our pollution threatens to destroy
us;] our politics are pathetic; our spirituality is
run-down and close to expiration; our economics
border on world collapse. Transformation is
required, and there is no going back.[15]

Before finally seeing the fraud and deception of these mystic
beliefs, Brooke had been the highest Western disciple under Sai
Baba, the most revered superguru in India—with 20 million de-
vout followers. Whereas earlier conservationists learned about
psychic power manifested in occult spiritualism and concepts of
reincarnation,[16] Brooke lived it:

* This is called *syncretism*; all religions lead to the one, true religion.

** Secular humanism is the religious belief or philosophy that upholds the su-
premacy of human beings rather than God or any abstract or supernatural
being or system. Man has evolved and is the measure of all things. Although
most people are not fully aware of the tenets of secular humanism, it has pre-
dominated in America since the 1940s and 1950s.

We were persuaded that total awareness was
possible: about nature, the cosmos, and man—
from the spiritual to the mundane. . . .
[We wanted] command of occult realities that only
a fraction of our world even knew about.
In short, I and my contemporaries believed
in the reality of cosmic consciousness, or superconsciousness, or enlightenment. . . .
Superconsciousness, I believed, could more than
encompass the range of intellectual knowledge.
. . . the superconscious one was able to know
all . . . things with an infinite depth after having
attained full awareness of "the Self."

. . . It was already plain to see that the elevator
shaft of consciousness went from the lower
floors of the animal world to the incredible levels
of man's greatest achievements. If this shaft continued to the vast levels of angels, higher beings,
and beyond, then by speculative extension the
mystics were right and human potential did not
stop until it arrived right at the seat of godhood.
. . . Consciousness had stages as well. . . .

The entirety of racial knowledge was welded within
every cell. Within [my] mind lay the vast
collective unconscious containing every[thing].
. . . Then one day, [while on drugs] I experienced it
all—in a glimpse, a split second in eternity. . . . I
saw a doorway into a new universe. It was a pinpoint of light. . . . At the barrier of the pinpoint
of light—*I entered the eternal present. All thirteen billion brain cells within me seem to turn inside out. . . . Each cell recites one of my former
names, and I as a nation hear the thirteen billion
names of my subjects and former earthly identi-
ties on the wheel of reincarnation. Once I enter
the pinpoint of light, all ties with the world vanish.
I enter the Unborn.* [17] (Italics original)

Brooke lived the New Age counterculture movement. In his book *When the World Will Be As One*, he relates not only what the counterculture movement was all about, but also how the movement translates into the politics of today. The book is must reading for anyone who wants to understand the full implications of the movement.

In Theosophy, Zen Buddhism, Vedic Hinduism, and other Eastern religions, these ideas crystallized into New Age advocacy of supernatural powers of astral travel (out-of-body travel) and the ability to psychically control events. Brooke relates his own experience while involved in New Age mysticism:

Implicit in soul travel among the living—those who have bodies to leave—is soul travel among the dead, whose souls can freely range through other planes without need of bodies. Implied in this is soul travel from life to life, incarnation to incarnation, hence *reincarnation*. . . . And what is the reason for reincarnation? The answer is central to Eastern thought itself. We reincarnate up the evolutionary ladder for the purpose of ultimate perfection and self-realization into pure consciousness. When consciousness realizes its identity with ultimate consciousness, and the mystery of being is over, then the separate ego-self ceases to exist. Then the "true self" unites with the ocean of being, the godhead. . . .

As our past records of karma* are worked away, we evolve spiritually and climb the ladder of being. We are a composite of millions of former characters in the cosmic play.[18] It is the ultimate expression of **the divinity within us**. Out of our **evolutionary consciousness** will emerge the end of our illusion of separateness. Our own divinity is a key reason for **global unity**.

* *Karma* refers to the "debt" accumulated against a soul as a result of good or bad actions committed during one's life (or lives). If good, the reincarnation will be at a higher evolutionary plane. If bad, the reincarnation will be at a lower evolutionary plane.

We are unified anyway—divinely [as god]. [19]
(Italics original, bold italics added)

Such theosophically based thinking is still alien to the vast majority of Americans. A 1991 Gallup poll found that only 15 percent of Americans believe in reincarnation and spirit mediums. Yet, this modern-day version of gnosticism* is but a variation of the thread of gnostic thinking through mystic time. Taking many forms throughout history, the New Age version focuses on the notion that "I" have an "evolved consciousness"; therefore, "I am god!" Once a person takes this view, can the belief that he has absolute truth be far behind? Not likely. In fact, the possibility of obtaining absolute truth is a key tenet of theosophical belief:

The goal of all work done in the [groups of disciples] of any of the Masters** is *Truth*— on all levels and at all times. As disciples learn the . . . truth into which they are being steadily integrated, their esoteric usefulness and effective service will—as a group—**know what has to be done** and find eventually that it is done. [20]
(Italics original, bold italics added)

The theology of Theosophy and its influence on American and global events is discussed in greater detail in chapter 11. But suffice it to say the theology that one already *has* the truth can only lead to mistrust and denial of traditional science and rational thinking. Alston Chase, who was also involved in the environmental

---

* *Gnosticism* comes from the Greek root word *gnosis* = knowledge. Two extremes of gnosticism have prevailed through history. One form attempts to avoid contamination by material things by rejecting them; the other rejects traditional morality as some sort of conspiracy to restrict freedom. Both forms are seen in the New Age and Environmental Movements, sometimes in the same person.

** A Master is one who has evolved far enough, in his or her consciousness to be able to communicate with the life force of the cosmos, and therefore, truth. Masters are responsible for guiding humanity into the Aquarian Age. They can take the form of advanced extraterrestrial beings who purpose to save the earth from itself. The latter is a common belief for those who do not want to use spiritual expressions.

movement for a time, noted that "these environmentalists not only rejected modern science but also became suspicious of traditional canons of reason. It was, they suggested, only by mystical communion with nature that we truly understand her."[21]

David Brower, president of the Sierra Club until 1971 and founder of the Friends of the Earth, believes "that figures in themselves are merely indices. What matters is that they *feel* right." Brower bases reality on feelings. He distrusts experts and is also suspicious of education.[22] Not surprisingly, he is an advocate of Zen Buddhism,[23] which in turn is one of the foundations for theosophical belief.

According to theosophical thought, traditional science hinders the path to self-realization by producing an "over-development of the analytical mind," which must be subverted.[24] The material world "is an illusion,"[25] whereas reality is in the mind of higher consciousness.[26] Feelings *are* truth to mystic environmental leaders. Therefore, if they *feel* that Alar, acid rain, global warming, ozone depletion, and other catastrophes are destroying the earth, then they are. Any science that would suggest otherwise is incorrect. In fact, Brian Swimme and Thomas Berry note in the 1993 winter edition of *Amicus Journal* that traditional science cannot be used to save the earth. They say, "[Saving the earth] will require that we . . . return to the mythic origins of the scientific venture. . . . [This will] bring us deep into the realm of imaginative vision where we feel the *scientist must participate to some extent in shamanic* powers* . . ."[27] (italics added).

The *Amicus Journal* is published by the National Resources Defense Council (NRDC). It was the NRDC, as you recall, that perpetrated the Alar scare. If it was shamanic powers that revealed to leadership within the NRDC that Alar was poisoning America's children, then we have truly entered the twilight zone. Is this why Bill Ellen went to prison? Are we to depend upon shamans to provide medical science, agricultural science, atmospheric science, and the other sciences? Apparently so. Theosophy demands that: "Doctors should endeavor to break loose from the modern and traditional ideas of healing, . . . [and turn] to intermediaries between the plane of spiritual energy and the patient."[28] Is America ready to turn away from medical science and depend on what used to be known as witchcraft and shamanism for curing their medical

---

* *Shamanism* is the religious belief of northern Asia that good and evil spirits pervade the world and can be summoned through inspired priests acting as mediums.

ills? Could shamanism have found the cure for polio? For tuberculosis, smallpox, and other major killers?

Where is environmentalism taking us?

THE ROAD TO NIHILISM

Tangled circular reasoning often prevails in environmental logic. For the mystic environmental leader, nature is part of god—is god—through a web of mysterious fluxes with cosmic interconnections. According to theosophical doctrine "the exact extent, depth, breadth, and length of the mysteries of Nature are to be found only in Eastern esoteric sciences. So vast and so profound are these that hardly a few, a very few of the highest Initiates—those *whose very existence is known but to a small number of Adapts*—are capable of assimilating the knowledge"[29] (italics original). Consequently, science is seen as unable either to measure nature or manage her. Therefore, traditional science is seen as meaningless. Truth is in *feelings*. It is then but a short step to deceit without guilt. If traditional science is wrong, then there is no deceit in distorting science to say what they "know" to be the truth. After all, professes William Thompson, founder of the New Age Lindisfarne Association (an esoteric environmental think tank), "science fact is really a disguised form of science fiction."[30]

Continuing this circular reasoning, if nature is god, nature itself must be sacred and "all knowing." Thus, *nature knows best.* If nature knows best, then anything that man does must be less than best. That leaves only one conclusion. Traditional science is not only wrong, but the sanctity of nature must be protected from science. Chase explains: "If all nature was sacred, environmentalists said in effect, then nothing should be disturbed. The prescription for preservation was benign neglect. Nature must be protected from the depredations of man. . . . Because everything was sacred, believers in this ethic said, *nothing should be touched*"[31] (italics added).

The downward spiral into nihilistic* antihumanism doesn't stop here. Like a giant whirlpool, this belief system continues to suck its victims deeper and deeper into this dead sea of antihumanism. For out of these religious beliefs came the philosophical concept of *biocentrism*.

---

* *Nihilism* is the belief that everything is meaningless and absurd. It is the belief that conditions in the social organization are so bad as to make destruction desirable for its own sake, independent of any constructive program or possibility.

BIOCENTRISM

Biocentric* reasoning goes like this. If everything is god, then everything is equal. And, if everything is equal, then everything has equal, intrinsic value. Hence, mankind must change from looking at the world from a "man-centered" point of view (called anthropocentric), to looking at it from a "life-centered" perspective. This life-centered point of view is termed *biocentrism*. Biocentrism is rapidly becoming a favorite word of environmental leadership to express their belief that everything in nature has "equal intrinsic value." But it doesn't stop here. If everything has "equal intrinsic value" and "nature knows best," then the fragile balance of biodiversity "she" has created is threatened every time man does anything to disturb it.

Surprisingly, an atheistic belief can arrive at the same biocentric conclusion. If there is no god, then everything on earth is here by simple evolutionary chance. But does that make man better or not? If a person believes being at the top of the evolutionary heap makes him superior to the rest of nature, then he also may believe that he can use and abuse nature as he sees fit.

On the other hand, if an atheist believes that man is not "better" just because he is at the top of the evolutionary heap, then man can be no better than an amoeba. In fact, many activists within the environmental movement have come from an atheistic background. Regardless of the philosophical source, however, biocentric reasoning inevitably leads to a dead future for mankind.

The problem is this. If everything is equal because it is equally god, then man has no more value than a tree, rock, water, mouse, mosquito, rattlesnake, or bubonic plague virus. How then can one "part" of god own or destroy another "part" of god? Indeed, how can one "part" of god even manage another? The belief that Native Americans were pure and gentle and lived in harmony with the land upon which they lived is pervasive within environmental leadership. The implementation of the European concept of property rights as the settlers moved west was evil in the eyes of this leadership:

Stripped of their myths and stories, the lands
sacred to the native peoples were no longer a gift

---

* *Biocentrism*—bio = life, centrism = centered.

of the Great Spirit to be held in common; they
became real estate. The conquered territory
was divided up and bought and sold as private
property. . . . But whereas the old [ways] were
animistic, related to the spirit of the place, the
new one symbolized the imposition of a rational
order upon the untamed wilderness and its division into private property. . . . The results
are disastrous. The desecration of the world
now seems appallingly destructive. We need
to recover a sense of the sacred.[32]

To those placing their faith in the belief that nature is god, dividing god into "owned property" is an act of desecration that has led to the "ecological destruction" we are now witnessing. This belief in the sacred land sets up an unsolvable conflict with the Western concept of natural resource management and the ownership of property. How can man manage or own trees, water, soil, and rocks when he has no more *value* than those things he claims to own? He can't—at least not by using biocentric reasoning. Therefore, our laws must be "transformed" to be more compatible with nature's "rights." Thus, this philosophy helps explain the bitter attack by environmental leadership on property rights and the Fifth Amendment to the Constitution. Property ownership is a literal heresy to god/nature biocentric beliefs.

Biocentrism is like a "black hole," sucking all reason into the blackness of nihilism. Ultimately there can be no compromise for a biocentrist.[33] After all, if man has no more value than anything else in nature, then our human population is grossly out of balance with nature. With a population of about 5.5 billion people, mere human survival brutally violates the "rights" of other parts of nature.

Although many environmental leaders say they want to find solutions, they always find themselves in this biocentric trap. Even when they are successful in getting their laws passed—as they usually are—it never seems to be "enough." It can't be enough.

As long as the law or regulation continues to permit man to benefit at the expense of nature, no law, no regulation will ever be "enough." What has resulted is a war of attrition on proven conservation practices and the Fifth Amendment to the Constitution. In summary, there is no such thing as compromise to environmental leaders who hold to a biocentric philosophy. Biocentrism, by its very definition, permits no pro-human compromise.

Ironically, the biocentric blindness that causes these believers to glorify native cultures for their supposed harmonious life with the Great Mother Earth also has blinded them to the reality that those cultures never existed. William M. Denevan, cultural ecologist at the University of Wisconsin, Madison, found in an exhaustive study of early American cultures, that these early cultures caused more environmental destruction than the European-centered culture that followed them:

By 1492 Indian activity throughout the Americas had modified forest extent and composition, created and expanded grasslands, and [changed the landscape through] countless artificial earthworks. Agricultural fields were common, as were houses and towns and roads and trails. All of these had local impacts on soil, microclimate, hydrology and wildlife."[34]

In some cases these pre-Columbian Indians altered the environment more than the Europeans and their descendants have in the 500 years since Columbus landed.

Sarah O'Hara, of the University of Sheffield, and two British colleagues were able to determine through sediment sampling of Lake Pátzcuaro west of Mexico City that the Mayan civilization 3,900 and 3,250 years ago resulted in tremendous amounts of erosion. But that paled in significance to the damage resulting during the post-Mayan culture dominant from about 1,200 years ago until the Spanish arrived. Dr. O'Hara estimated that during that period the annual erosion topped eighty-five tons per acre per year! This compares to about two-and-a-half tons per acre per year today. Even highly erodible soils presently lose less than ten tons per acre per year.[35] Dr. O'Hara concluded that this finding "explodes the myth that the indigenous peoples of central Mexico lived in harmony with the environment and didn't practice environmentally damaging agriculture."[36]

DEEP ECOLOGY AND ANIMAL RIGHTS

In spite of these revelations, the biocentric myth continues unabated—with ever increasing malice. Biocentric beliefs have divided environmental activism into two camps, New Age (Shallow Ecology), and Deep Ecology. The New Age, or Shallow Ecology, approach holds that although man is of no greater "value" than other aspects of nature, humans have attained a higher level of conscious evolution. Once a person finally sees this "light of truth" through full "self-realization" he is supposedly able to become part of nature and work harmoniously with her. Through the "proper" use of technology and mystic communion with nature, man becomes a benevolent caretaker of nature. At least that is how the theory goes.

These beliefs appear to dominate the thinking of the vast majority of environmental leadership. They also disgust the self-appointed Deep Ecologists. To them New Age ecology is nothing more than man-centered effort for nature abuse "in a priestly garb."[37] New Age ecologists look to their Aquarian future, their New Age. Deep Ecologists look to the past.[38]

To Deep Ecologists, mankind is a type of cancer to the earth. Deep Ecologists may start with a call for greater "humility" towards nature, but sooner or later believers in biocentrism must come to the nihilistic conclusion that there really is no hope. By definition, in biocentrism there is simply no other choice. David Graber, Research Biologist with the National Park Service, expresses these beliefs in graphic terms:

> Human happiness, and certainly human fecundity, are not as important as a wild and healthy planet. I know social scientists who remind me that people are part of nature, but that isn't true. Somewhere along the line—at about a million years ago, maybe half that—we quit the contract and became a cancer. We have become a plague upon ourselves and upon the Earth. . . . Until such time as Homo Sapiens should decide to rejoin nature, some of us can only hope for the right virus to come along.[39]

Humans are a cancer to the earth—even those native cultures of a few thousand years ago. The only solution is to eliminate man! Or at least to reduce man's population to somewhere around 500 million from the 5.5 billion that exist today. The more radical groups such as Earth First!, Sea Shepherd, and Greenpeace, ascribe to these beliefs, which helps to explain their extreme militancy. David Foreman, founder of Earth First!, puts this rather succinctly: "We are a *biocentric warrior society*. . . . Forget about career, about family, about VCRs and power boats and get out and fight!"[40] (italics added).

Deep Ecologists call for a "greater humility towards nature." What they really want is for man to forgo all technology and go back to a hunter-gatherer society. They don't particularly care how: "Our culture finds it all but impossible to face up to the terrible fact that a large percentage of humanity in both the undeveloped and developed world may be subject to this kind of *ecological redundancy*. This is understandable: *mass starvation* is not a pleasant thought."[41] "*Individual suffering*—animal or human—[is] *less important* than the suffering of species, ecosystems, the planet"[42] (italics added). Likewise, Foreman's loyalty is to nature: "My loyalty is to the grizzly, the snail darter, the plankton. It's to the rocks and the streams."[43]

Foreman claims that it's not Earth First's intention that people get hurt. But he adds, "If someone gets hurt in the heat of the battle to defend the planet—well, so be it."[44] The quickest way to reduce the human population is to let nature take its course: "The worst thing we could do in Ethiopia [to eliminate starvation] is to give aid—the best thing would be to just let nature seek its own balance, to let the people there just starve."[45] As shall be discussed later in the book, this biocentric militancy is at the heart of a new ecological science called conservation biology.

There is some good news, however. David Foreman was sent to prison for committing ecotage (same as sabotage, except it's done to "save" nature). As a consequence, most deep ecologists are advocating voluntary efforts to reduce the earth's human population. Most encouraging, however, is that so far there have been no reports of *any* deep ecologists offering themselves as a sacrifice upon the altar of nature.

Another sometimes violent repercussion from biocentric absolutism is the animal rights movement. Such absolute biocentric views maintain that animals have equal values and rights, and therefore should not be domesticated, used for medical research, or eaten. Further, "animals have the 'inherent right' to survive as *their* nature demands," without interference from man.[46] Man is the only entity that recognizes moral boundaries. Hence, man should sacrifice his interests to entities that can't. Ultimately, it means that only animals have rights. Ironically, man is not able to follow his "nature" if that means eating meat, but animals must not have their rights restricted. Since nature consists entirely of animals, their food, and their habitats, to recognize "animal rights" man must logically "cede to them the *entire planet.*"[47]

Most environmental leaders are not as extreme as David Foreman and other deep ecologists. But that is the nature of belief systems. The expression of any belief, be it Christianity, Communism, Islam, or capitalism is highly variable, but centers on the key tenets of the belief. Biocentrism is a nature-based religion centered on those tenets discussed above. But it must be remembered that biocentrism is a slippery one-way street, the dead-end of which is represented by the extreme radical views of deep ecologists such as Foreman. A study of the demands being made by the more "moderate" environmental leaders and bureaucrats clearly reveals that they too are slipping headlong down this same treacherous road.

Modern environmental leaders have taken the giant step beyond the "looking glass" into the never-never land of fantasy and the absurd. Yet, even though they represent only a very small fraction of those of us who are concerned about our environment,[48] they have been successful in redefining environmental morality in America around their nature religion. Even some of those in America who follow one of the Eastern beliefs would not necessarily agree with what environmental leadership is doing if they understood it. Just who are these environmental leaders, and how have they made such a huge impact on America? And how have they managed to keep this "new" yet very old religion so quiet? Read on.

Outfits like Greenpeace attack big business as being faceless and responsible to no one. In fact, that description better fits Greenpeace than it does modern corporations that are regulated, patrolled and heavily taxed by governments, reported on by an adversarial press and carefully watched by their own shareholders. There's little accountability for outfits like Greenpeace. The media treat them with kid gloves.

Leslie Spenser, et al.
Forbes
November 11, 1991, 176

In a biocentric approach, the rights of nature are defended first and foremost on the grounds of the intrinsic value of animals, plants, rivers, mountains, and ecosystems rather than simply on the basis of their utilitarian value or benefit to humans. . . . To be religiously concerned about a set of moral values is to have faith in those values, to trust them as true guides to enduring well-being and peace.

Steven C. Rockefeller
"Faith and Community in an Ecological Age,"
in *Spirit and Nature*, 143–44

5

THE NATURE OF ENVIRONMENTAL LEADERSHIP

BIOCENTRISM IN ACTION

Bud McCrary is an environmental advocate who practices what he believes. He is also a victim of nature-worship and biocentric thinking by mainline environmental leadership.

McCrary owns Big Creek Lumber Company, which operates in that part of the world where environmental attention has been spotlighted—spotted owl country in northern California. He has a policy of careful selection harvesting. The Sierra Club, the Natural Resources Defense Council, and the Nature Conservancy have all cited his operation as exemplary of logging that doesn't trash the forest. In fact, the Sierra Club recommended him in 1990 for an award recognizing his forest conservation efforts.[1]

McCrary bought a 4,000-acre tract of redwood and fir forest in the Santa Cruz Mountains above Butano Creek in 1991. He planned to harvest only four "old-growth" trees per acre. But old is relative. They looked old because they were so big and healthy. In fact, almost all of the area was second growth forest—originating after heavy cutting in the 1950s. The trees in the tract to be harvested were only forty to sixty years old. The 378 acres of the parcel's true old-growth was to be placed in a conservation area— off-limits to the saw. The area had no spotted owls.

There was an initial collective sigh of relief from environmental leadership that the Butano would not be clear-cut of all trees. But one by one the Nature Conservancy, Natural Resources Defense Council, Sierra Club, National Audubon Society, Greenpeace, and Earth First! turned on McCrary. One by one they *all* joined the effort to stop him from harvesting *any* trees. Old is relative to one's values, and their values were biocentric. Court injunctions based in what is called conservation biology were sought.

Earth First! even resorted to sabotage by draining transmission fluid from Big Creek tractors in attempts to slow his crews. A coalition of radical groups, including Earth First! and Greenpeace, handcuffed and chained themselves to logging equipment. They even put their people on platforms in the trees to prevent the sawyers from felling the trees. They said, "We will defend the trees of Butano any way we can." Their intent? "To put Big Creek out of business in the Butano." Chances are that if you read about McCrary in one of the environmental magazines, he was painted as a villain who was devastating the tract with "more" exploitation.

Shocked at the viciousness of the attack on him, McCrary asked, "Is it immoral to cut down an old tree?" Daniel Barron of the Greenpeace/Earth First! coalition responded, *"Absolutely."* But why? These weren't trees of the sacred "ancient forest." Instead, Barron's reply represents evolving biocentric reasoning. Now the reason wasn't to save the ancient forest, but rather to save every tree of any age—under the guise of supposed abuse suffered during the earlier harvesting.

Suddenly, these forests now require several hundred years to permit them to recover their "natural processes." Typically, a forest of trees of this age supports 100 to 200 trees per acre. Taking 4 trees out per acre is about the same as plucking four hairs out of your eyebrows. To say that this will damage these ecosystems is absurd. But a reader back in Boston doesn't know that. All he knows is what he is told. And he is *not* told that these trees have to be big and healthy if they are big enough to be worth harvesting in fifty years—especially when it is economically viable to harvest only 4 trees per acre!

This is the reality of biocentrism in action. Nothing is ever enough. No matter how hard McCrary tried to find middle ground through collaboration with New Age environmental leaders, it was never enough. What was once proclaimed "good" by these leaders is now "bad"—in fact, downright evil. But McCrary is fortunate. So far he is only out the 8 million dollars he paid for the Butano tract—he didn't go to prison as Bill Ellen and others did. Meanwhile, expensive equipment lies idle and people are not working—all to the detriment of the local communities and economy. Why?

IMAGES

The stereotypic image Americans hold of an environmental leader is of a person willing to sacrifice for principles in a valiant effort to save the environment from destruction at the hands of the greedy multinational corporations. Supposedly outspent and outgunned by the corporations, environmental leaders struggle to carry forward the battle with the meager donations and dues from thousands of Americans who send in their $25 faithfully each year. They are the people with purpose clearly defined and ethics beyond reproach. Truth must, therefore, be on their side.

This image of environmental leadership is a myth of almost unbelievable proportions—a myth perpetrated and maintained by a well-oiled and extremely well-financed propaganda machine of the environmental organizations themselves, along with a little help from the media. In fact, environmental leadership generally outmans, outspends, and outguns their opposition many times over. The level of funding at the fingertips of these leaders *has* to be huge for them to conduct their activities across such a broad front: the agricultural industry, the forest products and paper industry, the commercial fishing industry, the chemical industry, the automobile/trucking industry, the solid waste disposal industry (they don't want them to find solutions), and even the golf course industry. In fact, as Bill Ellen found out, they are against any individual who violates their nature-is-god, biocentric view of reality.

A MINORITY

Radical environmentalists make up a very small percentage of the millions of Americans who call themselves environmentalists. In fact, as noted in the last chapter, it is likely they make up less than about 5 percent of all of us who identify ourselves as environmentalists. But these leaders occupy positions of incredible power. With the exception of a few radical organizations at the state level, most members of the environmental leadership found in national organizations at the national level are high rollers and appear to be involved in the new nature religion.

The vast majority of man-on-the-street environmentalists are concerned about the environment because of what they have heard, read, or seen coming from the national headquarters of environmental organizations. As we have seen, most of this information is so distorted that none of it can be trusted to provide solid information upon which to form opinions about the severity or even the existence of a problem. Tragically, the vast majority of Americans who contribute $20 to $30 per year to one or more national organizations don't know what these leaders are *really* doing.

Americans have a strong sense of justice and fair play, which is often the reason they give dues to these organizations. The majority of supporters would be enraged by the duplicity of the leadership within these groups if they knew so much human suffering was resulting from the relentless drive to implement, by law, their biocentric and religious ideology.

We do have environmental problems. But most of these, if not all of them, are manageable problems with rational solutions that are far more effective and far less costly than those proposed by the environmental leadership. In this regard, many state level environmental groups, even some national organizations, do not appear to be involved in this nature-based religion that leads to biocentric nihilism. They want to find collaborative solutions as much as any American. They will disagree with those in industry and other segments in the business world over how to resolve problems. But this can be healthy and necessary, if both parties approach the table with a willingness to collaborate. Most state environmental leadership appears to generally accept the premise that we must use natural resources to meet the needs of American people. Although there is evidence this may be changing for the worse, the majority of state leaders are still willing to seek collaborative solutions to find that balance between using resources and protecting the environment.

This is not the case for leadership in the national organizations. The myth that national environmental leadership has the best interests of Americans at heart and is beyond reproach in its honesty and ethics is simply untrue. Yet it continues unchallenged.

POWER, MONEY, AND GREED

The first crack in the environmental myth strikes at the very heart of the environmental power base—money. Although environmental leadership maintains a facade of poverty, the opposite is the case. Berit Kjos, in her book *Under the Spell of Mother Earth*, reveals that the top twenty-five national environmental groups[2] have a membership of 12 million and a budget of nearly $600 million annually.[3] Many members belong to other organizations, so the actual total number of people supporting these groups is less than 12 million. Ron Arnold and Alan Gottlieb in their book *Trashing the Economy* report that in 1993 membership had increased to 15 million, and income of the top twenty-five environmental groups had increased to nearly $700 million.[4] A separate analysis by Rogelio Maduro and Ralf Schauerhammer of 21st Century Science Associates reveals total annual budgets of more than $830 million for the top thirty environmental organizations in 1990 and 1991.[5] The December 1992 issue of *Money Magazine* reported that environmental groups took in $2.5 *billion* annually. Where does all this money come from?

There are more than 3,000 so-called nonprofit environmental groups registered in the United States. Even if the rest of these had budgets averaging only $500,000 per year, this would represent total budgets of an additional $1.5 billion on top of that reported for the top twenty-five to thirty. That's over $2.3 billion! And the Nature Conservancy by itself owns land equivalent to the size of the state of Connecticut, worth nearly one billion dollars![6] But this is only once source of revenue. Private foundations such as the Rockefeller, Ford, MacArthur, Mott, and dozens more provide grants to these groups in the hundreds of millions of dollars each year.[7] Foundation money often doesn't even show up on the balance sheet because it's funneled through the parent environmental organization to a front group that carries out the dirty work at the local level.

Many of the national environmental organizations were initially created using private foundation, tax-free money. The Earthwatch Institute, which played a leading role in the Earth Summit, was created using tax-free money from the Rockefeller Foundation.

The Environmental Defense Fund (EDF) was created in 1969 by Ford and other foundations. It was the EDF that pressured the Environmental Protection Agency to ban DDT, which was later found to be completely safe. In 1986 the EDF helped to draft California's first in a series of sweeping environmental regulations (Proposition 65) that severely restricted the use of chemicals in industry and agriculture.[8] During the early 1990s companies began to flee California because of overrestrictive regulations, costing thousands of jobs and wreaking havoc on the state's economy.

The Natural Resources Defense Council (NRDC) was founded in 1970 "with a massive infusion of funds from the Ford Foundation."[9] It was the NRDC that perpetrated the Alar hoax of 1989 that scared Americans into boycotting apples and causing the bankruptcy of many apple growers.

In July 1990, the Rockefeller Foundation provided a $50 million grant to its Global Environmental Program and others for the purpose of creating an elite group of individuals globally to implement and enforce international environmental treaties.[10] This played a big role in the Earth Summit in June 1992. The power behind these foundations and their respective grants to these environmental groups is staggering. The in-kind services and power brokerage provided by these foundations can literally double or triple their dollar contributions.

These sources of income don't even include the thousands of small $50,000 to $100,000 grants provided by governmental agencies such as the Environmental Protection Agency, Department of Energy, Army Corps of Engineers, and others. Maduro and Schauerhammer of 21st Century Science Associates provide this sobering comment: "Officially the U.S. Government gives away more than $3 billion a year in grants to support environmental groups and projects. . . . While vaccinations for children, and other crucial projects have been virtually eliminated from the budget, billions are available for studies of how man is fouling the Earth."[11]

Most of us would agree that some of this money goes to top quality research that will help us to define real problems—if the results are not ignored as they have been in the past. But much of it also winds up in the pockets of environmental organizations to conduct "special studies" on the alleged catastrophic effects of global warming, ozone depletion, farming, clear-cutting, and so forth.

In a speech given in 1980 entitled "Government-Funded Activism: Hiding Behind the Public Interest," Peter Metzger stated that most give-aways that benefit environmental groups began in the Carter administration when he "appointed several hundred leading activists [from the counterculture] to key regulatory and policy-making positions."[12] One of the better known activists was William Reilly, who administered the EPA under President Bush.[13] We are reaping their personal and ideological goals today. It is perhaps not so ironic that Bill Ellen's own income tax helped send him to prison.

The exact funding level of environmental organizations cannot be calculated because of the many hidden and unaccountable sources. But a fair estimate would place it at more than $5 billion annually. Some estimates range as high as triple that amount, but that is unlikely. Even at $5 billion annually, funding exceeds the gross national product of thirty-nine Third World nations![14] The economic power provided by that massive level of funding is what enables these national environmental leaders to "wage the war" on so many fronts simultaneously.

Although many of the environmental activists on the "front lines" operate on a shoestring, that is not true of their national leaders. The directors and presidents of the bigger national organizations draw annual salaries in the six-figure range, as high as $400,000 per year. Fringe benefits add substantially to that. While many of the troops had to eke out a way to the Earth Summit in Rio de Janeiro in June 1992, these leaders went first-class.

The image that our national environmental leaders are selflessly sacrificing their lives to serve all Americans is a myth. And when you add up the total spent in lobbying, litigation, and education by these national groups, you will find that all the multinational corporations in America (including the American Farm Bureau) don't spend anywhere near that amount conducting the same activities. In fact most of them are outgunned by a ratio of five or ten to one. Perhaps that would be justified if the catastrophes environmental leaders proclaim were real, but they are not. That makes little difference to environmental leadership, however. After all, they "really know" the earth is being destroyed— Gaia has told them. Besides, nature comes before man, so any biocentric strategy to protect nature is acceptable.

HONESTY AND ETHICS

If the myth of poverty shatters like a house of distorted mirrors shot with truth, the myth of honesty and ethics begins to smell like a road kill on a hot afternoon. That odor drifted out in an October 1992 Conference sponsored by the Environmental Grantmakers Association (EGA). The EGA operates as an activity of the Rockefeller Family Fund and helps to coordinate "hundreds of millions of dollars to hundreds of environmentalist political action groups ranging from Audubon to the Wilderness Society, some of whom pass through money to local political action groups."[15] Among the 138 funding "angels" who are members of EGA are various Rockefeller foundations, Abell Foundation, ARCO Foundation, L. L.

Bean, Chevron Companies, Ford Foundation, Hearst Foundation, Kellogg Foundation, John Merck Fund, Packard Foundation, Pew Charitable Trusts, and Procter and Gamble Fund.[16]

The 1992 Annual Meeting of the EGA was held at the posh Rosario Resort in the San Juan Islands off the coast of Washington. Little did the organizers realize that tape recordings made during the various sessions would expose EGA's strategy to impose their earth worship on America through lies and deceit.[17]

BIOCENTRIC REALITIES

Canadian zoology professor, activist, author, and public TV producer David Suzuki launched the Environmental Grantmakers by giving the keynote address. He set the tone for the meeting by focusing on biocentric philosophies: "*Economics is a very . . . species chauvinistic idea. . . .* No other species on earth—and there may be 30 million of them—has had the nerve to put forth a concept called economics, in which one species, us, declares the right to put value on everything else on earth, in the living and nonliving world"[18] (italics added).

According to Suzuki, economics and human well-being are second to the well-being of all other species. This biocentric ideology clearly reveals the blatant insensitivity of environmental leadership to landowners who are denied their land and workers who are denied their jobs because of the "rights" of other species. Con Nugent, a moderator in one of the sessions, agreed with Suzuki. He revealed environmental leadership's true mission and strategy: "We start with the *premise* that the current use of the earth by humans is unsustainable and that the damage is done through billions of micro-economic behaviors. What we do in this business . . . is *stop, modify, or transform* . . . behaviors at any place along the economic spectrum from raw materials to the landfill, *through law or through culture*"[19] (italics added).

Note that the assumption earth is being destroyed is not open for discussion. It is already presumed. Through intimidation and ever more restrictive laws, environmental leaders are in effect willing to risk destroying the American economy and shatter perhaps millions of lives on a unproven and highly questionable premise. Yet this premise goes unchallenged while they demand that everyone else in America go through major upheavals to conform to their view of reality. And that view of reality is to stop or transform our economy rather than find solutions within our existing economic system.

In the session on Environment and Spirituality (one of twenty-six sessions), the moderator set the tone of the meeting by restating David Suzuki's call for reorganizing our society around different values that treat the earth as sacred. Ann Roberts, EGA member and president of the Fund of the Four Directions, identified why this is needed:

The native peoples . . . carried the spirituality of this land. My sense is that one of the reasons that their spirituality speaks so strongly to us is that it is an echo of our very ancient roots. . . . If we go far enough back we can find our druid ancestors, or our celtic ancestors, or whoever they were, and those people understood how to live with the land. They understood being in relation to the earth, they understood reverence and respect for the earth. Somehow between then and now . . . those things got lost and we got disconnected from our indigenous knowledge. . . .

Out of that longing to not lose what we didn't understand was born the conservation movement in this country. At the same time we were ravaging this land out of the european traditions. . . . The earth became . . . a commodity, something to market, something to sell, something that was a resource for the building of our society. Civilization was seen as that which was the product of the control of earth, and the growth of humankind became the way of destruction. . . . There is no way that we can remake our relationship to environment as long as we regard the earth as a commodity, as long as it is something we *possess*, as long as it is something we wish to *control to use for our own purposes*. It isn't until we can . . . understand that it is not necessary for us to be at war with our origins with the earth, that we will be able to have success in our desire to preserve and live in this land in harmony.

Not until mankind gives up the notion that we can own (possess) land and use the earth's resources for our own purposes will we cease our war with earth and be in harmony with her. This "earth savior" view of reality is the heartbeat of many modern environmental leaders. It is often not expressed verbally, but it does form the earth saviors' view of right and wrong that is then reflected in policy and action. Throughout all of the sessions, there seemed to be great care taken to identify the destruction of America's environment with European ideology. To this group of powerful people, anything the European foreigners did throughout our history was bad. Never mind that America has one of the best environmental and stewardship records in the world. Harmony must be reestablished between man and the earth mother at any cost.

PEOPLE AND JOBS

Restoring harmony between man and earth provided some unique problems for the earth saviors in the remaining sessions. How can they restore harmony and keep jobs? How do they show concern for *people* and do what must be done? Some of the dialogue recorded during the sessions shows a near schizophrenic paranoia to develop a public image of concern for people and jobs, while in the next breath demanding that no action is too severe to "save" a species, an ecosystem, or the environment in general. The underlying purpose of the forestry session, for instance, was to develop strategies to shut down "extractive industries" such as logging, mining, farming, and grazing. Yet Debra Callahan, Director of the Environmental Grass Roots Program of the W. Alton Jones Foundation, exhorted environmental leaders in the Wise Use session to find "case studies where environmental regulation has in fact created jobs. . . . Give it a human face, you know, the same thing politicians do. They always tell stories about, you know, Joe Mahoney and his community, you know, blah."[20]

During the meeting Callahan lamented, "How do you say to someone, no, I don't want you to have your job? . . . We're not the radicals. And that is probably the most critical message for us to take away from this: we don't want people to be jobless, and we don't believe it has to happen."[21] But it is happening, and the environmental leadership can't find a way to stop it. In fact, one participant candidly admitted that environmental leadership realizes this is a class issue:

> This is a class issue. There is no question
> about it. It is true that the environmental
> movement, has been, traditionally . . .
> an upper class, conservation, white movement.
> We have to face the fact. *It's true. They're not
> wrong that we are rich*, and you know, they are up
> against us. We are the enemy as long as we
> behave in that fashion.[22] (Italics added)

That admission is one of the key truths that Americans don't realize. A Roper poll in 1990 revealed the top 11 percent of adults highly involved in environmental support or activism are white and in the upper half of the middle-income class. In their exhaustive survey of environmental organizations and membership, Ron Arnold and Alan Gottlieb found that though 80 percent of all Americans claim they are environmentalists, only 12 to 15 million belong to and support an environmental group. Members of the Sierra Club, for instance, have median annual incomes of above $40,000, and a third earn above $50,000. The majority have achieved more than four years of university work, and 88 percent hold professional managerial jobs.[23]

Environmental leadership of national mainstream environmental groups is "lily-white, highly educated, overwhelmingly professional, and well versed in the ways of power. The environmental leadership is not only found heading up well known organizations such as the Sierra Club, Audubon Society, or National Wildlife Federation, those very same people are also found in government, on the boards of directors of top corporations, in high society, and wherever else they [want] to be. Many of them live in Washington and saunter back and forth between leadership positions in environmental public interest groups and government agencies that control environmental issues."[24]

Arnold and Gottlieb conclude from this that: "We are looking at the higher if not elite ranks of American society when we look at the organized environmental movement's [profile]: better educated people of ample money and liberal privilege who benefit from—and are totally oblivious to—all the productive resources enterprises they try to destroy."[25]

And they know it. During the EGA meeting, participants appeared desperate to find a plan to make themselves appear to be more concerned than they really are about people and the economy.[26] They apparently had little success.

In yet another session of the EGA meeting, Donald Ross, a top EGA head representing one of the Rockefeller groups, finally admitted the obvious, that it is futile for environmental leaders to even try to take a pro-job position. How are we, he asked, "who have no experience of ever running a business, managing a business, or starting a business, gonna go in and advise loggers who have no high school education and are making $40,000 a year to convert to some other kind of economy in the middle of the woods that is gonna produce $15,000 a year at best, and expect they're gonna embrace it."[27]

Picking up on this theme, another participant recommended that environmental leaders should continue to take a hard-line approach: "If it means shutting a plant down, or it means stopping a pulp mill in Sitka or what have you, *that's what has to happen. . . .* There are *local communities that are going to go over the abyss* in the short run. . . . *It's gonna be either a different kind of economy or it's not gonna be there*" (italics added).[28]

Asked if there might be some way to compensate the unemployed and displaced citizens in dying communities, Bill Devall of the IRA-HITI Foundation for Deep Ecology suggested, "I think it's quite possible. It means taxing, taking back the enormous profits that these corporations have reaped. . . . And that means in some cases *confiscating their assets*"[29] (italics added).

These leaders may be surprised when they find out that there are no enormous profits to raid. There never have been—huge profits are a myth in most cases. The vast majority of stock in most companies is held by mutual funds that invest money from retirement funds for workers in other companies and businesses. The money that is not paid to stockholders is put back into expansion, new plant equipment, and ongoing expenses such as conformance to an endless stream of new environmental regulations. To raid these "enormous profits" would, in reality, kill the golden goose that provides income for most Americans' retirement funds. Indeed, if regulatory restrictions continue to strangle our economy there might not even be any corporate assets left to raid; many companies will be in bankruptcy. So much for job concerns. The *New York Times Magazine* says, "The major environmental groups have become industries unto themselves, with well-paid professional staffs wielding extraordinary influence on Capitol Hill and in federal agencies."[30]

So much for honesty, integrity, and ethics that environmental leaders demand of all those who oppose them, yet don't apply to themselves. Strategies focused on lying and deceit are becoming the biocentric rule, not the exception. And now that they have destroyed the Northwest, they are setting their sights on the Northeast and private property rights.

NEW TARGETS, NEW STRATEGIES

How does all of this work? Attending the EGA conference was Chuck Clusen, a political strategist working for Laurence Rockefeller's American Conservation Association and a major funder for the EGA. It is interesting that the EGA is also controlled by the Rockefellers. It is no coincidence that the Rockefeller name keeps coming up. You will note in the balance of this book the major role the Rockefeller family has played in promoting and funding the agenda and implementation of local and global environmental strategies.

Clusen proclaimed at the EGA conference that he is working on the "development of a campaign plan [for the Northeast] that will probably go on for a decade."[31] How big? Merely a 50-million-acre block of mostly *private land* stretching 1,600 miles from northern Maine to northern Minnesota! It's called the Northern Woods Ecoregion. It originally started in 1990 as a 26-million-acre block called the Northern Forest that extended from northern Maine to Upstate New York.[32]

The EGA is providing funding for developing collaboration among all of the mainline environmental groups to provide a massive assault on private land ownership in the Northeast and lake states regions. These include the Sierra Club, National Audubon Society, Wilderness Society and National Wildlife Federation, and many others.[33] Clusen revealed that the "environmental community has come together in a very large coalition called the Northern Forest Alliance [comprising] twenty-eight organizations. It has the major national groups as well as the principal state groups of these four states. . . . I have been working with them the last year and a half to not only develop the political strategies, but also to facilitate their development of a campaign plan. . . . This campaign should go on at least for a decade."[34] EGA membership funding is helping do it.

Clusen continues his discussion of the original 26-million-acre "Northern Forest" effort by identifying the magnitude of the job ahead because the majority of the land is privately owned: "In many ways this is a much more complex situation [than we have ever tackled before] because of the private ownership in total of eighty percent of these 26 million acres. . . . There's no way we are going to buy it all. We all know of the great interest in the Forest Legacy Easement Program* as well as traditional acquisition, but these will only be part of the solution. There is a lot of thought and work being done on how to take a forest industry that is dying, and make it viable. How to make a working forest ecologically sound and sustainable that is becoming less and less economic."[35]

This is a brilliant strategy to destroy the industry and landowners that support hundreds of thousands of families across the region. It contains the perfect concepts to weaken and destroy property rights. Who could be against sustainability? And who could be on the side of companies that don't manage their lands in a sustainable manner? Never mind that none of these allegations are true and that hundreds of thousands of lives will be uprooted. Doesn't the end justify the means?

How will a "sustainable use" strategy work? First, by breaking down the difference between public and private lands using *biocentric* philosophy. The key, apparently, is to focus on the "terrible importance of thinking of private forests in the context of public forests as well. Species don't know the difference where the property line goes. . . . What we need [to emphasize] are large areas connected on other areas so we begin to look at the landscape the way plants and animals look at the landscape."[36] Although true in part—wildlife can't see boundary lines—eco-leaders believe that unless the ecosystems are "natural" and continuous, plants and animals will be threatened. If these plants and animals are threatened by discontinuities caused by property lines and different owner objectives, then the property lines should be eliminated and property rights abolished.

A "habitat needs" requirement blurs property rights, making it easier to convince Americans that nationalization of private property is necessary to save "endangered" species.[37] Secretary of the Interior Bruce Babbitt is already pushing for "an ecosystem approach" to protect species.[38] Who could be against sustainable

---

* The Forest Legacy Program is one where the state identifies priorities for recreation or protection of unique areas, and the federal government buys those rights from the landowner, while the landowner keeps certain rights. There is considerable interest in using this as a partial vehicle for collaborative solutions.

use and ecosystem protection? Yet, as John Fay, an Interior Department biologist, admitted: "You can't get three scientists in a room to agree on what an ecosystem is."[39] By elevating the endangered species issue from species to ecosystems, the need for surrogate species such as spotted owls is eliminated. Finding one surrogate at a time is inconvenient. Apparently, 26-million-acre chunks would be far more satisfying.

In 1990, Michael Kellet, who was then New England director of the Wilderness Society, told a Growth Management audience at Tufts University: "What we're really talking about here is sustainability, sustaining planetary life support systems and part of that is maintaining undisturbed ecosystems. I think it's likely this [26 million acres] will all end up, most of this will end up being public land, not by taking away, but that will probably be really the only alternative."[40] Although there were no "official" tape recordings of this meeting, the talks were nonetheless recorded and can be verified.[41]

Adding to Kellet's New Age comments, Sandra Lewis of the Tufts University Environmental Studies Program proclaimed, "We're going to have to think big because we've got some very big global things happening, some effects that people feel may change the way we live *very, very dramatically*. . . . I don't think it unreasonable to think about 26 million acres as a possible *reserve* and furthermore, I think it may be an absolute necessity to think in those terms for survival and for preservation of biodiversity"[42] (italics added).

Brock Evans, vice president of the National Audubon Society, said at the Tufts meeting: "I don't agree that we can't get it all [the 26 million acres] back. . . . I don't agree that it shouldn't all be in the public domain. In fact I think it all should be in the public domain. . . . You might say I'm a twenty-five year veteran of the forest wars in the northwest. It's the same kind of situation as here. We should get all of it."[43] He said the Northern Forest effort "will be an even bigger campaign in the next few years than the Ancient Forest Campaign we're just going through right now in the Pacific Northwest."[44]

Evans continues: "Be unreasonable. You can do it. Yesterday's heresy is today's common wisdom. It happens over and over again. . . . So I would say let's take it back, let's take it all back."[45]

Evans later told Nancy Anderson, Director of the New England Environmental Network, "The first time people see [our efforts], they're gonna say this is impossible . . . but we change those impossibilities, that's all. Our whole business is changing impossibility."[46] According to Ron Arnold, "[Evans] knows what he is talking about and he can do what he says. He has trashed more of the economy and nationalized more private property with his persistent political changing of impossibilities than some socialist dictators did with tanks and guns."[47]

Never mind that these forests accounted for nearly 10 percent of the state gross product of Maine, for instance, and nearly half of the state's high-paying jobs. Such mundane reasons apparently matter little to environmental leadership. In public hearing after public hearing, they decried how private landowners were destroying the forests, and that the government should take control before this pristine land was totally devastated.

Not surprisingly, proposals from the Northern Alliance had no plans for saving jobs and forests once private forestland was nationalized. Not so, clamored these eco-leaders. They had a plan that would bring economic prosperity to the region. The plan was revealed in a speech given by Jeffrey T. Olsen, Director of Ecosystem Management for the Wilderness Society in Washington, D.C., at the October 1992 Annual Meeting of the Society of American Foresters.

Speaking before an audience of hundreds of forest resource professionals, Olsen proclaimed that ridding the region of the timber companies would allow the forests to return to their pristine condition. The resulting forests would be so attractive to highly paid professionals such as lawyers, financial consultants, doctors, and bankers that they would want to immigrate and live there by the droves. These wealthy benefactors would spread their wealth around to the native populations. This, assured Olsen, would benefit the natives far more than the timber companies ever could.

There appear to be a few gaping holes in this plan, however. Once these rich professionals moved to the backwoods of the north country, who would be their clientele? The reason these professionals live and work in the cities today is because that is where their clientele also live and work. Even if somehow this did work, do Olsen and the Wilderness Society really believe residents within the Northern Forest would be willing to give up their independence and become serfs and servants for a new genteel class?

So much for Environmental Economics 101 and the "psychic-spiritual solutions." This might even be humorous if the Audubon and Wilderness Societies weren't so deadly serious.

Concerns run extremely high among people living in this region. President Clinton nominated George Frampton as Assistant to the Secretary of Interior over National Parks and the Fish and Wildlife Service that oversees the Endangered Species Act. Frampton was president of the Wilderness Society and has publicly announced his commitment to implementing the Northern Forest Wilderness Plan. While Frampton was president, the Wilderness Society published a 300-page report that *Forbes* magazine describes as a "search-and-destroy strategy guide aimed at what its authors regard as a dangerous 'antienvironmental backlash.'"[48]

Divide and Conquer

To weaken the backlash, EGA strategists plan to use sustainability divide-and-conquer-tactics. In this case Clusen chose to separate the big timber companies from the small landowners: "There is a real difference between the industrial forest lands, which are owned by the big companies like Champion or Bowater or whatever . . . where there are real arguments with some of those companies about forest practices such as clear-cutting, use of chemicals, over cutting, etc. . . . The non-industrial private landowners have managers who really do care about the kind of forestry they're doing and what they're doing to the land overall."[49]

By using a divide-and-conquer strategy, environmental leadership can play on people's emotional distaste for clear-cutting and the use of chemicals as "unsustainable." The removal of most trees in clear-cutting *looks* as if it must be destroying ecosystems. The use of chemicals seems harsh and so unnatural that it is easy to visualize their destroying the environment. But study after study has shown these practices are environmentally safe as long as they are done properly. This anti-corporation smokescreen is a key strategy that masks the human tragedy resulting from what is clearly becoming an attack on human civilization itself. Ironically, what they don't tell the American people is that recent research is beginning to show that these practices may even enhance biodiversity—if done correctly.

Ironically, it is the paper companies that fund most of the research on finding better ways to environmentally manage their lands. Even with billions of dollars at their disposal, the only research most environmental organizations do is designed to provide the answers they need in order to stop all progress and development. This is what pseudoscience is all about. It has been increasingly used since the DDT "catastrophe" in the late 1960s and early 1970s to advance the nature-based biocentric agenda of environmental leadership. Some traditional scientists still holding to the rigors of the peer-reviewed scientific method are now calling this *voodoo ecology*. Most environmental leaders are not interested in finding better management approaches or solutions to problems:

> Ruthlessness and religion are a combustible mixture, the more so when combined with absolutist certainty. Greenpeace gives research grants but doesn't fund research on [finding solutions]. . . . Why? Greenpeace says its role is to *prevent* pollution rather than cleaning it up. It seems that finding solutions to the safe disposal of such wastes undermines the *Greenpeace objective of eliminating the industrial processes that create the waste.*[50]

This is not true with all groups. Although the John Merck Foundation has given large sums of money to environmental leadership to attack landowner rights in the 26 million acres of Northern Forests, it has also funded some high quality research. The John Merck Fund has joined with industry and others to fund a huge, well-designed three-year research study in Maine. Both the Merck Fund and industry are really going out on a limb by cooperating on this study. The study is designed to determine how much present harvesting practices in Maine affect the diversity of declining Neotropical migratory songbirds. This type of cooperation is to be applauded as the only way to really find solutions to environmental problems. Imagine the solutions that could be found if the billions of dollars spent annually by environmental groups went to these kinds of efforts to find solutions rather than developing secret strategies to "preserve nature" by locking up millions of acres of land.

Tragically, such cooperation is the exception, not the rule. Typically, whatever it takes to impress or scare Americans into siding with environmental leadership, will be used—whether there is any truth to it or not. In some cases environmental organizations such as Greenpeace actually manufacture their horror stories.

Greenpeace was taken to court in 1983 because their propaganda film *Goodbye Joey* was faked by its producers using paid animal torturers.[51] Ron Arnold and Alan Gottlieb detail account after account of Greenpeace fraud, from San Diego tuna fishermen to Norwegian sealers. After losing a fraud case in Norway, Greenpeace membership collapsed. Norwegian Greenpeace chairman, Bjoern Oekern, resigned and confirmed Greenpeace's fund-raising tactics, calling Greenpeace "an ecofacist group."[52] It was this type of lying and deceit that finally caused Ron Arnold to leave his position as Director of the Sierra Club's Northwest District and begin opposing all such national environmental groups.

But this type of lying is nothing compared to the smear campaign now waged against anyone who would oppose their efforts. The campaign to take the 26 million acres of northern forest away from private landowners has begun. Woe be to any hapless victim who deliberately or accidentally gets in their way.

SNAKE OIL AND CHARACTER ASSASSINATION

The Environmental Grantmakers Association strategy began in the early 1990s. Former Republican Governor of Massachusetts Francis Hatch has played a key role in making sure that the strategy works, no matter who gets hurt in the process.

Hatch is past chairman of the Conservation Law Foundation, a well-heeled environmentalist law firm backed by elite, old money and the Boston Brahmins. Hatch presently sits on the Board of Directors of the Environmental-Grantmakers-Association-funded Maine Coast Heritage Trust. The Maine Coast Heritage Trust was founded by Peggy Rockefeller—wife of David Rockefeller—who has access through the EGA to the various Rockefeller Foundations' grant monies. Hatch is also chairman of the John Merck Fund, which has pumped a million and a half dollars into preservationist activities and university environmental activism. More than half a million dollars have gone into these New England issues alone.[53]

Hatch has been a busy man. He channeled $50,000 of Merck money into the Conservation Law Foundation to "improve" forest management practices in Maine's northwoods. His first efforts were to focus the Northern Forest Alliance of twenty-eight national and local environmental organizations into a coordinated effort blocking Bowater/Great Northern Paper's efforts to secure federal relicensing of critically important corporate hydropower facilities on dams the company has operated for eighty years. The alliance has in turn helped energize a smaller group of local environmental and sporting/recreation bodies to put pressure on Great Northern to employ sustainable land use practices on their 1.2 million forested acres.

On the surface that doesn't sound so bad. Everyone is for sustainable use of resources. But true to the Environmental Grantmakers' strategy outlined earlier, "sustainable land use" it turns out, is the extortion of land for being allowed to stay in business. The company must give up *all* development rights for the 1.2 million acres and permit the environmental organizations veto power over how the land is managed for timber.[54]

Why should there be a linkage at all between relicensing a dam and the management of a company's forestland? The link is purely arbitrary. It is the same thing as linking the renewal of your automobile registration to demands by the Sierra Club on how, or even *if*, you can mow and take care of your lawn. If the alliance can pull it off, it would be a quick, tidy way to secure 1.2 million acres of the 26-million-acre Northern Forest goal by not paying a dime for the land, and letting the company continue to pay the taxes! Most people would call this legal extortion.

As if this were not enough, environmental lobbyists are pressuring the White House to appoint environmentalists to the Federal Energy Regulation Commission to force such concessions nationwide.[55] This is not to say that such relicensing should be permitted without careful review for potential environmental damage. But as the Environmental Grantmakers strategy clearly reveals, environmental protection is not the real goal. The real goal is to obstruct all growth and development. Using the guise of defending the public's best interest, environmental leaders are instead a very narrowly focused special interest group intent on ultimately denying the very same public any use of these resources.

Hatch also funneled $50,000 from the Merck Fund back to the Conservation Law Foundation (CFL) in 1991 "to require the Dept. of Commerce to develop a plan for reversing the decline of Georges Bank [the fishing grounds off New England] food fisheries."[56] The "plan" would have put Maine lobstermen out of business in droves. Ongoing CFL legal activism continues to incite the wrath of Maine fishermen.

At the same time, the Maine Coast Heritage Trust played the good guy in an apparent good-cop–bad-cop strategy. Working with the fishermen, they encouraged the idea that all of the fish and scallop declines are caused by upriver paper mills and forest harvesting. At an April 1993 Penobscot Bay Conference held to discuss the declining fish and scallop resources, Maine Coast Heritage Trust representative and seminar moderator Jay Epsy announced that "not all property rights are private in nature. There are public rights too."[57] According to the report, members of the audience nodded their heads in agreement. Although there is truth in this statement, the key in the strategy is to directly attack the fishing industry through the Conservation Law Foundation while the Maine Coast Heritage Trust helps turn the anger of the fishermen towards upriver landowners and paper mills.

There are real problems to resolve in this issue, but all this finger pointing does is to help divide any opposition the environmental leaders might otherwise encounter—a classic divide-and-conquer tactic. Finger pointing also blurs the distinction between property rights and public rights. Meanwhile Hatch, Rockefeller, the Conservation Law Foundation, the Maine Coast Heritage Trust, and the Northern Forest Alliance continue their strategy of taking all rights away from everyone. If the Environmental Grantmakers strategy is being followed, the sporting and recreation clubs and organizations now supporting these environmental groups will likely wake up one morning and find themselves being attacked by their former allies.

Some groups and landowners are already waking up to the threat these environmental groups pose. Not surprisingly, environmental leadership is following the EGA strategy and attacking citizen groups. Hatch used his Conservation Law Foundation Newsletter in the winter of 1992 to savagely attack the growing number of land rights groups. He headlined them as "A Motley Crowd of Deceivers" whose claims of takeovers were "outlandish, untrue claims of imagined federal intervention [that] are spread regularly by property rights groups fronted by industry-funded public relations campaigns."[58]

Readers of his piece had no idea who these people really were, what they were opposing, or why. They were identified only as a greedy bunch who want to exploit the environment, whatever the damage. Such accusations were not made in ignorance. The Environmental Grantmakers Association conducted an exhaustive secret study of these wise use/land rights groups in 1991–92 that clearly showed such accusations to be false. Truth apparently is irrelevant, however. Anything to win.

Were there plans for federal acquisition? You bet. In a parallel effort, the U.S. National Park Service and the Maine State Planning Board were caught secretly promoting a National Natural Landmark. The Landmark was intended to encompass more than eighteen miles of winding, privately owned coastal land in Washington County, Maine.[59] During a 1986–88 Landmark study (preliminary plans dated back to 1979) the two agencies adamantly denied it to the local citizens. Incredible? Secret surveys are a common tactic employed by our National Park Service to build a case for justifying a takeover without foreknowledge by the local citizens. When the truth was finally forced to the surface in 1988, the citizens brought the duplicity to the attention of Maine Senators Mitchell and Cohen. In an excellent example of bipartisan cooperation, the two senators strongly requested the Secretary of Interior to investigate in 1989. After efforts by the Park Service to throw up a smoke screen, the entire National Landmark Program was put into indefinite moratorium, pending review. Had that not happened, another big chunk of land would have been locked up—again without the environmental groups having to pay a dime. We would have paid for it with our taxes. The local citizens would have paid for it with their homes—many of which had been in the family since the area was first settled.

While all this was going on, the Maine Coast Heritage Trust independently developed a fifty-page report in 1987 outlining the need for preserving the beauty of this same area. The report decried the fact that private activity (people's homes and businesses) *interfered with the "visitor experience" of tourists* on their way through Maine to the Roosevelt Campobello International Park in Canada![60] In 1989, the National Parks and Conservation Association (another preservationist environmental group) used the Maine Coast Heritage Trust report in its eight volume report to the National Park Service for two new national parks in Washington County. That effort is still in progress.

The Environmental Grantmakers Association's strategy has many heads. In yet still another flanking move is the National Park Service's effort to "study" New Hampshire's Pemigewasset River to "show" it qualifies as a wild and scenic river. Once designated, the river and lands within a one-quarter-mile corridor on either side of the river fall under Park Service authority. The act allows the National Park Service to force local zoning to conform with National Park System requirements within the corridor. If local property owners don't comply, the threat of condemnation through eminent domain is used. One of the apparent front groups requesting the designation is the Merrimack River Watershed Council, a regional preservationist group. It should be no surprise by now that the council is funded by the Merck Fund (an Environmental Grantmakers Association member) through the Appalachian Mountain Club and the National Park Service.[61]

Cozy deal? When asked about this conflict of interest the council responded, "[Although] we are also an independent advocate for the study, we have played down any role as advocate in order to maintain the *appearance* of objectivity"[62] (italics added). Needless to say, the landowners along the river were not reassured by such transparent reasoning. In addition to the National Park and EGA funding, the council receives money through the Appalachian Mountain Club from the Merck Fund to counteract the land rights groups in New Hampshire. In spite of the duplicity, Hatch proclaims these land rights groups to be "stirred up by a drumbeat of deliberate misinformation that had been systematically spread by a small cadre of non–New Englanders."[63]

The blatant distortion of the truth by such environmental leaders almost defies imagination. And this is only a small example of the Environmental Grantmakers' strategy in the Northern Forest. In turn, the Northern Forest example is but one in a multitude nationwide—against agriculture, mining, fisheries, power production, manufacturing, golf courses, solid waste disposal, and even family homes. The magnitude of the assault is staggering.

Americans generally believe what environmental leadership says without a single question. Yet citizens are being mauled by the ideological and power agenda of these biocentric leaders and bureaucrats throughout America.

GREED OR SOCIALISM?

Some of the extremism from national eco-leadership is motivated by greed, power, and self-preservation. William Dodd, a director at the San Francisco office of Craver, Mathews, Smith & Co. and a fund-raising consultant for Greenpeace U.S.A., the Sierra Club, and the Natural Resources Defense Council, admits, "You need a sense of urgency, and you need an enemy."[64] Self-preservation is a powerful basic instinct—especially when your salary is in the six-figure range. So is the intoxicating effect of the power these leaders wield. Former New Age leader Randell Baer makes these statements:

> [These leaders] know the things people want to
> hear and therefore pander to their egos and con-
> spire to strategies insuring their continuing
> patronage. . . . The most extreme ensnare
> willing submissives to exploit . . . human
> weaknesses of all types . . . and perform all
> manner of other grossly manipulative and cut-
> throat practices to further their own vested
> interests. . . . To one degree or another, these
> leaders know that they have sold their souls in re-
> turn for the fame, power and money they enjoy."[65]

In addition, many environmental organizations support a "socialist, redistributionist society, which they claim is nature's proper steward and society's only hope."[66] There is considerable truth
to this, since a socialist, redistributionist philosophy is a key tenet
in theosophical theology.[67]

Greed, power, and a socialist agenda are certainly important
motivators in energizing the environmental leadership. But motivators cannot explain, by themselves, the incredible insensitivity
to human need and suffering that characterizes many environmental leaders and their agenda. Remember Willis Harman, Director of the Center for the Study of Social Policy at the Stanford
Research Institute, who spoke about noetic science to a group of
key leaders in the Jackson Hole meeting (See chapter 4)? This is
what he says about socialist versus religious agenda of national
environmental leaders:

> The Greens parties are sometimes misidentified
> as being on the left. "Left" is usually associated
> with tendency toward the welfare state, public
> ownership of critical industrial and service
> organizations, and strong emphases on
> egalitarian and human rights issues. Although
> Green politics is concerned with human rights and
> social responsibility, its primary focus is quite
> different from that of the classical Left.

What is sought is a balance of these values with a more holistic view, and with the feminine nurturing, cherishing, cooperative, conserving values. There is an emphasis on self-realization, transcendent meaning, and inner growth leading to wisdom and compassion. That there is a dimension of spirituality to Green politics seems unquestionable, yet there is a reluctance to identify the movement as such in so many words. The concept of "deep ecology" is one of the adopted ways of talking about spirituality in terms that are inoffensive to those who, for various reasons, eschew religious language. "Deep ecology" goes beyond the scientific frame-work to a subtle awareness of the oneness of all life . . . to the irrepressibility of its tendencies toward evolution and transformation."[68]

The ecological and socialist agenda *are* intertwined. But, as noted by Harman, both are driven by a religious agenda that goes far beyond traditional science. It is based in pseudoscience.

Creation is that which has, is, and will inexorably draw humanity and the ancient forest into the crucible of cosmic interrelatedness where the forest will mirror for humanity the consciousness of its own evolving self.

> Chris Maser
> *Forest Primeval*
> Sierra Club Books, xv

Conservation biology can be traced back to Thoreau, Pinchot, and Leopold. . . . In the late 70s, many academics in the "pure" sciences wanted very much to contribute to conservation—to be "relevant." Altruism was part of it. Care for the planet, appropriate and harmonious lifestyles, and a healthy environment were the lenses that focused the energies of a generation. . . . [But] if conservation biology becomes isolated in the mental world of academia, it will be of little use.

> Michael Soulé
> *Conservation Biology*, 4–5

6

THE SCIENCE
OF MYSTICISM

SPECIES VERSUS HUMAN RIGHTS

As he walked through his vibrant and healthy groves of Douglas fir, Donald Walker shook his head. A testimony to good stewardship for three generations, he was being threatened with a lawsuit from an environmental group. What went wrong? Right had become wrong, and wrong right. He had passed through the looking glass where reality is turned on its head and reason is lost in fantasy.

You've heard of spotted owls versus jobs in the Pacific Northwest. Donald Walker, Jr., is one of those victims we read about in the papers who lost his job because of the spotted owl. At fifty-five years old, Walker learned that finding a new job is impossible; logging is all that he has known. Yet, he has something that he is very proud of. Walker's family has owned a 630-acre tree farm for three generations. Over the past sixty years they have carefully harvested the trees for income, carefully replanting the harvested area or converting some land to pasture to graze a few cattle. His conservation practices are exemplary.

In spite of this laudable witness of good stewardship, he and two hundred of his neighbors received a caustic four-page letter from the Forest Conservation Council, an environmental organization, threatening that if he "cut any more timber on [his] land it would sue [him] for violating the Endangered Species Act."[1] The lawyer who wrote the letter proclaimed that what Walker and his family had been doing on their *private land* for sixty years is no longer legal.

WHEN IS A SPECIES A SPECIES?

Everyone has heard of the spotted owl controversy. Just as nobody wants to destroy *real* wetlands, nobody wants to cause the extinction of a species if it can be reasonably avoided. But species *do* become extinct *naturally.* In fact, 95 percent of all species ever existing on earth have already become extinct—naturally! Man has been responsible for an extremely small percentage of these. Even so, most of us would agree that does not excuse the uncaring demise of more species. Polls show that is what most people think the spotted owl controversy is all about—a few jobs versus the extinction of a whole species. It isn't. Instead it is being used as a surrogate for another issue—maintaining the cathedral-like sanctity of the "Ancient Forest" by totally preventing harvesting of any type, at any time, in any place. In his Sierra Club book *Forest Primeval*, Chris Maser provides this explanation:

I have set out with you on a humble journey
through a forest of a thousand years so you may
see that the forest primeval represents our
spiritual and historical roots as human beings.
. . . Having spent the greater part of my life in
and around the ancient forest, my personal
myth—my metaphor of the Eternal Mystery—is
as inseparable from the life of an ancient
Douglas-fir tree as the tree's roots in the
earth are from its crown in the heavens.[2]

The spotted owl is actually found by the multiple thousands from Mexico to Canada. When the so-called crisis first started in the mid-1980s, only 600 owls were known to exist in Oregon and Washington. Environmental leaders supported a 1986 National Audubon Society report by "owl experts" that a minimum of 1,500 pairs of spotted owls in California, Oregon, and Washington would be sufficient to preserve the species.[3] By 1990 the government's owl recovery team advocated a plan to protect 2,320 breeding pairs of owls. By 1993, 3,500 such pairs had been found, along with at least 9,000 individual owls.[4] But these same leaders who would have been happy (so they said) with 1,500 pairs of owls now say 3,500 pairs are not enough. As this book goes to press, new evidence suggests that there may be 8,500 owls in northern California alone.

It is ironic that as research continues on this issue, the greatest concentration of spotted owls is found, not in "ancient forests," not even in "old-growth forests," but in cut-over forests on a privately owned tree farm in eastern Washington, where the oldest trees are forty years old. Some of the highest concentrations of owls are found on 400,000 acres of land owned by the Simpson Timber Company, where only 2 percent is old-growth forest.[5]

Once on the endangered list, a species is rarely taken off. That is, of course, unless the species becomes so numerous it becomes a public nuisance. One of the few species ever taken off of a threatened or endangered list was the alligator, and only when the prolific reptiles started snapping up the neighbors' cats and dogs and otherwise became yard fixtures. Even the bald eagle, the species that precipitated the passage of the Endangered Species Act in the first place, has fully recovered according to the Recovery Plan. Yet mention removing the eagle from the endangered list, and environmental leadership goes ballistic. This, of course, does not mean the eagle and others on the list should not be protected. To the contrary. But that protection can be achieved through other laws. To keep species on the threatened or endangered list provides excessive protection at the expense of society and our economy. Of course, that is exactly what environmental leaders want.

As a species, the spotted owl never was in any danger of becoming extinct. The real issue centered on a new science called conservation biology. Conservation biology maintains that species are not species at all, but a group of genetic populations in which the genes of one population are unique and not found in other populations. Therefore, the spotted owls that live in the old-growth Douglas fir forests of the Pacific Northwest are supposedly different genetically than those, say, in Southern Oregon, Northern California, or Canada. Taking advantage of a provision within the Endangered Species Act that states, "The term 'species' includes any subspecies of fish or wildlife or plants, and any *distinct population segment* of any species,"[6] environmental organizations have successfully pushed to have the species listed as threatened. This listing is not to protect the species—it is not in danger—but rather, a gene sub-population that *might* be unique, even though the possibility is only a *theory.*

This theory has in no way been proven. In fact, there is an ongoing controversy within the community of genetic scientists whether the genetic expressions within one population are totally absent within another. There is strong evidence that the potential for *all* genetic expressions remain within populations even where they do not dominate, and even when those expressions are intentionally discriminated against in experiments.[7]

What is not theory, however, is the *fact* that tens of thousands of people are losing their jobs over the spotted owl. The resulting stress is destroying people and families. Unemployment is forcing people to abandon their homes and lose their life savings as they move elsewhere to try to find work. As they leave, towns and communities are dying. One might argue this would all be justified if the spotted owl were truly in danger of becoming extinct. But it is not. This real destruction to the lives of people is instead the result of an unproven theory that a genetic sub-population of owls *may* be in danger.

The problems do not stop with those families and communities whose lives and existences depend on logging on public lands. We are led to believe that the Owl Recovery Plan is focused only on the 6.4 million acres of federally owned land, and that private ownership is excluded from its provisions.

Any landowner who believes that could be in for serious trouble. The Endangered Species Act contains a provision that makes any "taking" of a critical habitat for an endangered species a criminal act subject to federal prosecution and imprisonment. Therefore, if a pair of spotted owls is nesting on, or adjacent to, private land, that landowner may not use his or her own land or cut his or her own timber without risking a possible "take" of the owls' habitat. Nor can the hapless owner change any feature of his land. As Donald Walker, Jr., has found out, the landowner continues to own and pay taxes on the land, but, in fact, it becomes a *de facto* wilderness that he or she may be able to walk through and pay taxes on, but on which he or she can do little else.

Advised to cut his timber before a legal precedent could be set, Walker responds:

We don't want to. We're conservationists. This tree farm is our home, and the trees are part of our way of life. We work with nature to grow a crop the nation needs. The crop is wood. It puts food on our tables. In 26 years of married life, we have never been late on a bill we owed. The pressure on us now is hard to describe. My wife won't even read a newspaper anymore, because it's filled with stories about loggers losing everything, and preservationists filing more lawsuits.

Where will it all end? Do people count anymore? Do private property rights still have any meaning in America? Who will compensate us for our loss? . . . So far I haven't heard from anyone except the property tax collector.[8]

As of this writing at least one of his neighbors has been taken to court. The trial is pending.

To hear environmental leaders talk, these lives are a small price to pay for maintaining the biologically diverse web of life in our forests. David Brower, former executive director of the Sierra Club and founder of Friends of the Earth, puts this in graphic perspective: "Loggers losing their jobs because of spotted owl legislation is, in my eyes, no different than people being out of work after the furnaces of Dachau shut down."[9] But should extreme rhetoric and unproven theories take precedence when the destruction of lives and communities are the direct result? Apparently Americans don't think so. A 1992 poll for the *Wall Street Journal* and NBC News revealed more than 50 percent of Americans polled believe that people should have precedence over owls, and only 34 percent believed the owls should take precedence. Had this latter group known that the issue wasn't over the species of spotted owl, but rather populations, and that *each pair* of owls locked up $96 *million* of lost timber revenues,[10] chances are that the pro-owl percentage would have been even lower.

Needless to say, the spotted owl isn't the only "endangered species" threatening people. The U.S. Forest Service decided to achieve a 1 percent improvement in grizzly bear habitat by reducing the allowable timber harvest on the Kootenai National Forest in Northwestern Montana and Northern Idaho by 43 percent—with devastating economic consequences to local economies. In Georgia, an elderly couple decided to sell some timber from their land to pay for medical expenses. They were stopped because the Fish and Wildlife Service (which administers the Endangered Species Act) found seventeen trees with "possible" abandoned red cockaded woodpecker nests—even though the family had lived there for eighty years, and no one had ever seen a woodpecker on their property. The Stevens kangaroo rat even received exclusive rights to land worth $100 million.[11] And the list goes on. The average annual cost of protecting each species? A mere $2.6 million.

Senator Mark Hatfield, one of the original authors of the Endangered Species Act, still supports the original concept of the act, but he believes it now goes far beyond what Congress intended. Hatfield states: "I . . . know that it [the Endangered Species Act] has come to be an environmental law that favors preservation over conservation. There is no question that the act is being applied in a manner far beyond what any of us envisioned when we wrote it 20 years ago. . . . But today the act is being applied across entire states and regions, with the result that it now affects millions upon millions of acres of publicly and privately owned land, and many thousands of human beings. . . . The fact is that Congress always considered the human element as central to the success of the ESA. . . . The situation has gotten out of control."[12]

It's not that we don't need endangered species legislation; we do. But it has been redefined by environmental leaders, through changes in regulations and court rulings, to say that a species must be saved at any cost—in either dollars or human lives. The way the law is presently interpreted will cause the extinction of more species than it will ever save. Why? The answer is simple. It is based on punishing people, rather than encouraging them to protect endangered species. If a person is found guilty of disturbing the habitat of an endangered species, he or she can be heavily fined and even sent to prison—just like Bill Ellen. Now, suppose you find the last pair of endangered cockroaches (the Puerto Rican cave cockroach *is* on the ESA list!) in your $140,000 home. Nobody else knows about them but you. If you report them you will not be permitted to use your home because you *might* disturb their habitat (this is the *law*). You would still, however, get the privilege of paying your property taxes. Now, for a $2.75 can of

Raid, your problem is over. You would (most likely) do what everyone else would do . . . good-bye cockroaches. Another species bites the dust.

The Endangered Species Act has to be changed to become incentive-based to be effective. But that will be difficult. Environmental leadership, by applying tremendous political pressure to interpret regulations its way, and by using litigation to change interpretations of regulations it doesn't like, has become the fourth branch of government—with more power to affect the lives of all Americans than Congress itself.

CONSERVATION BIOLOGY

When is an ecosystem an ecosystem? When it can be systematically used to stop any use by man. Though facetious, this is how the concept is often used in environmental debates. Ecosystems are tough to define. They may be as small as a bathtub or as big as the earth.[13] They are so difficult to define that they make the perfect concept to weave into legislation or regulations that can then be interpreted any way desired in court.

Ecology is the contraction of two Greek words: *Oikos*, meaning house or household; *logos*, meaning the study of in order to obtain knowledge about. Ecology is therefore the study of the relations of life to its environment, or habitat. In 1935 Oxford botanist A. G. Tansely suggested treating organisms and the habitat in which they lived as a system—an *ecosystem*. It was a fantastic idea, for systems can be measured. Tansely's idea quickly caught on, and ecologists, engineers, biologists, chemists, physicists, and every breed of scientist started to measure energy fluxes and flows, water cycles, and carbohydrate balances in attempts to define this system and to boil it down to mathematical equations.

Recognizing the value of such a concept, Aldo Leopold took the idea into the realm of ethics in his *Sand County Almanac*, where he suggested that land was not merely soil and rocks, but a community of which man was merely a member. Leopold developed a land ethic that included man within the boundaries of an ecosystem. How, Leopold asked, can we be good biotic citizens unless we understand our relations with nature? As was the case for Lynn White's paper on the so-called brutality of Christianity, Aldo Leopold's concept of land ethics became the banner of this new breed of environmentalists in their search for a science to prove what they already knew. The concept of ecosystems provided the vehicle.

ORIGINS OF CONSERVATION BIOLOGY

The idea of an ecosystem as a closed entity for study by scientists began to fail in the 1960s and 1970s. Ecosystems were not closed at all, but interconnected with other ecosystems. Although scientists continued to set boundaries for ecosystems for study purposes, in effect there were no truly definable ecosystems —all the earth was an ecosystem. Such discoveries delighted the new environmentalists. Taking the boundary-less ecosystem a quantum leap further, they began to use the ecosystem concept to describe the intricate and fragile web of life of their mystic theosophical beliefs. Gushing forth from their version of ecosystems, an increasing crescendo of new theories was put forth by the IUCN and others. The IUCN (International Union for Conservation of Nature and Natural Resources) was created by the United Nations and the World Wildlife Fund to develop a science with "a new ethic, embracing plants and animals as well as people."[14] This new science would eventually be named conservation biology, a name destined to echo through the halls of politics and justice.

Ecosystems, according to these young environmentalists, functioned like a finely tuned organism that nature had taken millions of years to evolve to its present level of complexity. Diversity was the key to stability, and if man were to act ethically, he could not threaten the diversity of these ecosystems with his harsh treatment of nature. To clear-cut a forest and plant crops fragmented that diversity. Indeed, to clear-cut at all must fragment the continuity of ecosystems to the point where species diversity was threatened. If man is destroying ecosystems, man is destroying the earth!

These emerging environmentalists, now given the stature of scientists, formed the Society of Conservation Biology in 1985 and began to publish a journal called *Conservation Biology* in 1987 —with the financial assistance of none other than the Alton Jones Foundation of the Environmental Grantmakers Association.[15] In the first volume of this new journal, Michael Ellman Soulé, founder and president of the Society of Conservation Biology, outlined the reason for creating the society and its journal:

The society is a response by professionals, mostly biological and social scientists, managers and administrators to the biological diversity crisis

that will *reach a crescendo* in the first half of
twenty-first century. We assume implicitly that
we are in time, and by joining together with each
other and with other well-intentioned persons and
groups, that the *worst biological disaster in the
last 65 million years can be averted.* . . . We
assume implicitly that environmental wounds inflicted by *ignorant humans* and destructive technologies can be treated by *wiser humans* and by
wholesome technologies. [16] (Italics added)

The worst biological disaster in the last *65 million years?* Wounds
inflicted by *ignorant* humans? Being saved by *wiser* humans?
Now that's an elitist statement for a supposedly professional
science group. Does it sound as though maybe they already have
the truth? That all the science that preceded them was irrelevant?
Not only irrelevant, but created and applied by ignorant humans?
But this attack on modern science doesn't stop here. In the first
textbook on conservation biology, Soulé goes on to say:

In many situations conservation biology is a
crisis discipline. In crisis disciplines, in contrast
to "normal" science, it is sometimes imperative
to make an important tactical decision *before one
is confident in the sufficiency of the data.* . . .
Warfare is the epitome of a crisis discipline.
On a *battlefield*, if you observe a group of armed
men stealthily approaching *your lines, you are
justified in taking precautions, which may include
firing on the men.* [17] (Italics added)

Does that sound like war has been declared on normal science and
traditional conservation practices? Funny thing though, although
war was declared, somebody forgot to tell the opponents. Science
was out, voodoo and pseudoscience were in. If other scientists disagreed with them, shoot them. If someone questioned why it is
necessary to act before we know for certain the proposed problem
is even a problem, proclaim the catastrophe is so large we can't

wait for science. Does all this sound vaguely familiar? It should; it has been happening since the mid-1980s. But that's not all. In the same textbook, deep ecologist Arne Naess (who started the deep ecology movement) proposes a strategy to win what they want. "Hundreds of wars," he suggests, "were glorified by reference to God, patriotism, love of mankind, and supreme justice. Likewise, it is easy to agree upon the *intrinsic value* of the richness and *diversity of life* on the planet Earth. What I therefore suggest," he continues, "is that those who are thought to be experts and scientists *repeatedly and persistently* deepen their arguments with reference to basic *value judgements*." Rather than being guided by scientific results, Naess suggests scientists should be guided by "their *normative philosophy of life* and [frame their arguments] in terms of millions of years of evolution and intimate global interactions" (bold italics added).

Naess concludes that as long as these so-called scientists stick to emotional, justice-filled concepts like "intrinsic value, the richness and diversity of life, and the interconnectedness of life developed over the millennia," no one can "articulate" an effective opposition.[18] He was right; biodiversity and intrinsic value now dominate all debate and have gripped the hearts and minds of the American people—all without conclusive empirical scientific evidence.

Where did most graduates trained in conservation biology find employment? Few would be hired by industry or agriculture, where they would actually have to earn a living on this philosophy. In fact, most graduates would probably shun such employment as supporting the enemy. The only employment likely to be open to them would be regulatory agencies, education, and environmental organizations. It should therefore be no surprise that we have witnessed many of our nation's governmental regulators and teachers assuming the mantle of savior of nature rather than servant of the people.

It also partially explains why our children are being taught that cutting trees, using chemicals, plowing the land, building roads, and so forth are bad and are destroying the earth. But the largest reason is still the fact that most teachers simply don't know—any more than the typical American—that the eco-horror stories are mostly false. Our teachers are so cash-starved for supplementary material that they willingly accept readily available, free environmental literature from environmental groups. In *Environmental Overkill*, Dixy Lee Ray quotes Jonathan H. Adler:

"Most classroom environmental information, including most that is listed at the Environmental Protection Agency clearinghouse, comes from literature and teaching guides drafted and distributed by the major environmental groups" ("Little Green Lies: The Environmental Miseducation of America's Children," *Policy Review*, July 1992). It goes without saying that such literature is terribly distorted by their eco-catastrophe dogma. We are educating a generation whose view of reality is that man is destroying the earth. And, as Naess promised, no one has mounted an effective rebuttal, because "intrinsic values" and "biodiversity" are motherhood issues.

Traditional scientists and conservationists have always known that biodiversity is important. But they were totally blindsided by the emotional impact of biodiversity as a philosophy of life. Many scientists have attempted to clarify what biodiversity is and is not, but most of this has been lost in the emotional rhetoric, just as Naess said it would be. It is almost impossible to define truth with facts and figures when that grain of truth is clouded with emotional hype.

SCIENCE AND CONSERVATION BIOLOGY

Biodiversity is one of the factors that must be weighed in developing conservation practices, but the world will not collapse if we plant a field of corn or clear-cut a portion of a forest to have a plantation of pine or spruce. In fact, those "one" species ecosystems can literally add diversity to the whole landscape. But it must be done in a balanced context.[19]

An entire forest in which every acre has a highly diverse structure in ages and species is actually homogeneous, not diverse, if every acre is the same.[20] How diversity is arranged across a landscape is as important as how it is structured in a single stand of trees or grass. Old growth, for instance, is not as critical to the spotted owl as is the structure of the coniferous forest providing the habitat. If a sixty-year-old forest has a vertical and horizontal forest structure similar to that of a 200-year-old forest, it will provide habitat for the owl.

Although ecosystems do interconnect, they are not the highly fragile webs of life portrayed by environmental leaders. Rather, the interconnections operate in a more linear fashion. In other words, if a forest is clear-cut right up to a stream in the headwaters of a watershed, then the sun can warm the stream, affecting its temperature far downstream but not in the next watershed. If too many watersheds are cut in such a manner, the temperature of the river the streams feed, and so forth, can be affected. This process of ecosystem linkages is called cumulative effects, not the web of life. Cumulative effects must be considered, but in reality the forest and other ecosystems are very dynamic and resilient. Anyone who has fought weeds in a garden knows the truth of this. Caution, respect, and care are essentials in practicing conservation—not paranoia.

After the above discussion, the reader might think that there is no place in science for conservation biology. That is not the case at all. Conservation biology is what is called a "systems science." It looks at landscapes and their interacting systems holistically. This approach to ecology is long overdue. Until the late 1980s most research and management of ecosystems were done on a community-by-community basis, ignoring the interactions between communities. Conservation biology theories provide excellent starting points in testing hypotheses about how whole communities and their environments interact with one another. In essence, conservation biology is an approach that ecologists should have had fifty years ago. But so far that is all it is—an approach. Very little research has actually been conducted to prove the theories one way or the other. Certainly, there has not been sufficient research to base policy upon.

In its short life, conservation biology has been considered theoretical in nature. In other words, it centers on postulations that cause and effect relationships exist for observed natural phenomena. In many cases conservation biologists summarize results from numerous studies, often having differing experimental designs that test widely differing hypotheses, into one overall theory explaining natural phenomena. For instance, in theory, fragmentation results when continuous forest or grassland ecosystems are interrupted by agriculture, housing developments, roads, clear-cutting, and so forth. The impact of fragmentation is likened to islands being separated by vast oceans where plants and animals cannot freely migrate. The theory of fragmentation is based on what is called island biogeography. The smaller the island and the more isolated the island is, the greater the instability.[21]

In spite of the warm fuzzies this theory provides, it hasn't been fully validated even in a true "island" context. There is no evidence to suggest that urbanization and forest clear-cutting function the same ways oceans do in creating fragmentation. It requires a tremendous leap of faith to take theories developed for

South Pacific islands and apply them to mosaic forested landscapes in America. Zimmerman and Bierregaard caution: "The equilibrium theory of island biogeography and associated species area relations have been promoted as theoretical bases for design of nature reserves. However, *the theory has not been properly validated* and the practical value of biogeographic principles for conservation remains unknown. Recent studies have shown that species-area data in the absence of autecological basis [the direct evidence of cause and effect by environmental factors] *provide no special insights relevant to conservation*"[22] (italics added).

The same is true for other aspects of conservation biology theory.[23] In spite of this warning, eco-leaders demand that hundreds of thousands of acres be set aside as "untouched preserves" in order to save biodiversity. These reserves must, according to them, be interconnected with broad corridors on natural (i.e., untouched) ecosystems to permit species to migrate. If this is not done now, it will be too late. But like reserves, there is no credible scientific evidence that such corridors would work. The December 1992 edition of *Conservation Biology* carried an article providing the caution that "no unified theory combines genetic, demographic, and other forces threatening small populations, nor is there accord on the relative importance of these threats." The IUCN theories for the need for refuges have been "increasingly heavily criticized . . . largely because local population extinction was not demonstrated."[24] The theory that reserves and corridors "facilitate movement is now almost an article of faith."[25] The authors of this article claim that "no thorough analysis of this sort has ever been conducted. Possibly the most that can be done today is to say that some options are much less likely to be important than others."[26]

That warning as it pertains to fragmentation of America's forests is being borne out by some of the first research actually done to test these hypotheses. One of the issues that is causing great concern in the scientific world is the decline of what are called Neotropical migratory songbirds. They represent many of America's favorite summertime songbirds. Many of them are quite colorful—the bluebird, the scarlet tanager, and many others. These birds migrate from Central and South America each spring to nest in North America. But the populations of species that reproduce in the interior of older Northcentral and Northeastern forests have been declining.[27] Scientists generally believe the decline is either because of the loss of winter habitat in Central and South America due to the exploitation of the tropical rain forests, or the fragmentation of North American forests due to clear-cutting and urban-ization.[28]

One of the first major studies to determine if forest clear-cutting may be contributing to the decline was started in Maine in 1992. Most encouraging was that this study was cooperatively sponsored by the forest products industry, the Fish and Wildlife Foundation, Jessie B. Cox Charitable Trust, and the John Merck Fund—institutions that had been at odds with one another on other issues. This very large study sampled a variety of forests—from those with no clear-cutting to forests over 70 percent clear-cut. First-year study results found that "regional avian diversity is likely enhanced by industrial forest practices that maintain a variety of successional stages of forest."[29] Although the authors caution there may still be fragmentation effects on critical species, such evidence was not obvious from the first year's results. Though not final, the early results are promising.

Cornell University scientists Thomas Litwin and Charles Smith found that a thirty-year decline and local extinctions of some species of Neotropical songbirds in central New York was not caused by fragmentation as was originally assumed. Instead, they were caused by the *loss* of the fragmentation that had been created by harvesting and farming early in the twentieth century.[30] In other, less comprehensive research, results have shown that at least 15 percent of the forest must be clear-cut to achieve maximum biological diversity of songbirds.[31]

What hard science is beginning to show is that forest harvesting, including the use of clear-cutting, not only has no negative effects on diversity, it can enhance it! This doesn't mean scientists won't find problems in future research. It also doesn't mean that farmers, foresters, and other land managers can throw caution to the wind. But it does show that traditional, careful management of our natural resources can be done while maintaining diversity.

LITIGATION AND ILLUSION

Much needs to be learned about the impacts of managing whole ecosystems. So far conservation biology is merely a set of theories built around the pantheistic notion that nature knows best because she has taken millennia to develop these fragile ecosystems. Yet eco-leaders and radical conservation biologists demand that if we don't have all the answers, we should do nothing. David Suzuki in his keynote address at the 1992 Environmental Grantmakers Association in Washington State asserted: "We know virtually nothing about the natural world. What person would dare to say we know enough about complex ecosystems to be able to manage and dare to duplicate them. This is the height of arrogance."[31]

Such an attitude is foolish. Even if we spent $100 billion a year investigating these theories over a fifty-year period, we still would have much to learn. We will never have all the answers. To do nothing is like saying we should stop treating all disease until we fully understand its full value to the survival of the earth. This biocentric point of view is totally nihilistic. We cannot survive without using our resources—there are *no* exceptions. Instead, we must proceed with care but diligence. We have learned much already and will learn more in the future. As we do we will continue to improve our stewardship practices.

In spite of the lack of proof that conservation biology theories have any validity, environmentalist advocates are using these theories without mercy in our judicial system. Multiple thousands of lawsuits have been filed, stopping golf courses, farming, ranching, mining, forest harvesting, and other industries throughout America. In 1990, the U.S. Forest Service received 1,154 appeals filed against proposed timber sales, compared to an average of 170 for the years 1983 through 1985. These appeals created a potential economic loss of $195 million in federal taxes and $179 million in dependent county payments (in lieu of taxes).[32] The Forest Service spent almost $60 million processing appeals during a six-year period.

In a lawsuit filed against the Nicolet National Forest in Wisconsin, the Sierra Club asserted that in order to save biodiversity, the forest must set aside 150,000 acres of land in a "natural reserve." In their deposition the Sierra Club based its case on the heavily criticized theory of island biogeography:

In developing a *rational plan for the preservation of diversity* we must be guided by an understanding of processes that **unfold on an evolutionary time scale:** the birth and death of species, waxing and waning of whole faunas and floras, and the invasive replacement of archaic assemblages by more modern ones. . . . *The intellectual cornerstone of these advances is a paper entitled "An Equilibrium Theory of Island Biogeography."*

> *. . . The number of species belonging to a single taxon such as birds, ants, or flowering plants, equilibrates on a given island at a level that is a function of the area and the degree of isolation of the island. . . . Similar effects are seen on "habitat islands within continents."* This is not for nostalgia; we desperately need to understand how mature ecosystems function, and *every road, every forest edge, every clearing, is a wall between us and that understanding.*
> (Italics original, bold italics added)[33]

This lawsuit is but one of dozens across the country. It could have been taken right out of the battlefield strategy in the textbook *Conservation Biology* quoted above.

Lest you think that these unproven theories will never affect you, think again. Conservation biology leaders such as Michael Soulé (founder of the Society of Conservation Biologists and the journal of *Conservation Biology),* David Foreman (founder of the radical group Earth First!), and Reed Noss (current editor of the journal of *Conservation Biology,* who was given a $150,000 grant by the Pew Charitable Trust, an EGA member) presented an extreme plan at the 1993 annual meeting for the Society of Conservation Biologists that would affect all Americans. This "controversial plan to protect North American Biodiversity," note Charles Mann and Mark Plummer in *Science* magazine, "calls for nothing less than resettling the entire continent." Called the *Wildland Project,* the plan "calls for a network of wilderness reserves, human buffer zones, and wildlife corridors stretching across huge tracts of land—hundreds of millions of acres; as much as *half the continent.*"[34]

Under the plan, one quarter of America would be turned into wilderness where all human activity would literally cease. Human activity on another quarter of America would be "severely restricted" where "most roads would be closed; some would be ripped out of the landscape. . . . The long-term goal . . . is nothing less than a transformation of America . . . to an archipelago of human-inhabited islands surrounded by natural areas."[35] Although most conservation biologists reject such extreme plans, many believe it is the only way to save species from extinction; "[this plan] can be viewed as the logical extension of the Endangered Species Act, which mandates that biodiversity must be saved no matter what the cost."[36] The cost would be staggering.

It is unlikely that such a plan could be legislated in its present form. But the National Biological Survey that Bruce Babbitt and George Frampton attempted to push through Congress in late 1993 throws the door wide open for a scaled-down version of such a plan. Though Babbitt failed in Congress, he claims he has the authority to implement the plan without Congressional approval. The fact that this plan is being considered at all shows what happens when a "nature-is-god" theory and biocentric blindness get ahead of valid science. Do you suppose Bill Ellen or Donald Walker would feel better knowing that their sacrifice is for the good of the Earth Goddess Gaia? Who or what is Gaia? Read on.

Because we are moving into a new mythic age, it is little wonder that a kind of mutation is taking place in the entire earth-human order. A new paradigm of what it is to be human emerges.... This would not be possible unless it were a call of subject to subject, if it were not an effort at total self-realization on the part of scientists.... The most notable single development within science within recent years ... has been a growing awareness of the integral physical-psychic dimension of reality.

Thomas Berry
The Dream of the Earth
Sierra Club Books, 132–33

The Gaia hypothesis is promoted by its growing army of adherents as a scientific revolution and the "new paradigm" of the biological and environmental sciences. It is touted by some as the "grand unified theory of biology."

Dorion Sagan and Lynn Margulis
Gaia Magazine, issue 3, 4–6

It is not surprising that the new paradigm, as it emerges in physics and in other sciences, will be in harmony with many ideas in spiritual traditions. ... It is becoming ever more apparent that mysticism, or the perennial philosophy, as it is sometimes called, provides the most consistent philosophical background to the new scientific paradigm.

Fritjof Capra
The Tao of Physics, 326

7

GAIA AND THE
WORLD OF MYSTICISM

WISDOM FROM WASHINGTON

Bruce Vincent listened with amazement. At a special information meeting, the U.S. Fish and Wildlife Service (FWS) had been explaining how they planned to "augment" the grizzly bear population in the Cabinet Mountains of Montana. The grizzly is an endangered species, and the augmentation effort was part of the recovery plan mandated by the Endangered Species Act. But Bruce had noticed a wide highlighted band on the FWS map that surrounded the Cabinet Mountains. The highlighted band included Libby, the town where he lives. When he asked what the band on the map meant, the FWS representative casually responded, "That is the human/grizzly conflict zone."[1]

"Is this going to be a problem for us?" asked Bruce.

"No, it shouldn't be," they replied. "People in Kodiak Island, Alaska have adjusted."

Starting to smell a fly in the ointment, Bruce's wife asked, "Am I going to be able to send my kid out to fish in the creek like my husband has his whole life?"

The response was evasive. "Well, yeah, but you might have to make some minor adjustments."

Adjustments? Apparently the solution was for parents to tie bells on their children. Bells go *tinkle, tinkle, tinkle,* which scares the grizzlies and they run away—most of the time. What about the bears that violate USFWS rules and decide to investigate these small humans rather than run away? Nonplussed, the USFWS responded, "If we have a bad bear we will deal with it." Needless to say, the townspeople didn't like the plan, and said so.

Still unshaken, the USFWS looked them squarely in the eye and chided, "I don't think you understand. We are here to tell you what we are going to do. We are here to tell you the plan that is being put in place. We are mandated by the federal Endangered Species Act. Congress has told us we have got to do this. We are here to tell you we are doing it. It is not something that is subject to a public opinion poll."

Libby, like most rural Montana towns, depends on campers and hikers and other tourists for much of its income. How many campers and hikers are likely to frequent the environs of Libby if they too have to wear bells that go *tinkle, tinkle?* But that is not the only environmental problem Bruce and his fellow citizens have.

The biggest tourist draw is the 96-mile long Lake Koocanusa. It so happens the chinook salmon is also an endangered species. And, Lake Koocanusa is being used by the USFWS as a giant toilet to flush the chinook up and down the Columbia River. The lake is now called Lake Who-Can-Use-It by those living in the area. The fluctuations in lake levels have "killed spawning beds," and "increased sedimentation in our river to the point where we are having no fish spawning." All "because of a single species downriver that has a recovery plan with blinders on it."[2] How could it be otherwise if those who would be earth's savior believe that Gaia is being destroyed?

GAIA

Conservation biology is only one aspect that is centered on the theology of the diverse web of life. Gaia, the brainchild of Dr. James Lovelock, is conservation biology elevated to the size of the earth.

Gaia, the Greek goddess of the earth, was coined by Lovelock in his book *Gaia* to describe a hypothesis that all living things on earth interact effectively as components of one superorganism. Lovelock is a highly respected independent British scientist who has worked in some of the most prestigious institutions in England and America. Lovelock's greatest scientific achievement was his invention of the electron capture detector (ECD), which is an extremely sensitive device that can detect chemicals as low as parts per trillion. Much of Lovelock's more recent work was done in collaboration with Lynn Margulis, a highly respected microbiologist.

In his theory, Lovelock proposed that the living systems of the earth can be regarded as a single unit that regulates the environment in such a way as to maintain conditions suitable for life:

> Gaia is an evolving system, a system made up from all living things and their surface environment, the oceans, atmosphere, and crustal rocks, the two parts tightly coupled and indivisible. . . . In this system, the self-regulation of climate and chemical composition are entirely automatic. Self-regulation emerges as the system evolves.[3]

Gaia is not just a simple combination of discrete living and nonliving elements, but rather a living organism, a self-sustaining system made up of complex interrelationships between living and nonliving elements. Through complex interactions the atmosphere, the oceans, the biota, the climate, and the crust of the earth are regulated at a comfortable state for life because of the behavior of living beings. "The only feasible explanation of the Earth's highly improbable atmosphere," explains Lovelock, "was that it was being manipulated on a day-to-day basis from the surface, and the manipulator was life itself."[4]

In the later 1980s this theory began to be accepted by an expanding group of scientists, especially those specializing in atmospheric physics. Carbon dioxide is one of the key drivers for Lovelock's theory, and it appears likely that the Gaia theory may be currently providing much of the scientific undercurrent for today's global warming fears. Lovelock parrots the eco-leaders' assertion that we can't wait to find out if global warming is a problem; we must act now:

> How are we to know what the Earth is as a
> system? How can we govern it if science is
> still decades away from telling us what it is?
> Should we wait for the deliberations of the
> plenary session of the all-science interdisciplinary
> congress? Or should we listen to thoughtful
> environmentalists such as Jonathon Porritt
> [director of the deep ecology group Friends of the
> Earth, England], who ask "can we afford to wait
> for scientific certainty before taking the obvious
> sensible action on environmental affairs?"[5]

As discussed earlier, it would be both arrogant and naive to wait for total proof before forming policy on every issue. But it is equally arrogant and naive to chase after every perceived crisis man can dream up. Evidence and support for global warming and ozone depletion in the scientific community is declining daily. Although there is still reason for concern about this issue, would it have been prudent to blindly react to these scare tactics and spend trillions of dollars on the "evidence" of a theory? Like conservation biology, the Gaia theory is based on "systems science." Lovelock and Margulis have put together an incredible set of interlocking theories about how various earth "systems" interact. Like a house of cards, theory is built on theory, none of it proven. It may seem logical, but that can be very deceptive.

At an earlier time in history, man also had a systems theory of the earth. It was a flat system—a fact that everyone could "see." And since the moon, the sun, and the stars revolved around the earth, it was the center of the universe. After hundreds of years this theory was proven wrong by another theory—the earth is round and merely part of the universe. Will the Gaia theory change our current theories of the earth the same way? It's hard to say yet. It can never be totally proven. And it will take a long time before sufficient research is completed to provide solid clues. The point is that theories are just that—theories. They should be used with extreme caution until they are validated.

GAIA AND MYSTICISM

The Gaia theory was ready-made for New Age mystics and environmentalists. It provided the means for taking their eco-catastrophe fears to the global level. In the Sierra Club book *The Dream of the Earth*, Thomas Berry celebrates: "One of the finest moments in our new sensitivity to the natural world is our discovery of the earth as a living organism."[6] To eco-leaders and mystic scientists, the earth is a delicate functioning organism, and mankind is slicing and dicing her. The Gaia theory provides the perfect weapon to "prove" man is destroying *himself* as well as earth. They hit the core nerve of every human being—the instinct for survival.

It suddenly became clear that Gaia was in danger, and that the human race could be destroyed as Gaia gets rid of the virus that infects her. Lovelock proclaims:

Gaia is Mother Earth. Gaia is immortal. She is the eternal source of life. She does not need to reproduce herself as she is immortal. She is certainly the mother of us all, including Jesus . . .
Gaia is not a tolerant mother. She is rigid and inflexible, ruthless in the destruction of whoever transgresses. Her unconscious objective is that of maintaining a world adapted to life. If we men hinder this objective we will be eliminated without pity.[7]

The threat to Mother Earth appears to be acting as a unifying catalyst among the otherwise diverse groups having New Age philosophies. Gaia is being threatened by global warming and pollution in a way that could jeopardize her survival. Man's reckless exploitation and overpopulation of the earth now threatens everyone, whether he or she is in the environmental movement, the goddess feminist movement, pyramid power, the occult, or self-actualization/human potential.

THE LINDISFARNE ASSOCIATION

There is another side to James Lovelock and Gaia that almost no one knows. Lovelock is also a member of the Lindisfarne Association, one of the most gnostic and metaphysical "ecological" New Age groups in the United States. It is headquartered at the Episcopal Cathedral of St. John the Divine in New York City.[8]

The 1992 *New Age Source Book* proclaims New York's Cathedral of St. John the Divine as a "leader among the growing number of churches and synagogues that are becoming more 'green' in the outlook and practices. . . . The cathedral sponsors ecological conferences that bring together heads of major religious denominations with environmental scientists and political leaders.'"[9] In addition to the Lindisfarne Association, the Cathedral of St. John the Divine sponsors such spiritually based ecology programs as the Gaia Institute and The Temple of Understanding. It has also sponsored the Joint Appeal by Science and Religion for the Environment, of which TV science guru Carl Sagan is cochair and Vice President Albert Gore played a key role. The Gaia Institute "aims to create 'mother goddess' cults throughout the west . . . and is a movement to create a new religion."[10] In addition to being Lindisfarne's founding director, William Thompson is editor of Lindisfarne Press and Books. The Sierra Club has also published one of his books.

To provide a sense of the activities within this New Age think tank, among the various topics that were discussed in Lindisfarne in early 1992 was the topic "Science Fiction, Mysticism, and Weird," in which Thompson states, "Science fact is really a disguised form of science fiction."[11] Also, according to Thompson's January 1992 newsletter, the Lindisfarne Association had just received a three-year grant that will allow him "to develop a program of research, lecturing, and writing concerned with the theme of 'The Evolution of Consciousness.'"

One of the Lindisfarne Books edited by Dr. Thompson is entitled *G-A-I-A, A Way of Knowing—Political Implications of the New Biology*, published in 1987. Various authors contributed to the book, including James Lovelock and Lynn Margulis, Lovelock's close associate while developing the Gaia hypothesis.* In the foreword, Thompson makes this revealing statement:

---

* Lynn Margulis worked very closely with James Lovelock in the development of the Gaia theory. Carl Sagan was her former husband and Dorion Sagan is their son (see opening quote of this chapter).

> People like to hang out together because they can
> feel their ideas growing fuller and richer on the
> vine. This book is just such a cluster of ideas that
> comes from a small group of people who have
> been hanging out together for the last six years.
> More than anything it is a work of intellectual fel-
> lowship that expresses the ideas, conferences,
> conversations, letters, and phone calls. [12]

Although Lovelock surely does not share every belief of Thompson's, this foreword does illustrate the overall commonality of
ideas. Lovelock even describes one of the services of "celebration"
at St. John the Divine as being both sensual and religious. [13]

Lovelock attempts to downplay his spiritual side. But his
mystic views about the role history has played in creating our current ecological problems appear to parallel those of Thompson. In
his own mystical terminology, Lovelock squarely identifies the
cause of the problems of earth today as stemming from the Judeo-
Christian worldview of natural resource utilization:

> At some time not more than a few thousand
> years ago, the concept of a remote master God
> (the Judeo-Christian God), an overseer of Gaia,
> took root. . . . [As these people moved west]
> they brought a sky god, a warrior cult, and
> a patriarchal social order. . . . The evolution
> of these [people] to the modern men who ride
> their infinitely more powerful machines of
> destruction over the *habitats of our partners
> in Gaia*, seems only a small step. [14]

Lovelock has a totally wrong understanding of the Judeo-
Christian God, and he cannot relate to a remote, all-powerful, all-
seeing male Yahweh, but he can relate to the femininity in Mary:

> Mary is close and can be talked to. She is believa-
> ble and manageable. It could be that the impor-
> tance of the Virgin Mary in faith is something of
> this kind, but there may be more to it. *What if
> Mary is another name for Gaia?* Then her capacity
> for virgin birth is no miracle . . . it is a role of Gaia
> since life began. . . . She is of this Universe and,
> conceivably, a part of God. On Earth she is the
> source of life everlasting and is alive now; she
> gave birth to humankind and we are a part of her. [15]

Note that his book entitled *The Ages of Gaia* is now published by Bantam New Age Books. Whereas Lovelock would have other scientists believe his Gaia theory is based on pure scientific motives, his association with William Thompson and the Lindisfarne Association would suggest otherwise. This will become clearer when Findhorn is discussed, because Findhorn reflects Thompson's true beliefs.

Although we must be open-minded in science, this theory has no evidence to justify its use in making national environmental policy, especially since it has such a ring of New Age mysticism about it. In spite of this, Vice President Gore puts his blessings on Gaia in glowing spiritual terms: "[Gaia] evokes a spiritual response in many who hear it. . . . The simple fact of the living world and our place on it evokes awe, wonder, a sense of mystery—a spiritual response—when one reflects on its deeper meaning."[16]

Though claiming to be a Baptist, the vice president reveals his spiritual beliefs by affirming that goddess worship "could offer us new insights into the nature of the human experience,"[17] and extolling the virtues of other pagan beliefs centered on pantheism, gnosticism, and mysticism. If humans are made in the image of God, as the Bible claims, it is perhaps, Gore postulates, the "myriad slight strands from the earth's web of life . . . that reflects the image of God."[18] It is unclear where Gore received his theological training, but these beliefs are clearly not Baptist. He says, "Armed with such a faith it is possible to resanctify the earth."[19] It is hard to believe, but even with that bizarre vision of reality, Mr. Gore believes he represents "traditional American values." Instead, he claims throughout his book that it is the rest of America that is not living in reality.

This belief system looks to Gaia, the living earth, to provide the answers. The web of life is merely a continuum of spiritual/matter shifts that is now being supposedly demonstrated by quantum physics. Quantum physics demonstrates that matter and energy cannot be separated at the subatomic level. Matter has no discrete boundaries. New Age environmental leaders have jumped on this as "evidence" that everything is "one." Ann Roberts told the audience at the Environmental Grantmakers Association in their 1992 meeting:

Science has at last brought us all the way around to understanding some things that native people and peoples who have stayed in connection with the earth have known since the beginning. That is that we are the same composition as the earth. . . . Our physics, which is our higher science, has come around to understanding that there is no boundaries [sic] between us. That we essentially are inter-beings. That there are no boundaries between me and these pieces of paper, or me and this table or me and any of you who are sitting here. . . . We are expressions of energy and that matter and spirit move in and out of each other without effort and it is us in our illusions that have set limits to that motion. Therefore, we can understand our inner being with the natural world, and we can at last know that spirit can dwell with matter and we do not have to deny the matter of our being or of this earth. . . .
If we lie on our apartment floor on the fortieth floor, and really listen we can be nourished and feel mother earth and her energy coming all the way up through those floors to us.[20]

What amazing theology! And they call it science. Well, it looks like we are back to Environmental Economics 101. No matter how hard environmental apologists try, the mystic approach always falls far, far short of reality. Inevitably, those who put their faith in nature religion always fall back to communing with nature for solutions. Nature must be allowed to set the example, to guide the way, for nature is truth, all knowing. To be in harmony with nature a person must evolve to a higher state of consciousness— cosmic consciousness. To be one with nature is to be endued with cosmic power. Power to create your own reality. Power to make the Sahara Desert bloom.

Can this be done? *Has* this been done? *Yes!* according to environmental writers. The example? Findhorn.

FINDHORN

Findhorn! That mystical place in Scotland where the human mind melds with that of nature to produce the bountiful garden promised by the mystics of old. Where the promise of abundance from nothing has been realized—giving substance to the hopes of all those who have put their faith and trust in the mystic worship of nature. Findhorn! Where as early as 1963, the nature spirits inhabiting that sacred place revealed:

At last, [you] no longer need to be controlled by events, but by your power of thought, you control them. You can bring about anything by your thoughts. That is why this new-found power can only be used when there is no self left to mar it . . . This is the secret of creation. **What you think, you create . . . We are one.** *Therefore, all that appeared impossible in the past is no longer so. Everything is possible.*[21] (Italics original, bold italics added)

And indeed, it appeared that the promise was kept. Findhorn did bloom, and bountiful crops were produced. According to Peter Caddy, the founder of Findhorn, forty-two-pound cabbages were grown, along with broccoli so large that each one would feed the residents for months.[22] All of this by communing with and working in harmony with the devas (plant angels who hold the pattern for individual species) and nature spirits (elves and fairies). When the Findhorn residents encountered real-world problems, the devas and nature spirits would identify the problems as originating from the "imbalances caused by man" by poisoning insects with insecticides, or by filling the atmosphere with "chaotic thoughts," and of course, unnatural "atomic radiation" from nuclear test explosions.[23]

Was there any proof of this? Alas, "We didn't even think to take photographs of these early phenomena."[24] Yet, outside witnesses agree that Findhorn did produce a luxurious garden out of very sterile soil and a harsh climate. But Findhorn residents readily admitted that the "overflowing garden did require a great deal of hard work. [We were] kept busy from dawn until dusk, and in this land near the midnight sun, those summer days were indeed long. Every square inch of soil was handled by each of us several times."[25] With this kind of intensive effort, it would be a miracle if the garden did not produce luxuriously.

Although this apparently met their food requirements, there was time for little else. After three years of backbreaking effort, participants "were still living on Unemployment Benefits" to provide their meager existence—old trailers, clothing, shoes, and garden tools.[26] Utopia at last!

It is easy to ridicule. Perhaps that is why Findhorn is always referred to in mystical expressions, rather than concrete facts. But there is a darker side to Findhorn, to which outward expressions are found repeatedly throughout environmental "catastrophe literature."

Planting, cultivation, and pruning can only be done at the direction of the devas and nature spirits. Not to consult and follow their directions is to break harmony with them, leading to the "butchery" of nature's creation. Three passages from *The Findhorn Garden* illustrate this:

The greatest care must be taken to refrain from any action that will give offence. This particularly applies to the nature spirits. . . . You cannot continue to expect cooperation from beings, many of whom *still doubt that man deserves their help.* (Italics added)[27]

The picture the devas give is that from their viewpoint the *world situation is critical.* The world of nature spirits is sick of the way man is treating the life forces. The devas and elementals are working with God's law in plant growth. Man is continually violating it. *There is a real likelihood that they may even turn their back on man, whom they sometimes consider to be a parasite on Earth.* (Italics added)[28]

[Man] *does not need to douse the earth with chemicals. He does not need to exercise brute force on the forms of nature to make them obey his designs. He must provide us [the nature spirits] free scope to work with him, in love, respect and cooperation. . . . Man's consciousness must expand to new insights and into deeper communion with nature. Out of this can come a communion with us, a mating, if you will, that will embody a divine power to transform our planet. . . . This is a reflection of the equally great creative powers that humanity holds within itself, an ability to completely manipulate matter through the power of thought and spirit. . . . But there must first be a loving awareness and sense of caring and communion with all life forms, mineral, vegetable, animal and human.*[29] (Italics original)

There it is. The bold threat that unless man does it nature's way, nature will lash back and destroy all of humanity. Only by working in harmony with nature, by doing it nature's way, can mankind survive. Nature knows best. There is also the carrot that has been sought after since man was created. Power. Unlimited power! God power! Do it my way, says nature, and you receive the ultimate reward—you become god! Do it your way, and you will be squashed!

The footprint of Findhorn is found everywhere in environmental literature—from the horror stories of ecological catastrophes at the hand of man, to the raw fear that we must act now before it is too late, to the suggestion that the only solution is doing it nature's way. Is this example any different from that found in the Sierra Club book *Well Body, Well Earth,* where we are told to consult with Gaia:

Because most people who live in an urban or suburban setting have little or no daily contact with
the Earth, we require something like visualization
to help us get in touch with our planet . . .
[where we] can be in touch with those forces in
the universe that . . . encourage health and
well-being. . . . Priestesses of Gaia were trained
in the art of visualization and had dedicated their
lives to a study of the spirit of the living Earth.
When asked to help a person solve a problem—
such as when to plant their fields or how to
influence the conception of children—the
priestess . . . consulted with Gaia.[30]

No wonder environmental leaders who believe in this nature/
god live in raw terror of their perceived environmental catastrophes. No wonder they can ignore science when research shows the
problem to be nonexistent or manageable. They know better.
They have the truth—from Gaia herself. No wonder they believe
"nature knows best." They have even developed entire pseudo-
scientific theories around it!

The modern day worship of nature is no different than that of
the pagan cultures throughout history. Once again we are living in
raw fear of what the nature gods will do to us if we don't obey
them. One can only speculate when sacrificial offerings will once
again be offered up to these gods and goddesses. Indeed, it was the
desire to establish these pagan beliefs in the Western world that
was a primary mission of Findhorn:

The concept of a spirit, an intelligence, a god moving within nature and ordering all its aspects, has
been dismissed as a myth and legend of simpler
cultures. It is Findhorn's role to bring the mythology to life again. This idea of a life and spirit in-
forming nature and directing its activities is *not*

> *new* within human culture; it is the *basis* for such
> philosophies as *[pagan] animism and pantheism.*
> The most sacred esoteric teaching throughout
> the ages have held that in understanding the inner
> and outer realities of nature, humanity can under-
> stand itself, and vice versa. [31] (Italics added)

Now comes the acid test. If Eastern mysticism is the answer, then why are the economies and environments of Southeast Asia, where Hinduism, Buddhism, Taoism, and Zen predominate, in such a state of disaster? Who has the better environmental record? America, using proven traditional conservation practices, or those cultures where mystic beliefs are put into practice? Nowhere does science back up their theories. Should America put its trust in unproven theories or in scientifically tested, proven safe, traditional conservation practices?

If it is the latter, then we are already in trouble. Mystic religious beliefs are rapidly becoming enshrined in law and regulation. Ask Bill Ellen or Donald Walker. Take a hard look at what is happening to the Fifth Amendment to the United States Constitution. Not only is the Fifth Amendment not protecting the constitutional rights of American citizens, but laws and regulations are being instituted on the basis of nothing more than unproven mystic pseudoscience founded in nature religion—not in proven science. This effectively circumvents the intent of the First Amendment to the Constitution: "Congress shall make no law respecting an establishment of religion, or prohibiting the free exercise thereof." The only thing missing that makes this religion unaccountable to the First Amendment is that there is no *established* "Church of Nature."

Nature has, during some hundreds of millions of years through numberless billions of experiments, worked out the ecosystems that were flourishing so abundantly when humans and human civilizations emerged into being.

Thomas Berry
The Dream of the Earth
Sierra Club Books, 65

Eventually we either must come to grips with the abusive regulations and test every new theory against known hard facts, or we will indeed revert to the Dark Ages economically.

Larry Burkett
Whatever Happened to the American Dream? 152

Fascism: *A political and economic system, strongly nationalistic, magnifying the rights of the state as opposed to those of the individual, in which industry, though remaining largely under private ownership, and all administrative political units, are controlled by a central government.*

W. D. Lewis, F. H. S. Canby,
and T. K. Brown, Jr., 1944
The Winston Dictionary, Advanced Edition
Philadelphia, John C. Winston Co., 351

8

ECONOMICS, CONSERVATION, AND SPIRITUALITY

THE CASE OF THE MISSING FLEET

It was obvious that the hundreds of demonstrators were angry. Very, very angry. Placards were in abundance, decrying "Greenpeace—Nazis of the 90s" and "Greenpeace already killed our jobs —yours is next!" and "Greenpeace is lying to you!" Greenpeacies aboard the *Rainbow Warrior* were stunned. Nothing like this had ever happened to them before.[1]

The *Rainbow Warrior* had steamed into San Diego on February 6, 1992, in a media ploy for a tough new law that would make it illegal to capture dolphins in any way. According to their literature, the 100-boat American tuna fleet berthed in San Diego was mercilessly killing dolphins to the point of extinction. But when they arrived in San Diego they found that the tuna fleet was missing—departed forever. It had already been forced to sell out, reflag, and scatter all over the world because of the "dolphin safe" movement pushed by Greenpeace and other groups several years before.

Dolphins are often associated with schools of mature yellowfin tuna, and are used as "scouts" to help tuna boats locate the schools of tuna. Unfortunately, the dolphins themselves can become entangled in the nets used to catch the tuna. Although dolphins were never in danger of becoming extinct, the tuna industry had made a tremendous effort in time, money, and new net technology to reduce dolphin mortality. Most modern catches killed no dolphins at all. But this was not good enough for Greenpeace and other earth saviors. They demanded zero mortality. Tremendous pressure was put on tuna cannery firms not to accept Western Pacific tuna. Once this was done, the tuna boats had no place to market their catch and the fleet vanished.

Though the fleet had long since left San Diego, its families had not. They knew the whole "dolphin free" campaign was a fraud. And they were enraged when the *Rainbow Warrior* brought their propaganda machine for a visit. The centerpiece that had convinced Congress to pass the strict "dolphin-safe" laws that destroyed the West Coast tuna industry was a video clip showing the merciless slaughter of a net full of dolphins to get the few yellowfin tuna also in the net. The video was supposedly taken surreptitiously by Samuel LaBudde, an environmentalist with Earth Island Institute, who had signed on a tuna boat as a mechanic and cook. But like the faked Greenpeace film showing the skinning of live baby seals, this video was also a fraud. Among the protestors was the wife of Angelo Souza, a former tuna boat captain who was now forced to fish in the Western Pacific. She confronted Greenpeace about this video:

I have been involved with the tuna industry for over thirty years. I have gone to sea with my captain husband. The vessel and crew in this video are not Americans. This is not how Americans work. The whole film is a fraud. It is an old boat with a new owner and an inexperienced crew. Even the film was rigged, it was spliced from two different trips. It's common knowledge among fishermen that Samuel LaBudde lied about that dolphin slaughter. It's not typical of anything. You're all a bunch of liars! And you've destroyed the jobs of thousands of innocent people with your lies![2]

As discussed earlier, lies and fraud are not uncommon tools used by the earth saviors. They believe they know the truth and that the end justifies the means. Once again fraud and grandstanding won over truth and common sense. A law was passed, and the American tuna industry is gone—probably forever. And another of America's renewable resources is no longer available. It now belongs to Japan and other nations, and Americans are paying more for an inferior product. Except for the tragic impact on tuna fishing and processing families and local economy, this is but a small blip on the total American economy. Who cares? It saved a few dolphins and didn't affect anyone else—or did it?

THE IMPORTANCE OF NATURAL RESOURCES

Environmental leadership insists that unless we put environmental considerations before economic ones, we will destroy the earth, and mankind along with her. More than two-thirds of all Americans believe these false claims of environmental leaders over scientists.[3] Most Americans apparently accept the story that the environmental cause is just, or environmental leaders would not be sacrificing their lives to save us all from destroying ourselves.

Such major changes to the very fabric of our civilization must not be taken lightly. Peter Daniels, a member of the International Monetary Fund, has outlined five critical keys to a nation's economic and political stability:[4]

1. A rich, modern agricultural base
2. A flexible and dependable energy source
3. A diverse non-energy natural resource base
4. A thriving technology base
5. A strong educational system grounded in the basics

All five of these are under attack by environmental leadership. If these leaders are permitted to continue unchecked, their attack on these fundamental components of our civilization will result in economic paralysis or, worse yet, collapse.

Our natural resources, for instance, are the raw materials for our nation's wealth and the engine that drives our prosperity. All wealth initially starts with our natural resources. Most Americans are unaware of it, but every paycheck in America is directly or indirectly dependent on our natural resource base. Ninety-nine sectors are listed in the Scientific American Chart of the input-output structure of the American economy; *all* ninety-nine are fundamentally linked to our natural resources.

Forest products alone indispensably influence eighty-eight sectors of the total United States economy! It doesn't take much thought to discern that the fabric of society would collapse overnight without the simple commodity of paper, let alone agriculture, fisheries, minerals, and petroleum. Less than 2 percent of all American adults produce enough food for not only our tables, but for millions of tables around the world. Americans spend only 10 percent of their income, and even less time, securing abundant food for their tables. Yet Russians spend nearly *two-thirds* of their income, and even more time, providing a marginal supply of poor quality food for their tables. America's abundance does not happen by your local grocer waving his magic wand!

Agriculture is the largest single renewable resource in America's economy. Its importance is obvious every time we eat a meal. Our dependable food supply—that we all take for granted—is directly the result of almost incredible advances in agriculture technology. In fact, the number of people fed by a single farmer has increased from six people at the turn of the century to nearly one hundred people today! And since the 1950s the amount of heavy equipment, seed, fertilizers, and pesticides required to feed one person has tended downward! Although the total amount of pesticides used in U.S. agriculture increased by about 100 percent between 1965 and 1982, it *declined* by nearly 20 percent between 1982 and 1990.[5] Changes in farming practices have also resulted in a 90 percent reduction in farmland erosion on typical soils and a 50 to 60 percent reduction on highly erodible soils![6]

Ironically, if it hadn't been for these advancements in safe conservation practices, it is estimated that "we'd already have plowed under [nearly] *one million square miles* of wildlife habitat for food production . . . since 1940!"[7] How big is one million square miles? Norman Borlaug, Nobel Laureate and Distinguished Professor of International Agriculture at Texas A & M University, provides the comparison. "If the American farmer were still using 1940s technology," Dr. Borlaug asserts, "the additional acreage that would have to go into agriculture to produce as much food as is being produced today with modern technology would be equivalent to all the land east of the Mississippi River!"[8]

This same technology has allowed an increasing number of acres of agricultural land to revert to forestland, where it provides increasing habitat for wildlife. It should disturb everyone that the very agricultural technology that has provided the preservation of the natural diversity of so many forests is criticized by eco-leaders as destroying the world.

Jay Hair, president of the National Wildlife Federation, proclaimed that "this big, booming business, agriculture, is also killing the world. I mean that literally." Jay Hair formed a partnership with Windstar, a New Age organization in Colorado, to teach Federation staff how to "integrate earth, mind, and spirit."[9] Using similar language, the Sierra Club accuses the Farm Bureau and other groups of conducting a "massive and brutally destructive anti-environmental onslaught."[10] Yet, the facts show just the opposite. Once again, attacks by the environmental leadership appear to be based more on biocentric hatred than fact and reason.

Mechanized and chemical-intensive agriculture is costly. Hence, part of the reason there has been a decline in the intensity of mechanization and chemical use in agriculture over the past several decades is the desire to reduce costs as well as the growing awareness of the need to be more environmentally sensitive. In fact, nearly 66 percent of the reduction in erosion has come from voluntary efforts, rather than law and regulation.[11] Tremendous research effort has gone into these efforts since the 1950s and 1960s. These efforts have intensified in recent years under an umbrella called "sustainable agriculture." Sustainable agriculture of this type is based in science and bears little resemblance to environmental concepts carrying the same name discussed later in the book.

We should be proud of our farmers. They have come a long way from the exploitive and sometimes abusive practices used in the 1800s and early 1900s. Think about how much forest and wildlife habitat would have been lost if technological advances in agriculture had been prevented. Improvements can and will be made, but American farmers use some of the best practices anywhere in the world—so much so that we take the abundant food on our tables for granted and accuse farmers of exploiting the land, threatening wetlands and wildlife, and poisoning the earth.

Likewise, paper and forest products are the most cost effective in the world, permitting investment dollars to be allocated into other areas of the economy, stimulating growth and job creation. Although environmental literature implies that we are deforesting America, just the opposite is happening. Wild claims are made by environmental leaders that our National Forests are being overharvested. But less than 25 percent of National Forests are even *eligible* for harvesting. The rest is set aside for other purposes that prohibit harvesting.

On other American forestland, improved technology is permitting inexpensive forest products and paper. No one wants to see a return to the "timber baron" days of timber liquidation that occurred at the turn of the century. But that isn't happening today. Most forest landowners and timber companies are good stewards of their land because they realize a healthy forest is not only their future, but America's as well. There is no place else to go. In spite of what eco-leaders proclaim, our forestlands have actually *increased* by some *30 million acres* since the turn of the century—primarily because of the abandonment of marginal agricultural land as technology raised the yield per acre on other soil. Forest growth *exceeds harvest* by 37 percent, and net annual growth has increased by 62 percent since 1952. There is 30 percent more standing timber volume today than in 1952.[12]

As with agriculture, the bleak picture being painted by environmental leadership of America's forests is a gross distortion of reality based in deceit. This is especially true of clear-cutting. The Report of the President's Advisory Panel on Timber and Environment states: "If properly applied, clearcutting does not lead to soil erosion, nutrient-depletion, wildlife habitat damage, or stream sedimentation." Literally thousands of research studies demonstrate the safety of clear-cutting, done properly.

Simply stated, America has one of the best—if not *the* best—natural resource environmental records in the world. We have every reason to be proud. Improvement is always desirable, not only to enhance environmental protection, but also to improve efficiency in a cost-effective manner. But the *only* way this can be done is in a free market environment.

The efficient and wise use of resources depends on the freedom to own and manage those resources in ways that have been proven environmentally safe. Yet, the thrust of environmental regulation is taking direct aim at destroying the very rights that have provided Americans with one of the highest standards of living in the world. So far, much of the cost of the unnecessary environmental regulations has been hidden on the backs of landowners who are having more and more of their options taken away from them or more expensive options forced on them. We are beginning to see the costs reflected in inflation and recession, but the full impact cannot be determined because the regulations are rarely imposed in a way that can be measured.

THE RULE, NOT THE EXCEPTION

The Clean Water Act, the Clean Air Act, the Endangered Species Act, the Forest Management Planning Act, and multitudes more have resulted in similar horror stories. These acts are always passed with good intentions and have in many cases been highly successful in cleaning up the environment. But somehow, they are also leveraged by zealous groups to put nature ahead of people.

Ironically, while there may be some interconnections in nature that need greater protection, environmental leaders ignore the known interconnections in our economy that they are attacking with a vengeance. How could we build homes without wood or eat without food? Indeed, how could we even buy these items without transportation? And how could we have transportation without steel, plastics, and fuel? How could we live without electricity, and how could we have electricity without dams, coal, and oil? Who could afford restaurants, insurance, Barbie dolls, Nintendos, kitchen gadgets, and a host of minor necessities, conveniences, and luxuries if the bulk of our paychecks went to basic necessities such as food? Indeed, since no one would buy these "extras" anymore, who would employ those Americans who currently produce and provide services for these items that no one could any longer afford to buy?

Our economy is highly interconnected. An impact on any element of it ripples across our entire economy. The present unemployment rate and the inflation on some consumer goods are beginning to show the results of ignoring these interconnections. Within the first year of full implementation of the spotted owl recovery plan, for instance, the price of lumber doubled and tripled. In the spring of 1993 the price of homes suddenly took a big jump upward and out of reach for many families who would otherwise buy them. Or if families decide to scrimp to buy the home, they will no longer be able to buy that life insurance policy and microwave oven. That lowers the demand in other segments of our economy, and people are laid off.

In spite of the rhetoric emanating from environmental leadership that lumber price increases were not caused by the spotted owl, analysts disagree. Thirty-eight percent of our lumber comes from the West and half of this is impacted by the spotted owl. While Hurricane Andrew, wet weather in the South, and other market cycles contributed to the record price increase, many of these had already passed through their period of maximum impact when lumber prices sky-rocketed in 1993. It is impossible to say exactly how much of the increase was due to the owl, but analysts all agree the owl *did* account for at least 20 percent of the increase in lumber prices.[13] It may actually be much more. What is of greater concern to the analysts is the realization that we are near capacity in lumber production, and lumber shortages are a possibility in the future. Prices of lumber and homes will escalate dramatically unless artificial constraints on supplies are reduced.

THE COST OF REGULATION

The cost of regulation is almost beyond our ability to comprehend. For 1993, the federal budget for implementing all federal regulations exceeded $550 *billion*—exceeded only by the cost of social programs. It is estimated that 30 percent of the decline in American industrial productivity in the 1970s and 1980s can be traced to regulations imposed by the Environmental Protection Agency and the Occupational Safety and Health Administration.[14] Ex-governor of Washington Dixy Lee Ray points out in her book *Environmental Overkill* that "regulations have required $1.4 *trillion* to be spent since 1970 on cleaning up roughly 90 percent of industrial air and water pollution; the next 5 percent will cost an additional $1.6 trillion, amounting to another $25,000 per family of four."[15]

These data reflect only the cost to the government to regulate. What about the costs to businesses that are passed along to the consumer? These costs are hard to determine due to confounding effects of one action on another. However, William Laffer III, a nationally recognized economist, has reviewed the various estimates of numerous other economists and estimates that the "direct costs of regulation on the economy currently amount to at least some $636 billion to $857 billion per year, or between $6,565 and $8,869 annually per household!"[16] Regulations have benefits for their costs. However, even after subtracting the benefits, Laffer estimates the "net direct cost of regulation is some $364 to $538 billion per year, or between $3,762 and $5,561 annually per household."[17]

This is right out of your pocket. Do you think you could spend $4,000 to $5,500 better than Uncle Sam? Yet, in spite of this enormous drain on our economy, President Clinton's head of economic advisers, Laura D' Andrea Tyson, told a panel of congressmen that the United States is "an undertaxed nation." There is, she claimed, "no relationship" between a nation's tax burden and its rate of economic growth.[18] Incredible.

But it gets worse. The above figures merely include "direct" costs of regulation compliance to business and consumers. They do not include any of the indirect costs of regulation. Hidden costs include reduction in productivity and output caused by the direct costs, impacts on technical innovations, entrepreneurs throwing in the towel, and many other factors. The 1990 Clean Air Act, for instance, affects 150,000 small businesses from dry-cleaners to auto-body repair shops. In some businesses, the act will cost a small business between $10,000 and $15,000 just for the paperwork to get a permit, and the equipment to monitor emissions will cost another $10,000 to $50,000. To catch spray fumes, auto-repair shops have to buy equipment that costs $100,000![19] This will represent the death knell for tens of thousands of "mom and pop" entrepreneurs who can't afford compliance costs.

Guess who pays for the added costs when competition is removed from the "big boys"? If these are added, Laffer estimates the total cost of regulations could be "between $1.056 *trillion* and $1.969 *trillion* per year, or between $10,922 and $20,376 per household per year."[20] Economists Michael Hazilla of American University and Raymond Krupp of Resources for the Future, a Washington-based think tank, estimate the portion due to federal air and water legislation alone is $320 billion or $3,200 per family.[21] Though economists admit these figures are subject to uncertainty, they are staggering even if they are wrong by 50 percent. Regulations are killing America. It is estimated that environmental regulation alone caused the loss of approximately *4 million jobs* in 1990.[22]

No one is immune. Every American is affected when senseless regulations or lawsuits stop production, divert resources, or otherwise thwart entrepreneurs who would in different circumstances have contributed to the quality of life. That doesn't mean we should throw away all regulations and prohibit lawsuits. But most of those that are demanded by environmental leadership fall into the senseless category. They do little to help protect the environment—in spite of all the motherhood-and-apple-pie rhetoric to the contrary—and do much to damage the economy. National economist and author Larry Burkett reports in his book *Whatever Happened to the American Dream?* that the number of pages of regulations in the Federal Register went from 20,000 in 1970 to a whopping 87,000 in 1980 during the Carter administration. President Reagan brought it back down to about 50,000 during his term, but by 1993 it was spiraling past 70,000 pages towards the record set by Carter.[23] This translates into an increase from 16,500 federal regulations in 1954 to 200,000 today.[24]

Environmentalism is a story of innocence lost. It has become big business, more concerned with winning at any cost than with moral principle. The only thing separating environmental groups from the corporations they hate is that environmental groups don't have to compete in the real world and are not regulated, scrutinized, and investigated by endless governmental agencies and investigative reporters trying to catch them with their hand in the till. Environmental leaders can do with impunity what corporate leaders cannot even think of.

Environmentalism is destroying the American dream. The dream that each generation will have a better life is already lost. That hope was smashed with the counterculture. Now eco-leaders are taking direct aim at individual freedoms—those supposedly guaranteed by the United States Constitution. Step by step, law by law, regulation by regulation, these freedoms are being stripped away. After doing a study on the impacts of regulations, economist Burkett observed:

> Invariably, [regulations] hit small business with rules too complex for the most skilled engineers to understand, laws too complex for the government's own attorneys to explain, and a gestapo-like police force that can violate nearly every constitutional restriction placed on the government with impunity.[25]

Regulation and the taxation that feeds it is out of control. But it's not a tale only about costs and human tragedy. One of the worst consequences of environmental mania is that we are turning ourselves into a police state. Dixy Lee Ray laments:

> Today the number of law enforcement personnel assigned to carry out the edicts of all the new environmental laws must rival the number of traditional police. In the name of 'protecting our environment,' we not only have officials scouring

> the country for violators of environmental regula-
> tions, but neighbor is being set against neighbor
> to spy upon and report any suspected breaking
> of the myriad of environmental rules.[26]

One can only assume that this is by design. During the October 1992 meeting of the Environmental Grantmakers Association, Debra Callahan made it clear that the tool of choice for bringing about their economic and social transformation is regulation: "It's about individualism versus the Federal government, it's Federalism—the right to regulate." Like Alex Dolgos, the U.S. Army Corps of Engineer's "enforcer" who filed the charges that eventually put Bill Ellen into prison, these leaders openly admit that the federal government must have absolute, unchallenged power over its citizens. Rather than government "for the people," they believe people must serve the government.

Under greatest assault by this regulate-to-the-death mentality is the Fifth Amendment to the United States Constitution, which protects the rights of all landowners. Under the Fifth Amendment, no land shall be "taken" by any state or federal agency without just compensation to the landowner. But as discussed in chapter 4, land ownership is heresy to environmental leadership. To make regulation seem more palatable for the masses, Callahan suggests the concept of constitutional "takings" outlawed by the Fifth Amendment be changed and "called 'givings,' where in fact environmental regulations protect the public interest."[27] And who defines what is in the public's interest? They do, of course.

Supporting Callahan on this issue, representatives of the federally funded National Trust for Historic Preservation admitted, "We have to defend regulation. . . . Is there a way to play the game here so that the facts of the issue that's before a court . . . or legislature are in fact things that play our way to broaden the support base for property regulation?"[28]

Like the Environmental Grantmakers Association, the National Trust for Historic Preservation is becoming a "secretariat of sorts for a group that includes groups like National Audubon, Environmental Defense Fund, National Wildlife Federation and others" to promote regulation.[29] The objective of this regulation is to provide total power to the government, which in turn is highly influenced and progressively controlled by eco-leaders. The definition of fascism is worth repeating:

> Fascism: A political and economic system,
> strongly nationalistic, magnifying the rights of the
> state as opposed to those of the individual, in
> which industry, though remaining largely under
> private ownership, and all administrative political
> units, are controlled by a central government. [30]

Perhaps the expression "ecofascism," coined by conservative Rush Limbaugh (radio and TV talk show host), is an appropriate expression of environmental leadership's true political agenda. There is a nice fit between the political ideologies of fascism and the religious theology of Theosophy held by many of the eco-leaders.

INSTITUTIONAL STABILITY

Let us recall that a pattern has emerged revealing the strategy of environmental leaders, from a growing number of national environmental organizations and from federal regulating agencies themselves. First these leaders create the *perception* of an environmental holocaust by manufacturing plausible horror scenarios based to a small degree in truth. Once the "catastrophe" is raised to the level of hysteria, environmental leaders use the sense of urgency to demand that legislation be passed *now*, before it is too late. Several key elements govern their lobbying efforts. Though they call it "conservation," in reality they demand that the law be centered on *preservation*—i.e., the elimination of *all* use. Simultaneously, they demand that the law use regulations employing government control to achieve solutions rather than incentives that encourage individual creativity to find the desired solution.

Finally, the legislation must include provisions to allow "individuals" to *intervene* if they see violations of the regulations. This gives these environmental leaders the right for their organizations to harass and intimidate regulating agencies and citizens for stricter enforcement. It permits their own organizations to file lawsuits against anyone they perceive is violating what is, in essence, their own law. Most citizens are unaware that hundreds of millions of dollars are being squandered in frivolous lawsuits against government agencies and private citizens by environmental organizations using the very laws the organizations pushed into enactment.

These strategies have had a destabilizing influence on America's economic structure. Corporations and businesses must have a degree of assurance that investments they make today will survive long enough to pay for themselves tomorrow. The higher the risk or uncertainty, the higher the payback must be to justify the risk. The risk is determined within the framework of what is called institutional stability—the stability and predictability of the near and long-term political, economic, and legal institutions. The uncertainty created by constantly changing laws and regulations plus the good chance that what is legal today will incur litigation and uncertain penalties tomorrow destroys institutional stability. This makes it very difficult for businesses to build new facilities or expand when the future of that investment is clouded with so much uncertainty. As a consequence, recapitalization in America of our basic economic infrastructure is at an all-time low. Corporations and businesses are moving offshore or closing their doors, taking jobs with them.

Eco-leaders will claim that this is but another evidence of corporate greed. Greed certainly plays a role—as it potentially does with *every* human being—but greed is not the basis of this problem. Neither jobs nor money materialize out of thin air. Someone has to have the necessary money to invest in a company so it can expand to meet a growing market or retool to remain competitive. Now, let's bring the issue of greed down to your pocketbook. Let's say you decide to buy U.S. savings bonds for your children's college education or your own retirement. You could earn more if you invested in stocks and bonds. But you don't. Not because you're not greedy, but because you don't understand these complex markets and there is a *high risk* you can lose all your investment. So instead you invest in twenty-year U.S. savings bonds. Their returns are lower but assured. In other words, they are *stable*.

But wait. What if the government suddenly decided to reduce the national debt by reducing the interest it pays on your bonds — after you had already held them ten years. Now you won't break even with inflation. Or worse, what if they passed a law that nationalized not only your interest but part of your principle? Now you've really lost. You would have been better off buying that fancy car and at least having some enjoyment from your hard-earned money. Now you've unfairly been stuck with paying off someone else's debt! Should you invest again? If so, in what? The government assures you that this won't happen again—invest in America

—buy more bonds! But will you? How certain are you now that your hard-earned investment will survive long enough to pay off? It has nothing to do with greed but everything to do with wisdom—which depends on institutional stability. In effect, this is the sort of dilemma American businesses, companies, corporations, and landowners face as the consequences of environmental legislation.

Institutional stability is so important to companies that they have often been willing to accept unnecessary regulations just so they can forecast their costs—which they pass along to the consumer. Many also know that these regulations will force weak or new entries out of the market, thereby reducing competition. Some corporations even make huge donations to environmental groups in attempts to appease them. But, as we have already seen, biocentric earth saviors can never be appeased. As a consequence, though competition may be reduced, profit margins continue to narrow as potential consumers lose their jobs, and the ever-increasing avalanche of regulations continue to take their toll. All Americans come out the big losers.

Senator and past presidential candidate George McGovern found this out the hard way. McGovern was a staunch liberal who promoted many of the laws and regulations we have to live with now. After retiring from the Senate, he operated an inn in Connecticut and found he could not survive the regulations. "I wish," laments the senator, "that during the years I was in public office I had had this firsthand experience about the difficulties business people face every day. That knowledge would have made me a better U.S. Senator." McGovern then explains the impact these regulations have had on his business. "While I have never doubted the worthiness of these goals," he concludes, "the concept that most often eludes legislators is: Can we make consumers pay the higher prices for the increased operating costs that accompany public regulation and government reporting requirements with reams of red tape?"[31] The answer, the senator found, is no.

THE ROLE OF THE MEDIA

If all of this is true, why haven't we been told? The press has been strangely silent. Why? The media has been so silent that Americans have trouble believing anyone who would bring them the truth. It is not that the information is hard to get. Any good reporter or journalist can easily find and expose this deceit. So why isn't the other side being reported?

Part of the explanation, of course, is basic human nature. Just as environmental leadership must offer up scary "catastrophes" to get people to send $25 to their organizations, catastrophes sell more newspapers than the good news that Mother Earth is generally safe and sound. Greed and self-preservation is a strong driving force for any person or institution, whether it is an environmental organization, a newspaper chain or national network, a giant industrial corporation, or even a labor union. Ben Bradlee, editor of the *Washington Post*, said the news could go to perdition: "I'm interested in causes. *We don't print the truth.* We don't pretend to print the truth. We print what people tell us. It's up to the public to decide what is true."[32] With that editorial attitude, Americans will continue to be mere puppets manipulated by what the media wants us to hear.

This thinking may dominate editorial staffs across the nation, but it is doubtful. Rather, a far more likely reason the media has been so one-sided is probably that most of the reporters and journalists today grew up during or after the counterculture movement. Even if they weren't part of it, the "civilization is destroying the earth" dogma that flooded the news during and since the movement generates its own credibility. The psychology that "if you hear it often enough, it becomes reality" contains tremendous truth. Not only has this predisposed the media to believe it, but it has had the same effect on all Americans.

Contrary to some thinking, the media does have a responsibility to take an advocacy role, and it always has. The media has never been unbiased, nor should it be. What has happened today, however, is that it has allowed itself to become so blind to any idea that is contrary to the prevailing "truth," that it can't see the forest for the trees. This explanation is supported by statements from numerous reporters. For instance, Charles Alexander, science editor for *Time*, "freely admits that on this issue [the environment], we have crossed the boundary from news reporting to advocacy." Likewise, Dianne Dumanoski, environmental reporter for the *Boston Globe*, admits "there is no such thing as objective reporting. . . . I've become even more crafty about finding the voices to say the things I think are true. That's my subversive mission."[33]

By becoming *blind* advocates, many in the media have abandoned their journalistic responsibilities. And Americans are suffering as a consequence. The bad news is that this blindness still dominates the media. The good news is that this blindness seems to be gradually lifting, as more and more reporters are seeing through the grandstanding and deceit of environmentalism. One of the most famous of these is conservative radio talk show host Rush Limbaugh. His analysis and humor have done more to expose the deceit than any other mainline media outlet. Jim Robbins, freelance writer for the *Boston Globe,* exposed the religious and biocentric beliefs of the radical environmentalists. He even reported that such beliefs were held by many in such "mainstream groups as the Sierra Club and Audubon Society . . . though it is not an overt part of their politics."[34] *New York Times* environmental reporter Keith Schneider has also reported on the hypocrisy of environmental organizations.[35] Not surprisingly, these journalists have been viciously attacked by eco-leaders.[36]

THE WORST YET TO COME?

Mom and pop businesses and homeowners are increasingly running afoul of the growing power and unaccountability of regulators and eco-leaders bent on suing anyone who violates their biocentric view of environmental purity. These bureaucrats have the unchallenged power to prevent anyone from building on or using his property without permits from the mother agency. If these permits are available at all, obtaining them involves expensive consultants and years of waiting. And that assumes, of course, that people knew in advance that they were required to obtain permits. Some hapless homeowners have been forced to tear down their homes on dry land for violating unknown or obscure wetlands regulation. Others have had to restore or create swamps to avoid even worse penalties after running afoul of murky regulations. The bizarre misuse of power by the so-called "green police" has wiped out the life savings of many moms and pops.

If the unholy alliance between environmental leadership and government regulators is already putting people into prison for trivial and senseless reasons, dark days are ahead for anyone foolish enough to question the environmental crusade these leaders have launched. With this type of delusion at the highest levels of government, one can only imagine what is in store for America. If the Bill Ellens of the world are going to prison already, what is going to happen now that Vice President Gore has placed environmental extremists into key governmental positions and is throwing the door open to an avalanche of environmental regulation? Perhaps the word *eco-gestapo* will, in fact, describe the type of terror tactics that will be used in the future.

We do have environmental problems, but nothing to the extent Vice President Gore is claiming. Clinton's apparent compromise in the jobs-versus-owls crisis in the Timber Summit, April 2, 1993, brought forth a stream of vindictives from national environmental leadership that was "surprisingly strong even by their own standards" observed a *Washington Post* writer the following day. Jay Hair, president of the National Wildlife Federation, proclaimed that he "now knows what it means to be date raped." It is hard to understand this stance. After all, the president's decision did eliminate nearly two-thirds of the historic harvest in the Northwest, throwing another estimated 35,000 people out of work. If they felt "sexually violated" with that decision, what do you suppose they wanted that would have made them happy? Everyone's job?

This severe rhetoric apparently worked. During the summer of 1993, in the name of "finding balance," Mr. Clinton mandated a reduction in federal harvesting of timber in the West more severe than environmental leaders had demanded before the April Timber Summit.

Perhaps the eco-leaders should ask themselves: When the economy collapses, how are we going to afford to pay for environmental protection?

If environmentalists had a good replacement for our traditional, and proven, conservation practices, perhaps we could make the adjustment. The problem is, they don't.

We must be clear concerning the order of magnitude of the changes that are needed. We are not concerned here with some minor adaptations, but with the most serious transformation of human-earth relations that has taken place at least since the classical civilizations were founded. Human technologies should function in an integral relation with earth technologies.

Thomas Berry
The Dream of the Earth
Sierra Club Books, 65

Native Americans worshiped the Earth as sacred, and the European Americans treated what they called soil as a commodity to be owned. Whereas the Native Americans revered the earth, referring to it as Mother Earth, and had no concept of ownership, the European Americans drew imaginary lines in the soil, called them boundaries, and said, 'This is mine [to be exploited].'
. . . Such exploitation began to hack and hew at Mother Earth with an unrelenting sword whose epithet is the economics of extinction.

Chris Maser
Forest Primeval
Sierra Club Books, xv, xx

No person shall be . . . deprived of life, liberty, or property without due process of law; nor shall private property be taken for public use, without just compensation.

Fifth Amendment to the Constitution
of the United States of America

9

PROPERTY RIGHTS AND SUSTAINABLE DEVELOPMENT

ECONOMICS, PROPERTY RIGHTS, AND ENVIRONMENTALISM

I'm through; it's not worth it anymore." After spending some $13 million in projects that benefited the citizens in and around Bangor, Maine, Judson Grant had thrown in the towel. Growing disenchanted with the blizzard of regulations since the mid-1980s, his last effort had turned into a bureaucratic nightmare.[1] Grant had planned to build a gasoline/restaurant/car wash complex in an expanding area of Bangor. Starting in 1989 he spent a year securing all the necessary permits from the city and state authorities, including the Maine Department of Environmental Protection. At one time a wetlands, the site had been filled in for decades and there was no longer any standing water. Except, that is, for a few places where the water formed very small puddles on top of the otherwise dry fill for a few days each spring and fall. Tag alder and a few bulrushes had also become established on top of the fill—both of which are on the 1989 Federal Wetlands Species list.[2]

About halfway through construction, a Fish and Wildlife agent passed by. Having previously noted the tag alder and bulrushes, this federal employee reported Grant to the EPA for a Section 404 violation of wetlands. The EPA issued a cease and desist order and all construction was halted. Major design changes were demanded, along with an order to replace the "lost" wetlands with new ones—at Grant's expense.

After a $20,000 fine and agreement by Grant to all of the changes, Grant was once again allowed to resume construction. Winter had arrived, however, and all outside construction had to be postponed until the following spring. By the time Grant added up all of the costs of the delays, design changes, and fines, he had spent more than $250,000![3]

Such constricting regulations have a huge but hidden economic cost. What should take days or weeks to accomplish now takes months and years to work through the bureaucratic maze, plus the costs of expensive consultants. And as happened to Judson Grant, the landowner still doesn't know if he or she may have missed some obscure regulation that can add fines, delays, and additional costs midway through the project. That is, if the person manages to stay out of prison. Grant was perhaps more fortunate than he realized.

Multiply Grant's experience by tens of thousands, and you can start to appreciate the financial drag these senseless regulations are having on our nation's economy and each and every American. The cost is staggering.

THE ATTACK ON PROPERTY RIGHTS

Although environmental concerns have some basis in fact, when any nation bases its policy in fiction rather than scientific truth, it is only a matter of time before that society begins to collapse. The mindless attack by the Conservation Law Foundation, Sierra Club, National Audubon Society, and Wilderness Society against the commercial fishermen, landowners, and timber companies in northern New England is but a small example. Their "economic solution" is the kind of mythic hope that something will work just because they "think" it should. Nations are destroyed by accepting such irrationality as the cornerstone for policy.

An example of this can be found in the downfall of Communism around the world. The disintegration of the Communist empire was brought about by placing hope in an ideology that was doomed from the start because it was not based in reality. Instead, all truth in the USSR started and ended with its vast cadre of elite bureaucrats. It survived only as long as it was able to suck the lifeblood from its people. It should be sobering to every citizen to realize that many in America are demanding the same type of paralyzing bureaucratic central control.

In spite of the fact that central bureaucratic control has always proven to be a failure, the environmental elite are demanding a total restructuring of our economic system. The focus of their attack is on property rights. By controlling property rights, the management and uses of our natural resources can be controlled, not by proven conservation practices but by some mystical hope in metaphysics and spiritual communion with nature. Remember, to the everything-is-god beliefs of environmental leadership, no one should be allowed to own another part of god. To their way of looking at it, property rights are anti-god and should be abolished.

The biggest problem in the quest for abolishing property rights is that these rights are protected by the Fifth Amendment to the United States Constitution. This Amendment centers on the premise that the government cannot take private land for "the public good" without paying for it: "No person shall be . . . deprived of life, liberty, or *property* without due process of law; nor shall private property be taken for public use, without just compensation" (italics added). The right to own and use land with minimum constraints has not only played a large part in making our nation great, it is the best protection of the rest of our civil rights. To our founding fathers, property rights were every bit as important to a healthy and free society as the "freedom of speech" clause in the First Amendment. John Adams once said, "The moment that idea is admitted into society that property is not as sacred as the Laws of God, and that there is not a force of law and public justice to protect it, anarchy and tyranny commence. Property must be sacred or liberty cannot exist."

John Adams was correct. Property rights is a giant scale that balances the awesome power of the government with that of the people. Without property rights our remaining civil rights are an illusion. It is no coincidence that now that property rights are being assailed, tyranny has resulted. Once America gives its property rights to the federal government, we will have lost the only instrument that protects us from total control by the government. Like the feudal lords of medieval days, the federal government will have total control over every aspect of our lives. And the federal government is especially prone to rule by pressure groups.

The assault on property rights can be said to have been started by none other than the Rockefellers in 1972. During that year, the Rockefeller Brothers Fund sponsored a task force, which published a report entitled *Use of Land: A Citizen's Policy Guide to*

Urban Growth. The task force was chaired by Laurance Rockefeller, and the report was edited by William Reilly, who went on to become the administrator of the EPA under President Bush. The report has proved pivotal to the successful attack on property rights during the 1970s and 1980s. The thrust of the report supported the premise that development rights of private property should be at the discretion of the government for the good of society. Environmental protection areas would be protected "not by purchase but through the police power of the federal government."[4] In other words, although people could own and pay taxes on land, they could use and develop it only by permission of the government through local and regional land use and/or planning commissions. It is no accident that in recent years such commissions have proliferated—usually having total autonomy from the people they regulate. History records an interesting tea party in Boston held by those who had somewhat similar complaints about nonrepresentation. That is why the Constitution is supposed to protect us from that type of tyranny today.

The history behind the Fifth Amendment dates back to the English Magna Charta. It is based on the fundamental principle that freedom to own and use land wisely, and without government interference, is at the heart of the economic well-being and freedom of the nation. One only needs to look at the various governmental models that exist in the world to note the successes of those nations having strong property rights provisions, and the poverty of those that do not. Certainly, other factors are at work also, but as Calvin Coolidge once affirmed, "Ultimately property rights and personal rights are the same thing."

This belief has been reaffirmed by numerous Supreme Court decisions throughout America's history—until the late 1960s. Although sometimes abused, the Fifth Amendment has worked well for "takings" that involve highway rights-of-way and condemnation efforts. However, it has been almost totally ineffective in protecting landowners from the gradual erosion of landowner rights for supposed "environmental protection."

In 1922 Justice Holmes ruled that "while property may be regulated to a certain extent, if regulation goes too far it will be recognized as a taking."[5] But what is "too far"? In determining whether the Fifth Amendment applied in a litigation process in the 1970s and 1980s, the courts would determine if "the rights of the individual" endangered the rights or the safety of other people (i.e., a nuisance). If the government could define the land use as a "nuisance," then the "good of the many" would legally prevail over land rights. Through a series of court decisions, the definition of nuisance was so ambiguous that almost anything qualified. The courts shifted the basis for reviewing a "taking" from one of nuisance to one of "public good, or public trust."[6] The public trust doctrine historically was one in which land or water could only be put in trust for the public good by the courts. Once this shift was made, the government could regulate and restrict use on private property at will without any interference from the courts, and without paying for it:

> The public trust doctrine is the perfect tool
> to avoid paying [for private land]. With no
> economic penalty to be borne for their actions,
> the environmental movement's incentive is strong
> to eliminate every last scrap of private property
> in America. Environmental lawyers have pressed
> literally hundreds of cases in recent years
> invoking the public trust doctrine for
> environmental protection, expanding the
> concept of "essential for public use" to
> encompass virtually all private property.[7]

This was made all the easier by another ruling. Before a "takings" could be claimed, the court directed that the landowner had to demonstrate he or she had exhausted every effort to obtain permits and find alternative uses for the land. This could take decades and money most people don't have.

Very few people would deny that there are times when the environment is legitimately threatened and property rights should be limited. But what defines the point of damage? From a biocentric viewpoint, *any* disturbance to the environment where man benefits at the expense of nature threatens the environment. Lawsuits are constantly being filed to prevent landowners from managing land in a nonbiocentric manner. The fact that there are legitimate concerns has made it easy for environmental leaders to extend the process to situations where the threat is more imagined than real. There simply have been no scientifically based guidelines for the courts to follow. So the courts have had to make up their own guidelines on what seems right—something environmental leaders have become expert at doing through the use of conservation biology.

For more than fifteen years the courts have backed the government—"It is a nuisance (i.e., not in the public good) because they said it is." The effort has progressively stripped tens of thousands, perhaps hundreds of thousands, of landowners of the right to use their land in a prudent fashion. As long as the landowner could use his land for "something," it would not be considered a "taking." With the 1989 redefinition of Federal Wetlands Jurisdiction, for instance, many landowners saw what was previously dry uplands turned into wetlands, leaving them with only a fraction of the land for use. No compensation is offered those who lost the use of their land, yet they are still expected to pay their property taxes. Donald Walker, Jr., Judson Grant, and tens of thousands of other Americans have found this out the hard way.

THE LAND RIGHTS MOVEMENT

A backlash against environmental extremism is rapidly growing. A mushrooming number of landowners, land managers, and natural resource users are becoming frustrated over the never-ending attack by environmental leadership and government regulators bent on "saving the earth." Called by various names such as "land rights," "multiple use," "wise use" and others, these grass-roots groups are forming almost monthly because citizens are fed up with having their property rights systematically stripped from them.

Interestingly, these land-rights/wise-use groups are often accused of being as radical as some of the environmental groups. Some of them probably are. What Americans do not realize, however, is that environmental leadership has defined the playing field for the land-rights groups. Claiming to desire solutions, eco-leadership bring *nothing* to the collaborating table, while the landowners and small businesses bring their very lives and livelihood. Eco-leadership repeatedly negotiates "solutions," only to then claim the "solutions" are not enough.

Sickened by such tactics, landowners and managers have come to call this the "*50 percent rule*." Innocent landowners who want to find collaborative agreement give 50 percent of their rights away, believing that such compromise will be enough for environmental leaders. Environmental leaders give nothing. Once agreement is reached, the landowner is stunned to find that "enough" apparently is not enough after all. These same environmental leaders are after the next 50 percent until the landowner has nothing.

Any good negotiator knows that when one side tries to collaborate for win/win solutions and the other bargains for win/lose (i.e., winner take all), those who collaborate *always* lose. That is exactly what has happened to the landowners and resource managers who have tried to work with eco-leaders. This deception is tragic because the vast majority of environmentalists want to find solutions. A 1992 Gallup poll found that 75 percent of Americans believe the environment can be protected while using natural resources for man's benefit. But as long as national and radical state level environmental leadership is guided by biocentric thinking, issues will continue to be polarized, and collaborative solutions will continue to be impossible.

It should come as no surprise that environmental leadership decries land-rights/wise-use groups as being affiliated with the Moonies, backed by big industry, and part of a ultraright wing fanatical Christian sect that is bent on destroying the environment.[8] Nothing could be further from the truth. The vast majority of people joining these grass-roots organizations are everyday Americans coming from a wide background of professions, interests, and personal beliefs. It is ironic that although environmental leadership knows this, they are continuing their all-out smear campaign, calling these groups "fronts," extremists, exploiters, and so forth. In doing so they have trapped themselves in an enormous media manipulation effort.

Remember the October 1992 annual meeting of the Environmental Grantmakers Association? Debra Callahan, Director of the Environmental Grass Roots Program of the W. Alton Jones Foundation, explained she had previously thought of the resistance to environmentalism as coming from "command and control, top heavy, corporate-funded, front groups."[9] That is not, however, what the study found. Lamenting, Callahan continued:

What we're finding is that wise use is really a local movement driven by primarily local concerns and not by national issues. . . . And in fact the more

> we dig into it having put together a fifty . . .
> state fairly comprehensive survey of what's going
> on . . . we have come to the conclusion that
> this is pretty much generally a grass roots
> movement, which is a problem because it
> means there's no silver bullet.[10] This is
> happening in every single state.[11]

Callahan, whose own foundation distributes more than $7 million annually to environmental organizations, admits, "Some of these grass roots groups are dirt poor."[12] Contrary to the very-well-financed environmental organizations, the grass-roots groups receive little to no money from industry and operate on a shoestring—almost always depending on their own personal resources to carry on their efforts. Few, if any, land-rights/wise-use leaders appear to be in the fray for personal gain by desiring to exploit natural resources. Ironically, Callahan identifies the true stewards of the land in her continuing analysis:

> What they're [the land rights/wise use groups] are
> saying out there is 'we are the real environmental-
> ists.' We're the stewards of the land. We're the
> farmers who have tilled the land and know how to
> manage this land because we've done it for
> generations. We're the miners and we're the
> ones who depend for our livelihood on this land.
> These guys [environmentalists] live in glass
> towers in New York City. They're not environ-
> mentalists, they're elitists. They're part of
> the problem and they're aligned with big
> government and they're out of touch.[13]

Callahan is right; most landowners do tend to be very environmentally conscious. They want to use scientifically proven conservation practices as the basis for land use policy rather than pseudoscience and mythic "feelings." This message is so alarming that Callahan admonished those in attendance, "This means that this is something that is going to have to be confronted . . . across the country in different ways. . . . What people fundamentally believe about environmental protection is that no it's not just jobs and no it's not just environment—why can't we have both? The high ground here is capturing that message. And when Joe Sixpack hears that message he goes, 'you're right . . . people oughta be able to work, and the environment oughta be able to be managed.' The minute [property rights/ land use] people capture that high ground, we almost have not got a winning message left in our quiver."[14]

Unfazed by Callahan's report and the facts about property-rights/wise-use grass-roots organizations, environmental leadership attending the meeting decided to continue their smear campaign: "We must continue revealing the extreme positions of the wise use movement. We need to expose the links between wise use and other extremists: The Unification Church, The John Birch Society, Lyndon LaRouche and others."[15]

The national press is beginning to tumble onto this blatant deceit. In November 1992, Keith Schneider, *New York Times* environmental reporter, spoke at a forum entitled "The Wise Use Movement" sponsored by the Society of Environmental Journalists. Schneider observed:

I find it almost laughable that in the environmental press—the Audubon magazine, the Sierra Club magazine and others—the rap on the Wise Use Movement is that it's corporate funded. Well the largest corporate donation, that I know of, in the environmental movement is the million dollars that General Electric gives to the Audubon Society. . . . For the Audubon Society magazine to be criticizing the Wise Use Movement for corporate funding seems to me to *be just the height of hypocrisy. . . . The property rights groups that I know of have no corporate funding at all.* They're basically "mom and pop" type community environmental groups. . . . It's the restrictions on property, the *constitutional issue,* that's driving the heart of the movement. And that's I think what we need to watch.[16]

Such blatant deceit from environmental leaders suggests they are either guilty of the same greed they accuse multinational corporations of having, or they are trying to throw up a smoke screen to cover their own religious extremism. More likely it is both. In other words, we don't care about the truth and business-as-usual. Is it any wonder landowners and resource managers can trust little that is said by them?

We have indeed passed through the looking glass, where right becomes wrong and wrong becomes right. Every American should be alarmed that the Fifth Amendment to the Constitution provides no protection to Donald Walker from a "taking" by the federal government, yet the Endangered Species Act provides total protection to the spotted owl from a supposed "taking" by Donald Walker. Perhaps it is this type of injustice that Thomas Jefferson envisioned when he warned, "In questions of power, then, let no more be heard of confidence in man, but bind him down from mischief by the chains of the Constitution."

CONSTITUTIONAL VICTORY

There is hope, however. The courts are beginning to take a hard look at the abuses of the Fifth Amendment. In a 1992 Supreme Court case, *Lucas v. South Carolina Coastal Council,* the court rendered a decision in favor of Lucas. David and Martha Lucas bought two oceanfront lots in South Carolina for one million dollars in 1986. Surrounded by expensive homes on either side, Lucas planned to build a family home within a couple of years. In 1988, however, the state of South Carolina passed a Beachfront Management Act—under pressure from environmental leaders— prohibiting construction within a defined zone along the State Beaches.

Lucas's land was within the zone, and there was no way at that time for him even to get a special permit to build. The fact that homes were already established on either side of him didn't matter. Believing this to be a Fifth Amendment "taking," Lucas went to court. He won in the lower court, but the state appealed. Much to his dismay, the South Carolina Supreme Court found that Lucas could still use his land for "picnicking and camping," therefore his case was not a "taking." The two lots became the most expensive single-use picnic site in America. Taken all the way to the Supreme Court, the highest court in the land finally ruled in July 1992 that it was indeed a "taking," and the South Carolina

Supreme Court reversed itself and ruled that the state must either permit Lucas to build his home or reimburse him for his losses.

The case is significant because it ruled that Lucas did not have to exhaust every possible avenue to obtain a permit. But, more important, it shifted the burden of proof of a nuisance to the government, rather than the landowner:

[Regulations] requiring land to be left substantially in natural state, carry with them a heightened risk that private property is being pressed into some form of public service under the guise of mitigating serious public harm. . . . We emphasize that to win its case South Carolina must do more than proffer the legislative declaration that the uses Lucas desires are inconsistent with the public interest. [17]

Although the Lucas case was a significant victory for the Fifth Amendment, it cost Lucas more than $750,000 to fight it in court. Very few people who are systematically having their property rights stripped from them can afford to do battle with the government. The government usually wins by outlasting its opponents— using taxpayer dollars to fight the taxpayer! Even so, our Constitution may yet prove to be the undoing of the environmental leadership's attack on property rights.

But before everyone takes a collective sigh of relief, there is something we all should know. Environmental leadership has already embarked on a strategy to do an end run around the Constitution. It's called "sustainable development," and not only is it being used as an instrument to blur the distinction between public and private land, as in the case of the Northern Forest, it is the justification for what is rapidly becoming an open war on property rights.

The first salvo in this attack was the National Biological Survey Bill. This bill was the brainchild of Secretary of the Interior Bruce Babbitt (former chairman of the League of Conservation Voters) and Assistant Secretary George Frampton (past president of the Wilderness Society). It was put together in record time for a government agency during the spring and summer of 1993 and put on the fast track. Although the first target was likely to be the Northern Forest (see chapter 5), the bill worried landowners across America.

Babbitt and Frampton put together the perfect property rights assault weapon because it sounded so innocent. It was supposed to provide an inventory of ecosystems and species to permit sustainable development. However, according to Tom Lovejoy, Babbitt's science adviser, the National Biological Survey (NBS) would give the federal government absolute control over all development in America. "[The NBS will] map the whole nation for all biology and *determine development* for the whole country and *regulate it all* because that is our obligation as set forth in the Endangered Species Act"[18] (italics added).

Incredibly, during the Congressional Subcommittee and Committee hearings Babbitt and Frampton were adamant that landowners had no right to know when their land was being inventoried. Landowners were even denied their rights under the Freedom of Information Act to find out what the government had inventoried.

The decision of what was of biological significance was to be decided by federal scientists without any outside review. Discussions earlier in the book on wetlands and endangered species illustrate how arbitrary these decisions can be. By working in secrecy these federal scientists could develop a plan of reserves and corridors similar to those outlined in the Wildlands Project (see chapter 6) that lock up hundreds of millions of acres of land without any public participation—a grander version of what happened with the wetlands edict. The procedures used to collect and evaluate biological information in the Wildlands Project was chillingly similar to that in the bill.[19] Under this bill, millions of people could have awakened to find they had lost the use of their homes and land to reserves, corridors, and human buffer zones.

Although the bill sailed through various subcommittees, as landowners began to realize its horrendous implications, Congress was inundated with phone calls and letters from outraged citizens. On the day in October 1993 that the bill was to be voted upon, alerted Congressmen added key amendments that protected landowners and demanded that federal procedures would be reviewed by outside scientists. This was unacceptable to Babbitt. Even though Babbitt assured everyone that the bill was based on pure science and did not violate property rights, once the amendments were added he withdrew the bill.

This is how our political process is supposed to work. But the effort to neutralize property rights is far from over. Babbitt has indicated he has the authority to go around Congress to implement this plan. And the key to his success would be sustainable development. Not only was the National Biological Survey Bill centered on sustainable development, but so was the June 1992 Earth Summit at Rio de Janeiro. Why? Where did this new anti-property-rights weapon come from?

SUSTAINABLE DEVELOPMENT—THE HIDDEN AGENDA

Sustainable development. It has an appealing ring to it. It engenders a farsighted vision of the future whereby all development is scored on its ability to be sustained for future generations. Who can be against such lofty goals? If the concept is applied correctly, no one. However, we saw in previous chapters how sustainable agriculture and sustainable use have double meanings. Is the same true for sustainable development? The answer is a resounding yes. And, unless Americans are very careful, our Constitution could soon prove to be a worthless piece of paper that will protect no one.

THE BRUNDTLAND REPORT

Attempting to define sustainable development can be difficult, but the United Nations gave it a shot in the mid-1980s. After much waxing and waning, what has come to be known as the Brundtland Report was published in 1987. Named after Norwegian Prime Minister Gro Harlem Brundtland, who headed up the commission assigned the task, the definition can be summarized: "Fundamentally, sustainable development is a notion of discipline. It means humanity must ensure that meeting present needs does not compromise the ability of the future generations to meet their own needs. And that means disciplining our current consumption."[20]

That sounds simple enough, but there are some hidden traps that could destroy any nation's economy. For instance, if the definition was being enforced, say in 1960, America's budding electronics industry would be in shambles today. Most telecommunication at that time was by phone, transmitted through copper wires. At best, fiber optics were still in the experimental stage and yet unproven, and satellite communications were still a dream, the only known use limited to science fiction novels.

Copper is found only in limited supplies around the world. Increasing demand for copper was being caused by the rapid expansion of the electronics, telecommunications, and refrigeration industry. Copper was being depleted at alarming rates in the 1960s, and prices were at all-time highs. Forecasts were being made that copper would be depleted shortly after the year 2000 at that rate of consumption—even with recycling. Strict adherence to the above definition of sustainable development would demand that use of copper be cut dramatically—maybe by 80 percent or more. Yet, such a curtailment would have killed the technology development that gave us fiber optics, satellite communications, plastics, and composites that have dramatically *reduced* the need for copper.

The same story could be told for agriculture. Paul Ehrlich predicted in his 1968 best-seller *The Population Bomb* that there would be massive starvation in the world by the 1970s and 1980s. Not only did that not occur, but more food was available per capita during the 1980s than was available in 1960 when Ehrlich wrote his book. It wasn't (and still isn't) overpopulation or the lack of food that was the problem, but rather corrupt and dictatorial governmental policies and poor transportation systems.

Such Malthusian theories* have always proven wrong. Man has always developed alternative technologies to replace limiting resources. Yet, such Malthusian beliefs are fundamental to environmental mystic thinking. After all, if "nature knows best," then man cannot improve on anything nature does without irreparable damage being done.

Although time and science are proving these environmental theories wrong, we should not be careless and wasteful about using our natural resources—just the opposite. We should use them wisely, using good stewardship practices. In spite of these limitations, sustainable development as a guiding principle does have merit. The Malthusian pitfalls can be avoided if we don't allow ourselves to become trapped into dead-end mystic reasoning. Unfortunately, however, it appears that Malthusian dogma is not the most serious problem we have with sustainable development.

The saga of sustainable development has more twists and turns than a James Bond spy thriller. Far more serious is the fact that the Brundtland definition of sustainable development isn't the

---

* *Malthusian theories* pertain to the theories of T. R. Malthus, which state that population tends to increase faster than the means of subsistence, resulting in an inadequate supply of food and necessary goods. Therefore, populations must be limited by slowing growth or reduced by war, famine, or disease.

one really being used to form policy within the United Nations Environmental Programme. It is merely window dressing for public consumption.

THE STRATEGY

Many within the Brundtland Commission were unhappy with the tone and direction of the report, including Brundtland herself. They were upset because it did not accomplish what they had desired. The reason? The report had to be written from a man-centered point of view* to be palatable to the public. Brundtland maintains that the only way that people can realize "that living as we do will make it impossible for [our] grandchildren to live at all" is to make us accept it as "a religious belief."[21] Secretary General of the Brundtland Commission Jim MacNeill summarized his concerns in this way, "Much of what God created, man is now destroying. . . . The world's economic and political constitutions are *seriously out of step* with the workings of nature"[22] (italics added).

In short, what MacNeill is spelling out is that our economic and political foundations, our very Constitution is antinature and must be done away with or radically changed if we are to save the earth.

This should send chills down the back of every person in America. As faulty as it is, our constitutional form of government is perhaps the best ever devised by man, and is what has made this nation great. And it is being attacked by sleight of hand.

Just after the Brundtland Report was released, the Ethics Working Group was quickly created by the United Nations to develop the alternative definition of sustainable development. This alternative definition would provide the real working definition for developing UN environmental policy, whereas the Brundtland definition would provide the palatable definition to be used for public consumption. It was to include a "world ethic of sustainability for the transformation of human attitudes and values."[23] Under the leadership of the International Union for Conservation of Nature and Natural Resources (IUCN), the Ethics Working Group was to be a joint collaboration of the IUCN, UNEP (United Nations Environmental Programme), and the World Wide Fund for Nature (WWFN).

IUCN is composed of a union of more than 450 government and environmental organizations around the world. As discussed

---

* This is called *anthropocentrism*, which means man-centered as opposed to *biocentrism*, or life (nature) centered.

in chapter 6, the IUCN was given birth in 1980 by the United Nations Environmental Programme, the United Nations Education, Scientific, and Cultural Organization, and the World Wildlife Fund. Its charter purpose was to develop "a new ethic embracing plants and animals as well as people" in developing global policy.[24] The IUCN has been the prime mover pushing conservation biology to the forefront of science.

The 1987 Ethics Working Group, headed by J. Ronald Engel, was a closed group of self-appointed elitists with a narrowly defined mission: define sustainable development around "a new moral conception of world order":

"Sustainable," by definition, means not only indefinitely prolonged, but nourishing, as the Earth is nourishing to life, and as a healthy natural environment is nourishing for the self-actualizing of persons and communities. The word 'development' need not be restricted to economic activity, . . . but can mean the evolution, unfolding, growth, and fulfillment of any and all aspects of life. Thus "sustainable development," in the broadest sense, may be defined as *the kind of human activity that nourishes and perpetuates the historical fulfillment of the whole community of life on Earth.*[25] (Italics original)

This definition, the group claimed, reflects "the spirit of Albert Schweitzer's 'Reverence for Life' and the biocentric and holistic perspective of . . . Aldo Leopold."[26] It is also right out of any New Age environmental handbook. Self-actualization is an expression used to indicate an individual's realized "god potential." "Communities" does not mean human communities, but rather the cosmic web of all life, including rocks. Evolution does not mean biological evolution, but the progression of higher states of consciousness through reincarnation until that "aspect of life" reaches its full potential in the highest of all conscious levels. The "historical fulfillment of the whole community of life on Earth" is merely a phrase that provides for the implementation of the philosophy that all things are god and have the right to evolve through reincarnation to their highest potential, and in bringing unity to the earth (see the lead-in at the beginning of the chapter).

It is this IUCN/UNEP/WWFN definition of sustainable development that is the key to understanding the environmental strategy being implemented on the local and global scale—a strategy having a one-two punch. The first punch uses the scare tactics of ecosystem or global environmental catastrophe to justify the need for radical transformation. The second punch uses sustainable development/biodiversity as the catalyst to neutralize America's Constitution. It is brilliant. If it works well, people will be begging to give up their freedoms to save themselves. This strategy could do in a few short years what would take environmental leaders perhaps decades to accomplish using normal litigation tactics.

The above definition is the basis for claiming that the forest practices used in the Northern Forests of the Northeast are not "sustainable." It is the basis for asserting that the use of chemicals and biotechnology in agriculture is not "sustainable." It is the basis for stating that golf courses are not "sustainable." It is the basis for scaring Americans into believing that Western civilization itself is not sustainable. By understanding this, America can understand why anything proven sustainable by science is not necessarily sustainable in the eyes of a New Age or deep ecology biocentrist.

By 1990–91, there was a growing acceptance by the public of environmental catastrophes. The terms "sustainable development" and "biodiversity" had also become household expressions as absolute "musts" in the quest to save the earth. The stage was set for the 1992 United Nations Conference on Environment and Development (UNCED)—more popularly known as the Earth Summit.

We can understand the Peace of Earth only if we understand the earth is a single community composed of all its geological, biological, and human components. The Peace of Earth is indivisible. This creative process is . . . groping toward an ever more complete expression of the [spiritual] mystery that is . . . leading to a supreme achievement: the global unity toward which all earthly developments were implicitly directed from the beginning. . . . This is the dream of the earth.

Thomas Berry
The Dream of the Earth, 223

This Constitution, and the Laws of the United States which shall be made in Pursuance thereof; and all Treaties made, or which shall be made, under the Authority of the United States Shall be the supreme Law of the Land; and the Judges in every State shall be bound thereby, any Thing in the Constitution or Laws of any State to the Contrary notwithstanding.

Article VI
Constitution of the United States

10

GLOBAL STRATEGIES

THE SUPER EPA

Ron Stevens lives in Memphis, Tennessee, where he owns an electrical repair shop. One day in 1987 Ron got the shock of his life. He received a bill from the EPA for $250,000 to clean up a Superfund site in Cape Girardeau, Missouri. So how did he get a bill for a quarter of a million dollars for damages in Missouri? Easy. He sold nine used transformers in 1977 to a parts distributor in St. Louis for $250. A few of these transformers wound up at the Missouri Electric Works in Cape Girardeau, which later became a Superfund site.* Transformers of that vintage contained oil with some PCBs, which can harm wildlife. According to Superfund rules, any party that contributed even an extremely small fraction to the problem can be held responsible for the entire cost of the cleanup. Ron was told he could either settle up for the $250,000 or face a lawsuit where he could wind up paying millions.[1]

---

* A Superfund toxic waste site is an area that falls under the Comprehensive Environmental Response, Compensation, and Liability Act of 1980. It is designed to clean up large hazardous waste dumps or spills that were created before environmental laws were in effect. Love Canal, New York, and Times Beach, Missouri, are two more commonly known Superfund sites.

Ron's case is common, not an exception. The EPA identifies a few companies it believes can shell out large amounts of money, then encourages them to sue others so that their share of the cleanup cost is spread among many. Those brought into the lawsuit are then encouraged to sue others, who are in turn encouraged to sue others, and so forth. Insurance companies, banks, private citizens (whose garbage may have gone into the landfill), and small businesses are all targets. A classic Big Brother tactic of "implicating your friends to save yourself." Such tactics used to be confined to gang lords and despots having dictatorial power over their subjects.

But these gestapolike tactics are not directed only toward those who actually or remotely contributed to the problem. They also extend to those having *nothing* to do with the problem. Mort Zuber of Hastings, Nebraska, found this out when he permitted the EPA to drill test holes on his land to determine the extent of contamination from a chemical leak originating in a factory across the street. Some thirty years earlier this now defunct factory had poured chemical solvents into the sewer system—a common and *legal* practice across America at that time. Apparently some of the solvent had leaked onto Zuber's property; since the factory had long ago closed its doors, Zuber got the bill. Comments Zuber: "It's as if they have pictures of you driving through an intersection 20 years ago. They say you didn't obey the stop sign. You say there wasn't any sign there. They say, well, there is now." So far, Zuber has spent $125,000 defending himself against this incredible but legal lawsuit.

Under the 1980 Comprehensive Environmental Response, Compensation and Liability Act (CERCLA), the EPA was authorized to sue polluters to recover the cost of the cleanup. It has turned into a lawyer's full employment law. It takes eight years of planning and studying before actual cleanup work begins. Only 157 out of 1,235 sites have been completed. Another 11,000 sites are pending. Originally thought to cost $44 billion for the entire cleanup, it is now costing $10 billion *per year*. This could increase to $20 billion per year by 2000.[2] Homeowners and businesses are having to declare bankruptcy. Many companies are closing their doors, throwing thousands of Americans out of work, and moving offshore to avoid the unbelievable risk of this type of EPA lawsuit. It is not because they are irresponsible. They just cannot afford the uncertain risk of having to pay for someone else's mess. Once again, institutional instability is costing America dearly in jobs and economic instability.

CERCLA is also destroying the recycling business. What trucking firm or company would want to assume another company's liability by buying that company's used chemicals to transport to a recycling manufacturer? This has the potential for affecting individual families as well. Take batteries, for instance. Who is going to want to recycle used automobile batteries if the recycler could be held liable for a spill or accident by any person or company to whom the battery once belonged or will be sold to after reprocessing?[3]

Cleaning up massively polluted sites was a good idea back in 1980. But "it has achieved its original purpose," according to Jay Lehr, a prominent hydrogeologist at Ohio State University in Columbus.[4] The process got out of control when the National Resources Defense Council pressured Congress in 1986 to restore Superfund sites to nearly pristine conditions, an impossible task. Remember the NRDC? It perpetrated the Alar hoax that destroyed hundreds, perhaps thousands of apple growers in 1989. The NRDC is now publishing articles demanding that traditional science be junked in favor of shamanism. Unless shamanism is the solution they claim (and it isn't), it is physically impossible to return any site to its pristine condition. The CERCLA of 1980 has become the Comprehensive Employment Repression, Crippling and Lunacy Act of 1986.

Environmental lunacy is gradually destroying America and the American Dream. If the tens of thousands of laws and regulations that have been created over the past thirty years had been suddenly passed over a two to three year period, there would have been a nationwide revolt. Instead, laws have been gradually enacted and expanded on the basis of false or exaggerated environmental catastrophes created by a vast environmental propaganda machine. America is like the frog in a gradually warming pot—we are being cooked alive and don't even know it.

This is just what is happening within America. Imagine the suffering and human tragedy that would occur if we had a totally insensitive *global EPA!* Hold onto your seats—that is exactly what environmental leadership is currently putting into place.

THE EARTH SUMMIT

Traveling to Rio de Janeiro during late May and early June 1992 was a tip-off for anyone aware of the true history and agenda of environmental leadership. Among those traveling to Rio were "long haired refugees from the '60s in Birkenstocks and tie-dyed shirts, yuppies in designer digs wearing Greenpeace buttons, and members of the press . . . [poring over] the latest briefings from Worldwatch Institute, Friends of the Earth, or the Business Council for Sustainable Development."[5] Rio itself did nothing to change that image. There was the famous statue of Christ the Redeemer with outstretched arms welcoming the pilgrims on the one hand. On the other hand, below the statue of Christ "pagan aboriginal rites and wacky eco-babble melded to form an incoherent spiritual 'faith'" that flowed through the crowd of those who rejected Him "for the green-theology mishmash of earth worship and New Age mysticism."[6]

Concerned attendees might have realized that the invocation of the Earth Summit was itself the Great Invocation of Theosophy. Knowing this would have helped explain the opening address of Maurice Strong, secretary general of the United Nations Conference on Environment (UNCED), more popularly known as the Earth Summit: "It is the responsibility of each human being today," warned Strong, "to choose between the *force of darkness* and the force of light. We must therefore transform our attitudes and values, and adopt a renewed respect for the *superior laws of Divine Nature*"[7] (italics added).

The "force of darkness" is New Age doublespeak and represents the historical Judeo-Christian culture and beliefs of America. The "force of light" based in the "superior laws of divine nature" ultimately means we must trash our constitutional rights protecting our individual freedom to own property, conduct business without intrusive government interference, and express our beliefs without incrimination. The divine laws of nature *will* be the law of the land, if Strong and his elitist colleagues have their way. So far no one is stopping them.

MAURICE STRONG AND THE NEW AGE EARTH EXTRAVAGANZA

Who is Maurice Strong, and how can he believe this? A wealthy Canadian oil industrialist, financier, and investor, Maurice Strong is no slouch. Among his closest friends are David Rockefeller, Lord Rothschild, and Pope John Paul II.[8] Not only was Strong secretary general of the Earth Summit, but he also helped create the United Nations Environmental Programme (UNEP) and still wields tremendous power in it. He also cochairs the very powerful World Economic Forum.[9]

It should surprise no one that Strong is a New Age mystic, and "a member of the Baha'i World Faith which proclaims the unity of all religions, the oneness of all people, and the coming of 'A Promised One.'"[10] Strong calls his New Age center and ranch in the Baca Grande of Colorado "The Valley of the Refuge of World Truths," where Strong claims "we feel a sense of unity with the cosmos." Strong's wife, Hanah, reportedly believes that her grandson is the reincarnation of an eleventh-century Tibetan Buddhist monk named Rechung Dorje Drakpa.[11] Strong is a personal friend of William Thompson, founder of the Lindisfarne Association. The Lindisfarne Association built a great temple to the sun god at Strong's Baca Ranch.[12] The Baca Grande Ranch "has become an ecumenical mini-UN with a monastery, ashram, Zen center," according to E Magazine reporter Anne Wingfield Semmes.[13] Strong believes that the "only way of saving the world will be for industrial civilization to collapse."[14]

This New Age threat to America and the Western world is not one to take lightly. Maurice Strong's vision of a sustainable future should shock every American out of lethargy:

It is clear that current lifestyles and consumption patterns of the affluent *middle class*—involving high meat intake, consumption of large amounts of frozen and convenience foods, use of fossil fuels, ownership of motor vehicles and small electrical appliances, home and work-place air-conditioning, and suburban housing—are not sustainable. A shift is necessary toward lifestyles less geared to environmental damaging consumption patterns.[15]

But wait, what about all of those empty buses circling between the hotels and the conference at the Earth Summit itself? Designed to hold forty-eight passengers, they consistently had fewer than five. So much for gas conservation and carbon dioxide reductions. And what about the conference site itself? Vast acreages of "ancient forests" were slaughtered and wetlands destroyed to build the complex and parking lots. Even more acres were deforested to produce the blizzard of paper issued at the summit each day. A steady convoy of young men pushed gurneys groaning under the weight of massive stacks of paper from the UN's photocopy/printing facilities to the press and information centers.[16]

Even worse, much of the time the huge glass doors to the plenary session were wide open, forcing the air conditioning to work overtime in the warm, humid air. Then there was the trash—mountains of it. Seven tons per day! Every day photocopy machines spit out one million photocopies with a shelf life of about twenty minutes. In all the garbage and trash that was produced at the summit, not one piece was recycled! Greenpeace was even caught using plastic cups. Apparently they forgot to bring the ceramic Greenpeace mugs they urge others to use.[17]

Such is the hypocrisy of using the New Age definition of sustainable development. The superior laws of divine nature demand that all middle-class Americans give up everything they and their ancestors have worked hard to achieve. One can only suppose that the current jet-set lifestyles of Strong and his contemporaries will continue. After all, they are the Superbeings called to save the earth. They have their multimillions of dollars; it is up to the rest of humanity—those less evolutionarily evolved—to make the needed sacrifices!

I'm being sarcastic, but there is a horrible truth in what I'm saying. Hypocrisy riddles the environmental movement. Environmental literature consistently demands that the middle class live more simply—living in a sustainable way on what they call a bioregional basis. Environmental solutions demand forsaking automobiles, modern intra- and international transportation, and most modern conveniences that call for the use of plastics, metals, and electricity. In other words, live the life of the Findhorn prototype. This has been the goal of theosophists for hundreds of years, as will be detailed in the following chapter. Meanwhile, the environmentalists themselves continue to jet around the world using everything they demand we give up.

Let's take a quick look at what a life governed by radical environmental principles would be like. The economic consequences of such goals are staggering. Not only would our quality of life regress by 100 years or more, but changes would inevitably result in massive unemployment and starvation. As noted earlier, America could not feed itself using 1940s technology, let alone 1800s technology. Americans would know firsthand what hunger *really* meant. Even if food were available, people would have no money to buy it. Massive unemployment of record levels would prevail as manufacturing industries closed. All those people who are now employed by companies that make or distribute air-conditioners, refrigerators, food processing, electrical appliances, wooden homes, and much more would be out of work. Where would they find work? Hoeing fields for crops after farmers are forbidden the use of equipment and chemicals? As ridiculous as that sounds, that is exactly what Edward Goldsmith, editor of the *Ecologist*, proposes.[18]

This is about as workable as Wilderness Society's economic boom for those living in the Northern Forest once industry is kicked out. Unless Americans wake up to the duplicity of the national and global mystic elitists soon, it may be too late to avoid a major hemorrhaging of our economy. If that happens it will result in a period of major suffering for all Americans. Ask Bill Ellen, Ron Stevens, Mort Zuber, the citizens of Libby, Montana, and tens of thousands of other Americans what this kind of life might mean.

GLOBALIZATION, THE REAL AGENDA

Headlining the news about the sponsored Earth Summit was the recurring theme of global ecological disasters. Global warming and ozone depletion led the list. Ignoring the growing scientific evidence that these are not catastrophes—indeed, they may not be problems at all—environmental leaders of all kinds scurried about proclaiming them as proven catastrophes. The media accepted much of it without question.

The centerpiece for finding solutions was sustainable development. Whether it was Agenda 21 (price tag $125 billion/year), the Commission on Sustainable Development, or the Biodiversity Treaty, the IUCN/UNEP/WWFN definition was interwoven throughout the fabric of these accords. Not blatantly, but in innocent sounding verbiage that can later be defined to fit their mystic viewpoints.

Lester R. Brown, who heads the highly influential environmental Worldwatch Institute, and who is also a member of the shadow governmental group Council on Foreign Relations, says of the Earth Summit's mission, "Building an environmentally sustainable future requires nothing short of a revolution . . . restructuring the global economy, dramatically changing human reproductive behavior, and altering values and lifestyles."[19]

Brown identifies the true nature and mission of the Earth Summit in the June 3 issue of *Terra Viva*, a special daily newspaper of the Earth Summit:

> One hears from time to time from conservative
> columnists and others that we, as the United
> States, don't want to sign these treaties that
> would sacrifice our national sovereignty. But what
> they seem to overlook is that we've already lost a
> great deal of our sovereignty. *We can no longer
> protect the stratospheric ozone layer over the
> United States. We can't stabilize the U. S. Climate
> without the cooperation of the countries through-
> out the world.* If even one major developing country
> continues to use CFCs, it will eventually deplete
> the ozone layer. *We can't protect the biological di-
> versity of the planet by ourselves. We have lost
> sovereignty; we've lost control.* (Italics added)[20]

In Gro Harlem Brundtland's opening comments during the plenary session of the Earth Summit, she asserted, "In order to reverse present negative trends, we must change the way we organize our societies. . . . Furthermore, the nation state is too small an area for addressing regional and global challenges related to the environment and development. . . . Narrowly focused national priorities will only hamper progress and stand in the way."[21] Denis Hayes, founder of Earth Day 1970, and now president of the Bullit Foundation, has suggested that "we may need a charismatic leader" to unite the people into a majority.

Brundtland called for "a revolution," a "new global partnership," and a "new global structure."[22] Former French Prime Minister Michel Rocard is even more specific: "Let's not deceive ourselves. . . . International instruments must be transformed into instruments of coercion, of sanctions, of boycott, even . . . of outright confiscation of any dangerous installation. What we seek, to be frank, is the legitimacy of controlling the application of the international decisions."[23] How might this restructuring occur? The March 6, 1992, *New York Times*, under the lead-in entitled "The New World Army," reports that the UN "Security Council recently expanded the concept of threats to peace to include economic, social and ecological instability."

Maurice Strong (UN secretary general of the Earth Summit) calls for such an expanded role of the UN to be enforced by "International Law" and to be funded through "global taxation."[24] But Strong laments, "This will not come about easily. Resistance to such changes is deeply entrenched." The institution of such international law and taxation can only be a "response to compelling imperatives and the inadequacies of alternatives," concludes Strong. In other words, the desired globalization can only be achieved if the citizens are terrified into believing that giving up national sovereignty is the only alternative.

The Trilateral Commission (TLC), a globalist organization founded by David Rockefeller in 1973,[25] recently published a book entitled *Beyond Interdependence: The Meshing of the World's Economy and the Earth's Ecology.* Two of the book's more notable authors were Jim MacNeill (the UN secretary general of the Brundtland Report) and David Rockefeller. As discussed in an earlier chapter, Rockefeller is the power behind the Environmental Grantmakers Association—an umbrella organization with 138 foundations providing hundreds of millions of foundation dollars to environmental groups each year. Rockefeller is also the North American chair of the Trilateral Commission and former director of the Council on Foreign Relations, 1949–85. Maurice Strong wrote the introduction to the book, in which he proclaims, "This book couldn't appear at a better time. . . . It will help guide decisions that will literally determine the *fate of the earth*." In the same book, MacNeill advocates "a new global partnership expressed in a revitalized international system in which an Earth Council, perhaps the Security Council with a broader mandate, maintains the *interlocked environmental and economic security of the planet*"[26] (italics added).

No small thinking here. These men and women are playing for keeps. They are calling for both the reduction or elimination of national sovereignty, and radical, sweeping economic changes—all to be enforced by the United Nations. These planning efforts are not being done on a shoestring either. The Rockefeller Foundation announced a tax-exempt, $50-million, three-year global environmental program in 1990. This program was funded "to create an elite group of individuals in each country whose role is to implement and enforce the international environmental treaties now being negotiated."[27] The goal was to have the structure in place by the 1992 Earth Summit.

The Earth Charter, which President Bush reluctantly signed at the June 1992 Earth Summit—and only after the language was watered down—reflects this thinking. According to early drafts,

Earth, with its diverse life forms, is a *functioning whole*. . . . The Earth community, of which humankind is [only] a part, functions in *interrelated cycles, processes, and systems* upon which life depends. . . . Progress . . . must foster a *sustainable and regenerative Earth order . . .* that contributes toward a *united, global, and harmonious* society. Education should promote the *consciousness* of the common heritage of humanity and the *integral connection between humankind and the larger world of nature.*

The principles of the free market, particularly when they are exercised by multinational corporations, must be exercised within the context of a *regulatory* framework designed to protect a *sustainable and just global economy.* Social structures and institutions at all levels must be *dedicated to achieving harmony among people, nations and the Earth.*[28] (Italics added)

Does this language sound familiar? It should. It is based on the IUCN definition of sustainable development and other IUCN "earth order" documents discussed in the last chapter.[29] Conservation Biology, Gaia, and quantum physics theories are interwoven throughout the document.

The Earth Charter will extend the "peacekeeping" powers of the UN to the task of protecting the global environment even in the absence of scientific certainty: *"Lack of scientific certainty shall not be used as a reason for postponing cost-effective measures to prevent environmental degradation"*[30] (italics added). Principles 8 through 12 reinforce the requirement for transfer of money and technologies to the Third World. Agenda 21 demands that the Western world share its resources—money and environmentally safe technology—with the Third World nations with no strings attached. Principle 13 establishes the framework setting liability and compensation for "the victims of pollution and environmental damage." The Sustainable Development Commission within the United Nations will be "empowered to have hearings, to have public proceedings, and receive evidence about the behavior and policies of countries around the world in order to assess whether and to what extent they are consistent with the agreements reached."

Reflect on what all this says. In essence, this global group of mystic elitists have given themselves almost absolute powers over our lives. They don't have to have any scientific evidence to force any nation, any local government, any individual to comply with their interpretations of "sustainability" as impacted by almost any issue, social or environmental.

How serious can this be? During a meeting with Maurice Strong, arch-environmentalist and New Age author and speaker Hazel Henderson[31] suggested that "economics is a form of brain-damage," and all economists should be forced into reeducation camps where they would be made to attend classes in biology, anthropology, sociology, et cetera, and then pass a test to prove that they had reformed. "They will not be able to be policy-making economists until they pass their sustainability exams," she asserts. Not to be outdone, one environmentalist friend suggested: "Look Hazel, you really need to line them up and shoot them all." Maurice Strong endorsed Henderson's proposal.[32] Henderson should be taken seriously. She is a member of the powerful Club of Rome, created in 1968 by New Age leader Aurelio Peccei, a prominent Italian industrialist. According to various writings by Peccei, the club's goal is to implement global solutions to bring world peace and prosperity. Peccei believes this could best be accomplished by communicating with nature and the collective unconscious of the human race.[33]

America has embraced this global agenda eagerly. President Bush attempted to do an end run around the entire farce. But the American press would not let him. He was intimidated and bullied into attending and then signing the various agreements and treaties. Once again, if there were reasonable evidence that these eco-catastrophes were happening, perhaps such action would be necessary.

THE HEIDELBERG APPEAL

Forty-six prominent scientists and intellectuals in the United States, including twenty-seven Nobel Prize winners, joined 218 scientists in other countries in an appeal to the heads of states attending the Earth Summit. They called their petition the Heidel-

berg Appeal after a conference held during April 1992 in Heidelberg, Germany, on hazardous substance use:

We want to make our full contribution to the preservation of our common heritage, the Earth. We
are however worried, at the dawn of the twenty-
first century, at the emergence of an irrational
ideology which is opposed to scientific and industrial progress and impedes economic and social
development. We contend that a Natural State,
sometimes idealized by movements with a ten-
dency to look toward the past, does not exist
and has probably never existed since man's first
appearance in the biosphere. . . .

We fully subscribe to the objectives of a scientific
ecology for a universe whose resources must be
taken stock of, monitored and preserved. But we
herewith demand that this stock-taking, monitor-
ing and preservation be founded on scientific criteria and not on irrational preconceptions. . . .
We intend to assert science's responsibility
and duties toward society as a whole.

We do however forewarn the authorities in
charge of our planet's destiny against decisions
which are supported by pseudo-scientific arguments or false and non-relevant data. [34]

What happened to this appeal from some of the most reputable
scientists in the world? Nobody listened. They were all too busy
"saving the earth."

In spite of the fact that hundreds of the top scientists in
America refute the "eco-catastrophe" theories that provided the
only reason for the Earth Summit, Vice President Gore and other
environmental leaders continue to tell Americans just the opposite. Americans have been led to believe there is universal agreement among scientists that these catastrophes are real and are
threatening our very survival.

THE SUCCESS OF THE EARTH SUMMIT

Was the Earth Summit successful? In public, environmental leaders say they lost too much for the agreements to be effective. But look at what the highly influential Worldwatch Institute proclaims behind the scenes about the success of the Earth Summit:

National sovereignty—the power of a country to control events within its territory—has lost much of its meaning in today's world. . . . International treaties and institutions are proving ever more critical to addressing ecological threats. *Nations are in effect ceding portions of their sovereignty to the international community, and beginning to create a new system of international environmental governance as a means of solving otherwise unmanageable problems.*

Paradoxically, one way to make environmental agreements more effective is in some cases to make them less enforceable—and therefore more palatable to the negotiators who may initially feel threatened by any loss of sovereignty. *So called "soft law"—declarations, resolutions, and action plans that nations do not need to formally ratify and are not legally binding—can help to create an international consensus, mobilize aid, and lay the groundwork for the negotiation of binding treaties later.* Agenda 21 [will be] an action plan on nearly all aspects of sustainable development [as it] emerges from the Earth Summit, . . . [It] falls into this category.[35] (Italics added)

Maurice Strong strongly agrees. "Agenda 21," according to Strong, will receive enough "high level political sanction [that its] potential for influencing and guiding the policies . . . of governments . . . will be substantial."[36] Scott Hajost of the Environmental Defense Fund was overjoyed that the creation of the UN "Commission on Sustainable Development" was accepted by Bush. The Environmental Defense Fund, along with three other environmental organizations, believed its creation was important because "it will provide a forum where *governments can be held accountable for their actions*"[37] (italics added). If you find this unlikely, consider how "world opinion" pushed President Bush to go to Rio where he signed agreements and treaties he did not think were in the best interest of America.

Many participants agree that "the Rio meeting was by and large a success. . . . Even if the agreements adopted by the Earth Summit fall short of what is needed, they do provide institutional mechanisms and benchmarks for holding governments accountable for progress in integrating environmental and development."[38] The Summit has redefined global politics.

Worldwatch notes that the next step is "a World Summit on Global Governance" in 1995—the fiftieth anniversary of the founding of the United Nations. Brace yourself, and hold on tight to your copy of the Constitution. If the elitists are successful, you will want to keep it to show your children and grandchildren the freedoms Americans enjoyed before the Gaia Environmental Regulatory Agency assumed control over every aspect of our lives.

One can only hope that the Senate has the wisdom to see through this charade and that they will not ratify any such treaties. But it will be difficult. There will be incredible political pressure brought against the Senate by environmental leadership and world opinion. But one can hope.

OF TREATIES AND CONSTITUTIONAL RIGHTS

If people are going to prison by actions of our own unaccountable and crusading bureaucracy, imagine what will happen if we are ever under the thumb of a global EPA run by elitist, self-actualized mystics such as Maurice Strong who have little regard for economists.

America took the first giant step toward this future when President Bush signed the watered down Climate-Change Treaty, the Earth Charter, and the Sustainable Development Agreements. Fortunately he did not sign the Biodiversity Treaty. As noted previously, biodiversity is itself a New Age environmental concept centered on the theology of the "web of life." Although it has a high degree of merit as a *tool* for understanding ecosystem functions and stability, it has limits in its application for anything beyond a tool. Certainly it cannot be the centerpiece of a treaty, since its ambiguity allows it to be made to mean anything the mystic elitists want it to mean. From a biocentric understanding of sustainable development, *any* alteration of biodiversity by man is not natural and is therefore damaging.

If such a treaty were signed, America would be bound to the decisions of an elite, mystically oriented group of people. These people would have godlike power to define the limits permitted for America to "sustain" biodiversity. In other words, the treaty would totally circumvent the Constitution of the United States. But then, that was apparently the plan all along. The Biodiversity Treaty could be used by the elite global environmental leadership to totally and legally gut the Fifth Amendment and any others that got in the way. Could this happen? Article VI of the Constitution reads:

This Constitution, and the Laws of the United States which shall be made in Pursuance thereof; and all Treaties made, or which shall be made, under the Authority of the United States Shall be the supreme Law of the Land; and the Judges in every State shall be bound thereby, any Thing in the Constitution or Laws of any State to the Contrary notwithstanding.

All national and state laws would be subservient to such a binding treaty. That possibility should give all Americans pause for thought and deep reflection. Where is environmental extremism taking America? Slowly but surely we are enacting this nature religion into law—it is rapidly becoming America's, and the world's, new state religion.

Even though there is an extremely high risk in losing our sovereignty and freedoms in signing such open-ended treaties, Vice President Gore pressured President Clinton to sign the Biodiversity Treaty in 1993 with even more give-aways than Bush would have allowed had he signed it in 1992. Although the treaty has not yet been ratified, Clinton signed it in July 1993. Gore continues to support all efforts to find "global solutions."

THE ENVIRONMENTAL MOVEMENT— SPONTANEOUS OR PLANNED?

Both the peace movement and the environmental movement have been driven by New Age ideology. In fact, they have been so intertwined that the two are inseparable on many issues. World unity demands peace, and environmental purity demands world unity. Yet, many wealthy industrialists depend on the war machine for their wealth and power. War or the threat of war has always had the effect of unifying the masses behind the government. How does one maintain power and wealth in peace? Simple. The war machine has to be replaced with something else. Preferably that something else could also be used as a springboard into providing an ironclad reason for dismantling the sovereignty of nations so that the new world order could truly be globalized. Now that's a big order. Is there evidence for such an effort? Sadly, yes.

THE IRON MOUNTAIN REPORT

In August of 1963, a group of fifteen experts in the fields of social science, history, economics, international law, cultural anthropology, psychology, psychiatry, mathematics, astronomy, and others met in secrecy at Iron Mountain, New York, to begin a process that would last two years. Iron Mountain is a network of underground vaults and offices near Hudson, New York, for corporations in the event of a nuclear war.[39] The objective of the group: *"To determine, accurately and realistically, the nature of the problems that would confront the United States if and when a condition of 'permanent peace' should arrive, and to draft a program for dealing with this contingency."*[40]

Over the next two years the group met many times in different areas of the United States, but never in government facilities. Leonard Lewin was given the report's manuscript by one of the group's members whom Lewin would identify only as John Doe. Lewin published the report with his own foreword. In the foreword Lewin emphasized that he did not agree with the "attitudes toward war and peace, life and death, and survival of the species manifested in the Report. Few readers will. In human terms it is an outrageous document . . . [but] it appears to explain aspects of American policy otherwise incomprehensible by ordinary standards of common sense."[41]

The Iron Mountain group concluded that war not only unified the people, but was *the* stabilizing influence of nations: "The war system makes the stable government of societies possible. It does this essentially by providing an external necessity for society to accept the political rule. In so doing, *it establishes the basis for nationhood and the authority of government to control its constituents*[42] (italics added).

As the group progressed, a worldview of total amorality emerged. War to them had become essential to the survival of nations: "War is not . . . an instrument of policy utilized by nations to extend their expressed political values or their economic interests. On the contrary, it is itself the *principle basis of organization* on which all modern societies are constructed"[43] (italics added).

War acts as brake, throttle, and rudder to a nation's economy: "[M]ilitary spending can be said to furnish the only balance wheel with sufficient inertia to stabilize the advance to [those] economies. The fact that war is 'wasteful' is what enables it to serve this function. And the faster the economy advances, the heavier this balance wheel must be."[44]

Then comes the ultimate in the group's idea of state control and stability:

The arbitrary nature of war expenditures and of other military activities make them *ideally suited to control* these essential *class relationships.* . . . Until [a substitute] is developed, continuance of the war system must be assured, if for no other reason, among others, than to *preserve whatever quality and degree of poverty a society requires as an incentive,* as well as to maintain the stability of its internal organization of power.[45] (Italics added)

This cold, calculating group not only believed that peace destabalized nations, but that there must be a *class system* where the *poor are kept poor* for the good of the nation (and, one would assume, the upper power structure). Remember, this was written just as President Johnson's Great Society was being launched. According to this philosophy, the American people are merely pawns to be kept loyal and in bondage—like serfs to the knights of the realm during the medieval days.

Given that as the background for what this group believed were positive social values for war, they next faced what to replace it with. They reviewed as possible replacements "a comprehensive social-welfare program . . . a giant open-end space research program, aimed at unreachable targets . . . an omnipresent, virtually omnipotent international police force, an established and recognized extraterrestrial menace, massive global environmental pollution, fictitious alternate enemies . . . new religions or other mythologies, and others."[46] They found every one of them lacking, at least in the near term:

> However unlikely some of the possible alternate enemies we have mentioned may seem, we must emphasize that one *must* be found, of credible quality and magnitude, if a transition to peace is ever to come about without social disintegration. It is more probable, in our judgment, that *such a threat will have to be invented*, rather than developed from unknown conditions.[47] (Italics added)

Once again, lies and deceit have put us through the lookingglass into the Alice in Wonderland of the absurd. This group would have liked to have found something that could have been implemented within ten years. But such a vehicle could not be found. The next best solution? *Invent* environmental catastrophes to build the fledgling environmental movement. But more time was necessary for this issue to attain credibility:

> It may be . . . that gross pollution of the environment can eventually replace the possibility of mass destruction by nuclear weapons as the principle apparent threat to the survival of the species. Poisoning of the air, and of the principle sources of food and water is already well-advanced, and at first glance would seem promising in this respect; it constitutes a threat that can be dealt with only through social organization and political power. But from present indications it will be a generation to a generation and a half before environmental pollution, however severe, will be sufficiently menacing, on a global scale, to offer a possible

> basis for a solution. . . . However, the mere mod-
> ifying of existing programs for the deterrence of
> pollution could speed up the process enough to
> make the threat credible much sooner.[48]

In other words, pass a lot of laws that cost a lot of money and don't really do anything for the environment. Does this sound familiar? Writer Franklin Sanders claimed the report directly affirmed or indirectly endorsed "war . . . human sacrifice, slavery, genocide, racist eugenics (including the substitution of artificial insemination for normal human procreation), a planned economy, fascist partnership between business and government, planned government waste, official opposition to medical advances, globalism, environmentalism, and even the new pagan Mother Earth religion."[49]

Could it be that the entire eco-catastrophe and fear-mongering campaign has been a gigantic hoax—a hoax perpetrated on the world for a small group of so-called superhumans who are called by theosophists the "Brotherhood of the Masters";[50] a hoax invented so that its perpetrators can gain global control and implement the new world order and a universal religion keyed on Theosophy? Preposterous! Not even Hollywood has had the imagination to develop such an outrageous plot for a movie—in an industry notorious for outrageous plots.

On the other hand, the report does exist. *U.S. News and World Report* called it the "book that shook the White House":

> The book set off a blazing debate . . . cries
> of "hoax"—and a "manhunt" for the author,
> or authors. . . . But nagging doubts lingered.
> One informed source confirmed that the "Special
> Study Group" . . . was set up by a top official in
> the Kennedy Administration. The source added
> that the report was drafted and eventually
> submitted to President Johnson, who was said
> to have "hit the roof"—and then ordered that
> the report be bottled up for all time.[51]

John Doe has never been absolutely identified. Speculation centered on a variety of people who might have been John Doe. Others claimed it was a fraud written by Lewin himself. *Time* magazine reported that "[Lewin,] after all, contributed political satire to the *New Yorker* and anthologizes it as well. Since he bears a long-standing grudge against think tanks and their war games, he may have decided to counterattack with some peace games."[52] Yet, as New Age critic Brooks Alexander notes in his review of *Iron Mountain*, there was no hint of satire. "Satire depends on a maximum gap between what is accepted and what is being suggested. And therein lies the weakness of the 'satire theory.' *Iron Mountain* isn't funny, because there is little if any difference between what it proposes and what is under discussion or already underway."[53]

If the report is real, Harvard economist John Kenneth Galbraith is the odds-on favorite for being either John Doe or the group's leader. Galbraith reviewed *Iron Mountain* for *Book World* (a newspaper supplement) under the pseudonym of Herschel McLandress. Although he did not own up to authorship in the review, he did acknowledge that he was involved in the project. Galbraith asserted, "As to the authenticity of the document, it happens that the reviewer can speak to the full extent of his authority and credibility."[54] Galbraith also asserted: "I would put my personal repute behind the authenticity of this document, so I would testify to the validity of its conclusions. My reservations relate only to the wisdom of releasing it to an obviously unconditioned public."[55]

Who better than Galbraith is in a position to know? Galbraith was another CFR member during the time David Rockefeller was its director.[56] The CFR's April 1970 issue of *Foreign Affairs*—just in time for the first Earth Day—contained an article entitled "To Prevent a World Disaster," by George Kennan, an eminent government policy planner. According to Brooks Alexander, Kennan made three points:

1. The eco-crisis is a global threat so great that it endangers life on earth;
2. The crisis should be controlled by a partnership between government and business, operating under a central, international Super-Agency to regulate environmental issues; and
3. The new crusade "must proceed at least to some extent at the expense of the . . . immensely dangerous preoccupa-

tions that are now pursued under the heading of national defense." In other words, the military threat will be phased out, and the eco-threat phased in, while national sovereignty is whittled away.[57]

Four years after the publication of the *Iron Mountain Report*, the highly influential Council on Foreign Relations, under the directorship of David Rockefeller, suddenly called the eco-crisis a threat to the earth. Rockefeller and the foundations within his sphere of influence began the massive funding of environmental organizations. As discussed earlier, they even created many of the more radical ones, such as the National Resources Defense Council and the Natural Defense Fund. The environmental movement was off with a bang.

It would be tempting to just pass all this off as seeing specters behind every tree. But in 1991 the Club of Rome, the globalist organization headed by New Age leader Aurelio Peccei, reinforced the unifying principle laid out by the *Iron Mountain Report*: "In searching for a new enemy to unite us, we came up with the idea that pollution, the threat of global warming, water shortages, famine, and the like would fit the bill. . . . All these dangers are caused by human intervention. . . . The real enemy, then, is humanity itself."[58]

Various members of the Rockefeller family have supported and been members of the Club of Rome in the past.[59] The parallels and correlations between the *Iron Mountain Report* and the literal unfolding of the strategy of that plan before our eyes stretches coincidence beyond the breaking point.

Whereas we really do have some *manageable* environmental problems, it is now apparent the eco-catastrophe was manufactured to further a much larger agenda. By 1990, about a generation and a half later, just about everything in the *Iron Mountain Report* had come true. The attack on our Constitution and national sovereignty was well under way. The environmental movement was draining our financial resources dry. Many Americans had been whipped into a state of raw terror—in fear of global ecological collapse. And President Johnson's Great Society had created a welfare system that was effectively locking the poor into the chains of poverty.

What is going on? Is there something that can tie this all together? Yes, there is, and it's called Theosophy—the religion of the counterculture and of the peace and environmental movements.

America is at risk.

[Theosophy] belongs neither to the Hindu, the Zoroastrian, the Chaldean, nor the Egyptian religion, neither to Buddhism, Islam, Judaism nor Christianity exclusively. The Secret Doctrine [of Theosophy] is the essence of all these.

Helena Blavatsky
founder of the Theosophical Society
The Secret Doctrine, vol. I:viii

Satan will now be shown in the teaching of the Secret Doctrine [of Theosophy], allegorized as Good, and Sacrifice, a God of Wisdom, under different names.

Helena Blavatsky
The Secret Doctrine, vol II:237

Interference by man in this civilization can disrupt the life forces of nature and the occult. Only in countries where there is no civilization can the power of nature be found—the world's soul.

Helena Blavatsky
Iris Unveiled, vol. 1: 210–11

A Study of the Plan . . . appears to be working out in the five kingdoms in nature. . . . The teaching connected with this . . . will be more definitely and academically occult in its significance . . . for it will be based upon information contained in The Secret Doctrine.

Alice Bailey
The Externalisation of the Hierarchy, 59

11

THEOSOPHY

A VIEW OF THINGS TO COME

Maurice Strong, secretary general of the Earth Summit, has a dream—a dream to write a book on how the environmental evils of the world could be corrected. Strong outlined a portion of his proposed book in the May 18, 1992, *British Columbia Report*, following an interview with Jim Johnston:

What if a small group of world leaders were to conclude that the principal risk to the Earth comes from the actions of the rich countries? And if the world is to survive, those rich countries would have to sign an agreement reducing their impact on the environment. Will they do it? The group's conclusion is "no." The rich countries won't do it. They won't change. So, in order to save the planet, the group decides: Isn't the *only hope for the planet that the industrialized civilizations collapse?* Isn't it our responsibility to bring that about? This group of world

leaders *form a secret society to bring about
an economic collapse.* [1] (Italics added)

In an earlier interview with Daniel Wood of Canada's *West* magazine, Maurice Strong related how, in his hypothetical vision of the future, these economies could be destroyed. Daniel Wood reports what Strong told him:

"Each year, the World Economic Forum convenes in Davos, Switzerland. Over a thousand CEO's, prime ministers, finance ministers, and leading academics gather in February to attend meetings and set economic agendas for the year ahead."

With this as a setting, he then says, "What if a small group of these world leaders were to . . . form a *secret society* to bring about an economic collapse? It's February. They're all at Davos. These aren't terrorists. They're *world leaders.* They have positioned themselves in the world's commodity and stock markets. They've engineered a *panic* using their access to stock exchanges and computers and gold supplies. They jam the gears. They hire mercenaries who hold the rest of the world leaders at Davos as hostages. The markets *can't close.* The rich countries . . . " and Strong makes a slight motion with his fingers as if he were flicking a cigarette butt out the window. "I probably shouldn't be saying things like this," he says.

I [Daniel Wood] sat there spellbound. This is not *any* storyteller talking. This is Maurice Strong. He knows these world leaders. He is, in fact, co-chairman of the Council of the World Economic Forum. He sits at the fulcrum of power. He is in a position to *do it.* (Italics added)[2]

Of course this is mere fiction. Or is it? Truth sometimes is stranger than fiction. As Daniel Wood remarked, Strong *is* in a position to do it. As discussed in the last chapter, Strong is a close personal friend of David Rockefeller. It is, if you recall, the various Rockefeller foundations that sponsor the Environmental Grant-makers Association, whose members in turn funnel hundreds of millions of dollars to environmental groups. Strong is the power behind the UN Environmental Programme and International Union of Conservationists for Nature and Natural Resources, which played a strong role in developing conservation biology and the mystic development of sustainable development behind the Earth Sum-mit—all of which was heavily financed by the various Rockefeller foundations.

But that is only the tip of the environmental iceberg. Strong, like other powerful political and financial figures around the world, really believes that the Western world is destroying the earth. Many of these are New Age environmental extremists. Maurice Strong is also a close friend of Peter Caddy, who founded and directed the Findhorn Community in Scotland, and William Thompson, who founded the Lindisfarne Association in the Cathedral of St. John the Divine. Thompson, in turn, works closely with Caddy and James Lovelock of Gaia fame. Through the Lindisfarne Association, Thompson built the Babylonian Sun God Temple for Strong's New Age community on his Baca Grande Ranch in Colorado.[3] The potential international intrigue behind this network of environmental globalists makes Ian Fleming's James Bond spy thrillers of the 1960s pale in comparison.

Can such intrigue be real? One of President Clinton's favorite professors at Georgetown University, Caroll Quigley, suggests it is. Quigley, a Harvard professor emeritus before his death, provides details on an international network dedicated to creating a world system of financial control in his 1966 book magnum opus, *Tragedy and Hope: A History of Our Time*:

This network . . . has no aversion to cooperating with the Communists or any other group, and frequently does so. I know of the operations of this network because I have studied it for twenty years and was permitted for two years, in the early 1960's to examine its papers and secret records. I have no aversion to it or to most of its aims and have, for much of my life, been close to it and to many of its instruments. . . . Their aim is

> nothing less than to create a *world system* of
> financial control in private hands able to dominate
> the political system of each country and the
> economy of the world as a whole. The system was
> to be controlled in a feudalistic fashion by the
> *central banks of the world acting in concert,* by
> secret agreements arrived at in frequent private
> meetings and conferences.[4] (Italics added)

Quigley's book itself has an aura of intrigue surrounding it. Its publisher, the Macmillan Company, withdrew the book from the market almost immediately after its release. The book was even withdrawn from library shelves. Former New Age advocate and author Tal Brooke possesses one of the few remaining books of Quigley's, which he details in his book *When the World Will Be As One.* It makes for fascinating reading.

During an interview with *Quest* magazine, William Thompson seems to also affirm such a possibility. Thompson claims "there is a ruling class at the time that communicates through oral means, face-to-face . . . and at the bottom there is an underclass. So it's almost like a return of the Vedic (Hindu) caste system." This "oral" class Thompson continues "has the right accent, and has wealth. . . . The rich get richer and the poor poorer, and the smaller ruling class just rules the masses through pageantry and illusion."[5] This elite is instituting a new planetary religion, admitted Thompson: "We have now a new spirituality, what has been called the New Age Movement. . . . The planetization of the esoteric has been going on for some time. . . . This is now beginning to influence concepts of politics and community in ecology. . . . This is the Gaia (Mother Earth) politique . . . a planetary culture." The old world is over, Thompson concludes, including: "the independent sovereign state, with the sovereign individual in his private property."[6]

Both Quigley and Thompson make far-out and serious assertions. They imply there is some sort of grand conspiracy afoot. Are they telling us the truth, or are they merely spinning more mystic webs, and by doing so discrediting any grand conspiracy theorists who may quote them? Americans love conspiracies on the silver screen, but pooh-pooh them in real life.

Whether there is a grand conspiracy or not is not the point. Proving conspiracies is nearly impossible, and innocent people can get hurt in the process. What is certain, however, is that America has already moved far beyond the altruistic goal of merely having a clean environment. We are dealing with the reality and consequences of basing our society around Gore's "central organizing principle of the environment." It is no longer hypothetical. The blatant deceit in declaring that environmental catastrophes exist is real. The Earth Summit and its goals are real. These men and their agendas are real. The power and influence they wield is real. The legislation and regulations they have produced are real. Real people are suffering as a consequence of these self-appointed leaders. Real people are going to prison at the hands of these earth saviors. These are innocent people with families, no different from any other American.

America's human suffering has just begun. Imagine the suffering we will all face if the economy becomes so unstable under the regulatory and redistributionist burden that it collapses, as Maurice Strong's not-so-fictional book outline proclaims. A growing number of leading economists today are beginning to believe such a collapse is no longer a matter of "if," but "when." Economist and author Larry Burkett makes this sobering observation:

> It is hard for the average, law-abiding citizen to imagine the consequences of national bankruptcy on our country. Just consider the anger, frustration, and potential violence, if millions of Americans see their lifetime dreams evaporate and they lose their jobs, their homes, and even their retirement savings. The flame of resentment will probably be lighted by the inner-city poor who see their subsidies cut to the bone and inflation rob them of all hope. But it is the anger of middle-class America that represents the greatest threat. They may not riot. Even worse, they may vote in a "dictator."[7]

What drives these men (and women) of power? Why are they so insensitive to the suffering they are creating? As noted, the one thing that appears to be a common thread behind this network is the little known but apparently powerful belief system called Theosophy. Secret societies such as Theosophical Society and Lucis Trust played catalytic roles in promoting the theosophical-based counterculture and New Age movement in the 1960s and 1970s. Although most adherents of Eastern mysticism in America have never heard of Theosophy or view it as an unimportant sideline of their belief, it nonetheless appears to be the one common denominator. It was no coincidence that the invocation of the Earth Summit was from the "Great Invocation" of Theosophy:

From the point of Light within the Mind of God, let light stream forth into the minds of men. Let Light descend on Earth. From the point of Love within the Heart of God, let love stream forth into the hearts of men. May Christ return to Earth. From the centre where the Will of God is known, let purpose guide the little wills of men— the purpose which the Masters* know and serve. From the centre which we call the race of men, let the Plan of Love and Light work out. And may it seal the door where evil dwells. Let Light and Love and Power restore the Plan on Earth. [8]

Who could ever be against such a goal? Isn't love and light (knowledge) what we all desire? And shouldn't we be against evil? But this allure is the stuff from which cults have sprung forth through the ages. The promise of love, esoteric knowledge, and supernatural power have seduced men and women of all classes and intelligence. It is no different today. Understanding the doctrines, goals, and activities of Theosophy throughout the centuries explains much about the modern environmental movement.

THEOSOPHICAL ROOTS

As quoted at the head of this chapter, Theosophy is a mix of Eastern and Western mystic beliefs. It is all of them, yet it is none. It is esoteric (secretive) and can only be known through a series of

---

* Masters are supposedly humans with highly evolved abilities to consciously communicate with the nature world and the cosmic ether (web of life). Ascended Masters are those so highly evolved they no longer need human bodies to exist. The relative pecking order is termed the "Hierarchy."

stages and secret initiations by those who show themselves to be worthy students. It is centered on the belief that everything is god, the cosmos is a highly interconnected web of life, and superhuman knowledge and psychic power is attainable. As outlined in the Great Invocation, it is supposedly the path to love, knowledge, power, and global peace.

The Theosophical Society was established in 1875 by Madame Helena Petrovna Blavatsky and Colonel Henry Steel Olcott.[9] Of the two, Blavatsky dominated the society through her two highly esoteric and occultic books *The Secret Doctrine* and *Iris Unveiled*. *The Secret Doctrine* is considered the New Age bible.[10] Blavatsky supposedly exhibited psychic abilities at an early age. While visiting the United States she became intensely interested in spiritualism and astral projection. She eventually promoted psychic phenomena such as supernatural dematerializations, spirit manifestation, and trance mediumship.[11] Progressive involvement with the occult and Eastern mysticism and metaphysics eventually led her to create the Theosophical Society with Colonel Olcott.

Upon Blavatsky's death at the turn of the twentieth century two women, Annie Besant and Alice Bailey, took the leadership in the society. Besant remained in Europe where she deepened the mystical and occultic nature of theosophical beliefs to an increasingly receptive European culture. Alice Bailey continued the slow development of Theosophy in the United States in the midst of an unreceptive Christian culture. She gradually distanced herself from the more radical European Theosophical Society until she broke away entirely by splitting Lucifer Trust Publishing from the Society. Needless to say, the name Lucifer Trust was not well received in the Christian culture of America, and Bailey soon renamed it Lucis Trust. Lucis Trust still flourishes today and has published the prolific writings of Alice Bailey.

The Theosophical Society and Lucis Trust are almost totally unknown to most Americans. Although the primary objective of Theosophy has always been to change Western civilization back to its Babylonian belief system, Lucis Trust and the Theosophical Society have used the the peace movement and environmental movement in America as vehicles to make the change. The Theosophical Society, in fact, still plays a central role in EcoNet, a computer network for environmental organizations to share ideas and strategies.[12] Lucis Trust, started by Alice Bailey back in the first quarter of the century, has a membership of 6,000 that encompasses the political Who's Who of America. Past and present members include Robert McNamara, Donald Regan, Henry Kissinger, David Rockefeller, Paul Volker, and George Shultz.[13]

Certainly, not all members of Lucis Trust understand its religious implications, but neither are these men naive. Such membership gives credibility to the claims of global power that this belief system wields. In fact, Foster Bailey, Alice Bailey's husband and coleader in Lucis Trust, adds yet another twist to the international intrigue Quigley and Thompson described above. Bailey describes how an occult hierarchy oversees an astute force of international financiers, businessmen, and educators who are master manipulators:

> The occult Hierarchy of the planet functions in a way which is a bit analogous to the way any great international, powerful corporation functions in the world today. . . . If an international business concern decides to undertake expansion and investment in a new part of the world, they have to have capital, they have to have the personnel, they have to study the problems involved, they have to lay their plan so that an investment of so many millions will in a certain number of years produce sufficient profits to justify it.
>
> The [occult Hierarchy] are under the necessity of adjusting their developments to the existing government whatever it may be, good or bad, and that part of the world in which they're proposing to operate. They study the people and the language as well as the sources of raw material, availability and quality of labor and transport problems. They send out scouts and they test reactions to their plans. Finally, when they are ready, they move forward. The Hierarchy functions like that.[14]

Does the *Iron Mountain Report* discussed in the previous chapter sound like something a group like this would produce? Such an assembly would have to be dismissed as pure fantasy if there weren't so many things happening today that provide pause for deeper consideration.

What is Theosophy? Why does it have so much power when so few have even heard of it? Simply stated, to understand Theosophy is to understand environmental and global politics. Yet, in studying Theosophy, it is important to understand that, like any belief system, not everyone who believes in these things believes them in exactly the same way. In fact many environmental leaders may not understand their beliefs as being rooted in Theosophy. There is considerable variability: from those who are merely enamored with the concepts of Gaia, the cosmic web of life, and "nature knows best," to those who accept these tenets lockstep. According to theosophical literature, it really doesn't matter who knows and who doesn't as long as its agenda is advanced. And that agenda is pervasive from local to global claims of environmental destruction. So just what is the theology behind the nature-is-god teaching?

NATURE

To the theosophist, nature is sacred, and true harmony with nature cannot be obtained in civilization as we know it today: "Interference by man in this civilization can disrupt the life forces of nature and the occult. Only in countries where there is no civilization can the power of nature be found—the world's soul."[15]

Because nature is esoteric, modern-day science that focuses on proving cause-and-effect cannot define the reality of nature:

[Modern science] cannot, owing to the very nature of things, unveil the mystery of the universe around us. . . . [Only] the *occultist, arguing from metaphysical data and by probing the inmost secrets of Nature, can transcend the narrow limitations of sense, and transfer his consciousness into the . . . sphere of primal causes.*[16] (Italics added)

In other words, civilization disrupts the web of life, and, therefore, Western civilization must revert back to a simpler way. Only the theosophical elite can understand these mysteries. Shamanism is the only answer to mankind's problems. Can there be any doubt why New Age physicist Brian Swimme writes in the Natural Resources Defense Council's *Amicus Journal* that shamanism must become the heart of science if the earth is to be saved?[17]

In these beliefs was the militant modern environmental movement born. But these are merely the first absurdities of Theosophy. It gets worse.

Blavatsky maintains that there is no room for both Theosophy and science. She asserts that those who continue their journey in mysticism "have no choice but either to blindly accept the deductions of Science, or to cut adrift from it, and withstand it fearlessly to its face, stating what the Secret Doctrine teaches us, being fully prepared to bear the consequences."[18] In other words, a person can accept scientific reality, or he can accept these mystic beliefs, *but not both.*

But Americans would not accept anything *less than* science to justify major policy changes. Therefore, environmental leaders had to use something that *sounds* like science to convince citizens that the earth is being destroyed. Hence, conservation biology, the Gaia hypothesis, and other forms of pseudoscience were created.

The anticivilization beliefs dominating modern environmentalism stem from theosophical and other Eastern beliefs that evolution occurs through reincarnation. According to theosophical belief, it is a sacred process found in nature, which civilization interrupts. This evolutionary process begins with the "Monades, or the Souls of Atoms" that evolve until they take on solid form. "Here," as Blavatsky explains, "losing their individuality in the mineral kingdom, they begin to ascend through the seven states of terrestrial evolution to that point where a [conscious] correspondence is firmly established between the human and *Deva* (divine) consciousness."[19] Devas, as you recall, are the divine beings with whom those at Findhorn communicated.

Such higher consciousness is what these enlightened believe they have obtained. Hence, many today have redefined the New Age movement as the "Consciousness movement." This also explains the militancy of Sierra Club author Thomas Berry when he warns:

Every being has its own interior, its self, its mystery, its [holy] aspect. To deprive any being of this sacred quality is to disrupt the larger order of the universe. We have made our terrifying assault upon the earth with an

> irrationality that is stunning in enormity. Reverence will be total or it will not be at all. [20]

This is dangerous stuff. The raw ingredients of these theosophical beliefs about nature and truth lead to one nihilistic conclusion: The only solution to save earth is to trash our economy and civilization. Yet as revealing as these passages are to the understanding of the modern environmental movement, they are nothing compared to *how* they are being implemented by what is called "The Plan."

THE PLAN

Of all the key theosophical players, Blavatsky and Bailey had by far the greatest long-term impact. Bailey was even a more prolific author than Blavatsky, writing more than two dozen books, all published by Lucis Trust. All of these, she claimed, were really authored through mental telepathy and automatic writing by a mysterious Tibetan Master named Djwhal Khul. These books provide the outline for what Bailey called the "New World Order" and the ushering in of the New Age—the Age of Aquarius. Throughout her books she referred to the process of implementing the New Age and New World Order as "The Plan." [21]

The vast majority of the verbiage in her books is directed towards achieving love and harmony in mankind and between mankind and nature. All of us, in one way or another, are for love and harmony. But it is *how* it is supposedly achieved by this belief system that is of critical importance. And that is the esoteric key that The Plan provides.

The Plan, according to Bailey, has been in existence since the days of Atlantis, gradually being implemented by the Masters through those holding theosophical and other Eastern and Western mystic beliefs. Central to this process is Lucis Trust, of which David Rockefeller and other big hitters have been members. It is now time, she claims, to "grasp the opportunity to bring to an end the long silence which has persisted since Atlantean Days; the Masters can now begin to undertake to renew an ancient 'sharing of the secrets.'" [22] Throughout their books both Bailey and Blavatsky trace the roots of Theosophy to the Rosicrucians, Knights of the Templar, the Jewish Kabalists, Greek and Egyptian mystics, Buddhists, Babylonian and Chaldean mystics, Aryans, back to the superhumans of Atlantis.

UNITING MAN AND NATURE

According to The Plan, man (Aquarius is the sign of man) is in the process of evolving into his "higher Self" where he consciously becomes one with the cosmos and the web of life.[23] This will occur when the psychic power generated by humanity reaches the point in which the Great Invocation is finally realized:

When the thought behind the Great Invocation can be carried high enough in the consciousness of those using it through a joint effort of the world disciples and the Hierarchy of Light, then the Spirit of Peace can be invoked. . . . Thus the third great planetary centre, Humanity, becomes creative and magnetic, and two divine aspects— intelligence and love—will reach fruition . . . making it possible for the first aspect and the will of God (understood by humanity as the Plan) to be consciously carried forward on earth in conformity with the activity instituted at Shamballa.[24]

This event is variously called Omega, Harmonic Convergence, Fusion, The Turning Point, Mind Convergence, and others. When this happens mankind (Aquarius), the Hierarchy (a name covering the working disciples of all degrees having esoteric power),[25] and Shamballa (the center of god's will) will be united in peace and harmony. The Triad will have been made complete and the New Age will have dawned. "Humanity will then for the first time enter upon its destined task as the intelligent, loving intermediary between the higher states of planetary consciousness, the super-human states and the sub-human (nature) kingdoms. Thus humanity will become eventually the planetary saviour."[26] This "soul infusion" of the Triad will supposedly precipitate the kingdom of god, usher in the "one universal religion," and "give birth to a new kingdom in nature."[27] As this happens, the kingdom of god is finally revealed to all people to be in reality the kingdom in nature.[28]

Is it any wonder that the Great Invocation was used at the Earth Summit? Maurice Strong and others appear to believe that if we all *think* warm and positive thoughts we can usher in the New Age through mystic power. Environmental activism locally and globally is bent on totally dismantling our economy and then re-structuring it around Gore's environmental central organizing principle of America and the world so that this can happen.

Note in the above quote that humanity supposedly is the third planetary center. Corollary triads exist in the planets. According to Blavatsky, the planetary triad is composed of Earth (Gaia), Venus (Lucifer or Satan), and the Sun (Shamballa).[29] The Great Invocation will cause the fusion or mating with the Sun and Gaia, Mother Earth. This is the apparent purpose of the Sun Temple that was built by the Lindisfarne Association at Maurice Strong's Baca Grande Ranch in Colorado. Maurice Strong and others are financing it with hundreds of millions of dollars of their own money, and are coercing American citizens, the federal government, and United Nations to finance even more.

In a rather revealing twist, Bailey defines the occult numerology of the nature-based triad to be 666. Both Bailey and Blavatsky claim their esoteric mystic theology is supported by the Bible. Yet, the number 666 happens to be one of the darkest symbols of the Christian Bible. The number 666 is the number of the Beast, or Antichrist, described in Revelation 13, who reigns over mankind during the seven-year Tribulation.* Bailey attempts to explain away this dark biblical sign by claiming it represents materialism in the Bible, but is "divine" in the context of the triad: "Like all other divine qualities, it [the triad] has its material counterpart, and that is why 666 is regarded as the number of the Beast or of materialism."[30]

Although materialism is certainly undesirable, the Beast described in Revelation and Daniel is not materialism, but rather a person who forces all people to receive a mark to show their allegiance to him.[31] What is so astounding is that Bailey actually claims that theosophical followers will indeed receive a mark—except that the theosophical mark is one of salvation. Bailey maintains that those initiated into the New Age will receive what is termed "'the mark of a Saviour' and it will embody the mark or indication (the signature as medieval occultists used to call it) of a new type of salvation or salvage."[32] Bailey claims this mark as a outward sym-

---

* The often-misunderstood concept of the Tribulation comes from the discourse Jesus gave about the great tribulation or distress that would accompany the latter days before His return in Matthew 24, Mark 13, and Luke 21. According to biblical scholars, this fascinating event will last seven years (Daniel 9:27) and be accompanied by persecution and distress unknown since the beginning of time (Daniel 12:1, Matthew 24:21).

bol of a new type salvation where man becomes god, and one with nature. The Bible, on the other hand, says that all those who receive the mark will lose their chance at salvation.

Can these men and women really believe in this? Are they willing to stake America's future on it? If they are truly theosophists the answer is a resounding yes. In fact this is the key to understanding the New World Order.

THE NEW WORLD ORDER

Throughout all of her writings, Bailey claimed that The Plan called for a "New World Order" to usher in the New Age. But before the New World Order could be established, there had to be peace: "In the preparatory period for the new world order there will be a steady and regulated disarmament."[33] The Plan called for a group of powerful men called the "Brotherhood"* to establish this peace by the year 1975.[34]

Bailey wrote the preceding quote in 1957. Now we have the advantage of hindsight. Although the Vietnam War was concluded in 1973, the potential for true peace was not possible until 1989–92, with the dissolution of the Soviet Empire and the Soviet Union itself. Think of the propaganda that would have generated if the spectacular circumstances of the demise of the Soviet Union coincidently would have occurred in 1974–76 instead of 1989–92. On the other hand, it is more than interesting that the purpose of the Iron Mountain meetings in 1964–66 was to implement peace within ten years. The only reason it wasn't implemented was the lack of a mechanism to accomplish a socio-economic replacement for war within that time period.

According to Bailey's dating, the return of the Christ[35] and the implementation of the New World Order will fully begin in the year 2000 and the New Age will be fully implemented by the year 2045.[36] This New World Order will have three outward manifestations: (1) a one-world government, (2) a forced education system based in mysticism, and (3) a one-world religion based in Theosophy.[37]

This New World Order is socialist in its basis. It so happens that Theosophy is one of the oldest socialist beliefs around. Every-

---

* "The Brotherhood is a community of Masters who are swept by the desire to serve, urged by a spontaneous impulse to love, illumined by one pure Light [light in Theosophy is Lucifer, the morning star], devotedly fused and blended into groups of serving Minds, and energized by one Life. Its Members are organized to further the Plan which They consciously contact and with which they deliberately," Alice Bailey, *Discipleship in the New Age*, 23.

thing in the New World Order will be shared: "The *new world order* will recognize that the produce of the world, the *natural resources of the planet* and its riches, *belong to no one nation* but should be shared by all. There will be no nations under the category 'haves' and others under the opposite category"[38] (italics added).

Global redistribution of wealth and resources was the central theme of the 1992 Earth Summit. Many saw this as merely the continuation of the old leftist social agenda in a green garb—"green on the outside and red on the inside." It is not—at least not in its basis. Rather, it is a very old form of socialism coming from the religious left. It has been around a lot longer than modern socialism, Marxism, or Communism. Since all men are part of god, all men are *literally* equal and have equal rights to what others produce. This "what is mine is mine, and what is yours is also mine" philosophy is evident from the judicial philosophy of "public good" used to attack property rights in our courts, to Agenda 21 of the Earth Summit.

Men will have equal access to nature's resources, not because of any right of superiority mankind may feel, but because these resources are being offered by the earth herself: "The mineral wealth of the world, the oil, the produce of the fields, the contribution of the animal kingdom, the riches of the sea, and the fruits and the flowers are all *offering themselves to humanity. . . .* They belong to everyone and are the *property of no one group, nation or race*"[39] (italics added).

This, of course, is the message of Findhorn. Or is Findhorn a message of Theosophy? In any event, according to the theology of the theosophical religious left, property rights and even national sovereignty must go. As discussed in previous chapters, the attack on property rights by national environmental leaders has been escalating to a point of all-out war over the past two decades. The Rockefeller/Strong plan at the UN-sponsored Earth Summit assaulted both property rights and national sovereignty at the global level.

It would be naive to say that The Plan is being implemented lockstep, or is the basis for some sort of conspiracy. The Christian Bible has a plan of evangelism too. Different denominations often cooperate in planning evangelistic missionary efforts. Yet, no one calls these efforts a conspiracy. There is also considerable difference in how these efforts are actually implemented. Even those who consider themselves "evangelical" Christians interpret the biblical commands differently. Like Christians and advocates of all belief systems, theosophists themselves will have differing interpretations of what and how theosophical ideology should be implemented. Nonetheless, all evidence suggests a major effort to implement common goals by the year 2000. If so, Americans can only expect the assault on property rights and the United States Constitution to get worse.

The Plan permits the continuation of some national sovereignty, but in practical terms it will be in name only.[40] The ruling global body would be centered in what The Plan calls an "economic league of nations." According to Bailey, this ruling entity could be the United Nations since it has demonstrated its "potency of spiritual values" and is laying down those "foundations which will guarantee a better and more spiritual way of life."[41] Whether the ruling entity will be the United Nations or some similar group, the people of the earth will be administered by blocking out the earth into economic and political zones:

A world divided into "blocs" for mutual aid and economic sharing. . . . Such blocs would be cultural and not militaristic, economic and not greedy, and they could provide a normal and progressive movement away from the separative nationalism of the past and towards the distant creation of the One World, and the One Humanity. . . . A world in which there would be no war and in which men could live at peace with each other and in security . . .[42]

Bailey wrote this in 1957. In 1973 the Club of Rome, the futurist group of industrialists, scientists, economists, and others —led by New Age founder Aurelio Peccei[43]—published a report entitled *Regionalized and Adaptive Model of the Global World System*. This report defined ten such political/economic blocs.[44] Peccei claimed this "multilevel hierarchical system (based in theosophy) divides the world into ten interdependent and usually interacting regions of political, economic or *environmental* coherence"[45] (italics added). The report exhorts that "a world consciousness must be developed. . . . The basic unit of human cooperation and

hence survival is moving from the national to the global level."[46]
Club of Rome directors Aurelio Peccei and Alexander King proclaim:

> Philosophers have, from ancient times, stressed
> the unity of existence and the interconnection of all
> the elements of nature, man and thought. How-
> ever, their teaching has seldom been reflected in
> political or social behavior. . . . The winds of change
> have begun to blow. A keen and anxious awareness
> is evolving to suggest that fundamental changes
> will have to take place in the world order and its
> power structures, in the distribution of wealth
> and income, in our own outlook and behavior.[47]

Indeed, the winds of change are blowing. Does all of this seem
a little familiar? Like maybe the European Community, the North
American Trade Agreement, the Earth Summit and its redistributionist plans, and others around the world that have been in the
headlines the past few years? The fact that economic blocs are
being created doesn't automatically make them bad. We are, after
all, in a global community, and we do have global responsibilities.
But it's the agenda *behind* the Earth Summit and the creation of
these blocs that should concern every American.

The hippies of the counterculture and New Age movement
have been most active in two areas, the peace and environmental
movements. Whether they knew their doctrine to be Theosophy
or something else, they have been busy, though certainly not
knowingly or perfectly, implementing "The Plan."

GROUPS

The evidence of this religion is everywhere. Yet most of those
who subscribe to it in one form or another call it something besides Theosophy. Many have never even heard the word *Theosophy*. So how could it be so prevalent in such a short period of
time? Because Theosophy depends on secrecy, even within its
own circle of believers. It is not important to theosophical leaders
whether this belief system is called Theosophy or something else,
as long as its initiates believe in its general precepts. That is the
way of the occult and esoteric religions. The initiates never know

what the higher "truths" are until they have been prepared (pre-conditioned) to receive them, at which time they are initiated into the next secret level.

Theosophy defines "three grades of workers."[48] The first group comprises general disciples who have of "their own free choice realised the immediate and coming need of humanity and have pledged themselves to serve."[49] These represent the vast masses who join groups out of concern for whatever cause the group is pushing. They also include those who are marginally or fully into Eastern mysticism but have no knowledge of the higher truths of Theosophy. These masses are, according to Bailey, "working in the dark."[50]

Many in this first group who follow Hinduism, Buddhism, and other Eastern beliefs may believe in the oneness and harmony of nature, but would not agree with the militancy of Theosophy. In fact, they may truly be open to collaborative solutions. This matters little to Bailey and other theosophical leaders—as long as they are contributing to the overall effort to implement "The Plan." Although these people would personally stop far short of theosophical goals, all that is needed is their cooperation at the broader level to implement "The Plan."

The second group is much smaller. They "act as intermediaries in the working out of the Plan in the world and they hold themselves in readiness to go anywhere when requested."[51] They are the various disciples of Theosophy, including Blavatsky and Bailey. This second group and the next, the Masters, are part of the so-called occult Hierarchy referenced by Foster Bailey earlier in this chapter. The third group represents the inner few and are the Masters of the Brotherhood. "They work primarily upon the inner side. Their activities are confined largely to the mental plane and to the scientific use of thought. Thus they guide Their workers and helpers and influence Their working disciples and the world disciples."[52]

In order to implement "The Plan," thousands of "seed groups" have supposedly been established having functions ranging from telepathic communicators, trained observers, healers, educators, political organizers, religious leaders, scientific servers, psychologists, and financiers and economists.[53] The best analogy to this effort might be the efforts of Christian churches to send missionaries to work in foreign lands, except that the theosophically based groups were established in great secrecy. "Such potent group interplay and group relation," according to Bailey, "[provide] an *emerging world unity [that] can be seen in embryo*. . . . There will (through these . . . groups) be set in motion on earth a network of spiritual energies which will facilitate the regeneration of the world."[54]

Literally thousands of these groups have been created over the last seventy-five years or so. They include thousands of environmental groups, peace groups, mystic Christian groups, and others.*[55] Several of those founded by Bailey through Lucis Trust[56] during the 1920s and 1930s include the Arcane School of esoteric studies, which focuses on the so-called "full-moon meditation" assemblies. Local Arcane School gatherings can be found in most larger cities throughout America. Lessons are administered by correspondence.[57] Among the more often mentioned groups started by Lucis Trust is the New Group of World Servers: "The slow and careful formation of the New Group of World Servers is indicative of the crisis. They are overseeing or ushering in the New Age. They are present at the birth-pangs of the new civilisation, and the coming into manifestation of a new race, a new culture and a new world outlook."[58] The Triangles within Lucis Trust consist of hundreds of meditation groups consisting of three people who "simultaneously imagine triangles of light as they recite the Great Invocation for the return of 'the Christ.'"[59]

Another major group spawned by Lucis Trust is World Goodwill, which until 1990 was headquartered in the United Nations building in New York City.[60] The purpose of World Goodwill is to work towards implementing "The Plan."[61] The 1982 World Goodwill Newsletter outlined its environmental policy:

The entrenched materialistic state of mind which has characterized humanity, especially since the birth of the industrial age, is directly reflected in the present dangerous situation. We have felt

---

* Within the New Age itself there is the Arcane School, Association for Humanistic Psychology, Association for Transpersonal Psychology, Association for Research and Enlightenment, Astara, Chinook Learning Center, Club of Rome, Esalen Institute, The Farm, Greenpeace, Hunger Project, Institute of Noetic Sciences, Findhorn Foundation, Lindisfarne Association, New Group of World Servers, Ken Keyes Center, Lucis Trust, Pacific Institute, Perelandra, Planetary Citizens, Planetary Initiative, Self-Realization Fellowship, Sierra Club, Sirius Community, Tara Center, Theosophical Society, Windstar Foundation, World Goodwill, to name a few.

> free to destroy and pollute our environment re-
> gardless of the consequences to the Earth. Only
> recently have we begun to realize that any organ-
> ism, even a planet, can become so diseased that
> its survival is threatened. We have now reached
> that point. . . . Present-day farming techniques
> are fast becoming recognized as a life-threatening
> environmental hazard [due to pesticide] and ferti-
> lizer use. . . . The solution may be found in small-
> scale, high yield, organic farming practices, . . .
> recycling, . . . and non-polluting energy using solar,
> wind, tide, geo-thermal and fusion power. . . .

> The hope lies largely in . . . recognizing that
> humanity is only part of a greater whole. For us
> to begin to interact in a harmonious fashion with
> all the kingdoms in nature will necessitate vast
> changes in our present mode of living. . . . As
> we become more aware of our essential unity
> with all life, we will one day find it contrary
> to human nature to violate the environment.[62]

This transformation, according to the newsletter, should all occur by the year 2000—the same year the christ is supposed to return and the New World Order, established according to Bailey's Plan discussed above.

NETWORKS

Planetary Citizens was created by United Nations Assistant Secretary General Robert Muller and United Nations consultant Donald Keys at the direction of United Nations Secretary General U-Thant. U-Thant remained honorary chairman for several years and was succeeded by Norman Cousins (*Saturday Review*), who remained honorary chairman until his death in 1992. Cousins was also a member of the Club of Rome. Donald Keys remains as chairman of Planetary Citizens. Keyes dedicated his book *Earth at Omega: Passage to Planetization* to Djwhal Khul, supposed author of Alice Bailey's "Plan." New Age teacher/leader Willis Harman, president of Stanford's Institute of Noetic Sciences, and New Age powerhouse Maurice Strong, founder of the United Nations Environmental Programme and secretary general of the United Nations

1992 Earth Summit, are among Planetary Citizens' strongest supporters.[63] Planetary Citizens investigates innovative economies,
ecologies, and lifestyles needed for the New World Order when it
comes—including a networking survey of "alternative communities" such as Findhorn.[64]

Both Peter Caddy, founder of Findhorn, and Findhorn board
of directors David Spangler helped to develop Planetary Citizens'
agenda. William Thompson, founder of the Lindisfarne Association, not only is active in Planetary Citizens, but also publishes
Findhorn's books. And James Lovelock, of Gaia fame, is a member
of Lindisfarne.

Computer networks exchange information between all of these
organizations. PeaceNet and EcoNet were founded in 1984 and
were formerly linked through the creation of the Institute of Global Communications in 1986. IGC then funded the development of
EcoNet, ConflictNet, HomeoNet, PaganNet, and others. Most environmental organizations use EcoNet to maintain interorganiza-
tional communications and stay current on each other's activities.
At the core of EcoNet, with one of the biggest "conferences," is
none other than the Theosophical Society.[65] From this can come
the seeds of cooperation and strategic planning.

Those involved in this nature/higher consciousness religion
really believe the cosmos is highly interconnected. That remains
to be proven. But the interconnections of these groups and people
is truly spectacular.

We are fortunate to have the freedoms in America that we do.
Those who hold these "nature is god" theosophical beliefs have
every right to do so under our Constitution. The Constitution,
ironically, was based in the Christian belief that human rights
must be protected from men in power who will subvert the rights
of those they rule, given the opportunity:

We have no government armed with power capable
of contending with human passions unbridled by
morality and religion. Avarice, ambition, revenge,
or gallantry, would break the strongest cords of
our Constitution as a whale goes through a net.
Our Constitution was made only for a moral and
religious (Christian) people. It is wholly inadequate
to the government of any other—*John Adams.*

> . . . The entire Bill of Rights came into being
> because of the knowledge our forefathers
> had of the Bible and their belief in it:
> freedom of belief, of expression, of assembly, of
> petition, the dignity of the individual, the sanctity
> of the home, equal justice under the law, and the
> reservation of the powers to the people. . . . I like
> also to believe that as long as we [hold to the spir-
> it of the Christian religion], no great harm can
> come to our country—*Earl Warren, Chief Justice
> of the United States Supreme Court.*
>
> The basis of our Bill of Rights comes from the
> teachings we get from [the Bible]. I don't think we
> emphasize that enough these days. If we don't have
> a proper fundamental moral background, we will
> finally end up with a . . . government which does
> not believe in rights for anybody except the State!
> —*Harry Truman, President of the United States.*

How right our forefathers were. As the Constitution goes, so go our freedoms—and the American dream. If these modern men of power and theosophical beliefs are successful in neutralizing the Constitution, there will be no freedom for any belief but their own. America could easily revert to medieval feudalism—with the elite mystics as lords of the realm who, with superior wisdom, rule over their serfs.

Is there any evidence that such doctrine will really do these things? Tragically, yes—in one of the greatest black marks of the twentieth century.

It is worth remembering how long we waited before finally facing the challenge posed by Nazi totalitarianism and Hitler. Many were reluctant to acknowledge that an effort on the scale of what became World War II was actually necessary, and most wanted to believe that the threat could be wished away with trivial sacrifices.

> Vice President Albert Gore
> *Earth in the Balance*, 272–73

Many of the great regulatory and enforcement agencies of the United States are beginning to adopt the pose of the medieval churches, with regard not for what is true or right, but rather for what defends their notions of the intent of regulatory laws or their established policies and for what supports their own delusions of power, omniscience, and infallibility! The beleaguered scientist with evidence of the fallibility of these agencies, or the triviality of a program that they regulate, or of the underlying faults in their regulations can only recant his findings [if he wants any more research support].

> Dr. John Isaacs,
> then director of the Institute
> of Marine Resources
> at the University of California,
> in testimony given to the
> Water Resources Subcommittee
> of the House Committee on
> Public Works, May 24–25, 1978

12

LESSONS FROM THE PAST

THE ECO-GESTAPO

John Pozsgai couldn't believe what had happened. This was America, home of the free, where even an immigrant from Hungary could start with nothing and through hard work build a good business and life. Now, because he cleaned up some junk tires and started to build a garage, he was sent to prison and robbed of his life's savings. This was just what he remembered happening to his neighbors under the Nazi Gestapo and Communism!

Immigrating in 1956, Pozsgai built a small business running a truck repair shop out of a small building behind his home in Morrisville, Pennsylvania. In 1991 Pozsgai purchased a fourteen-acre tract across the street to expand his business. Since it had been used as a dump for twenty years, John's first effort was to clean up 7,000 old tires, along with an assortment of rusting car parts, and to replace them with clean dirt and gravel. The property is not a marsh, swamp, or bog, and Pozsgai was told by state officials that he needed no permit.[1]

However, since a mostly dry streambed was adjacent to the cleanup in progress, and since skunk cabbage and sweet gum trees were present, Pozsgai's land fell under the 1989 wetlands jurisdiction definition.[2] The EPA obtained a restraining order to prevent the deposit of the fill, whereupon Pozsgai immediately erected barricades to keep the contractors he had hired from dumping any more fill. But, alas, Pozsgai did not camp out on the site to forcibly stop the contractors.

Several contractors who had not yet gotten the word drove around the barricades and deposited their loads as prescribed in the contracts. The EPA videotaped these contractors placing the clean dirt on the land, and the video tapes were used to convict Pozsgai of violating forty-one counts of the "Navigable Waters" provision of the Clean Waters Act. Now bankrupt, he was fined $202,000 and sentenced to three years in prison. He was also ordered by the court to restore the land—not to its previous state—but to a pristine condition.

Paul Kamenar of the Washington Legal Foundation noted that Pozsgai's sentence was "the longest unsuspended jail term imposed in the history of the United States for any environmental crime, including the dumping of extremely toxic and hazardous wastes and where people were even injured and killed."[3] As in Ellen's case, the prosecuting attorney had this to say about environmental crimes: "A message must be sent to all landowners, the corporations [and] the developers of this country that light sentences for environmental crimes are a thing of the past."[4]

Perhaps those who have been hapless victims of environmental lawsuits and criminal prosecutions are correct. America is rapidly evolving towards a totalitarian state with an eco-gestapo to enforce its myriad environmental laws.

THE HOLOCAUST

Sadly, much that comes from environmental groups today is, at best, sensationalized, groundless opinion based on half-truths, even outright lies. It is being fueled by a national and global agenda beyond fiction. Contrary to what is believed by the majority of Americans, most scientists either disagree with, or have strong doubts about, environmental catastrophe theories. Just as the *Iron Mountain Report* recommended, the eco-catastrophe "substitute for war" had to be invented.

Vice President Gore claims we must make the environment "the central organizing principle for civilization."[5] Whether by chance or design, the two examples he used to describe how this might work were both based in the old organizing principle of war

—World War II and the Communist threat of nuclear war. In exactly the same way as outlined in the *Iron Mountain Report*, Gore maintains that to build loyalty to a cause has "historically been secured only with the emergence of a life-or-death threat to the existence of society itself."[6] To this he adds a little extra twist of fear: "This time however, the crisis could well be irreversible by the time its consequences become sufficiently clear to congeal public opinion—*if not panic*. . . . It is essential, therefore, that we refuse to wait for the obvious signs of impending catastrophe, that we *begin immediately* to catalyze a consensus for this new organizing principle"[7] (italics added).

KRISTALLNACHT

Do you sense a little old-fashioned, high-pressure sales job here? Generally, the higher the pressure, the less reality is in the product being sold. In the case of eco-catastrophe there appears to be no catastrophe. Vice President Gore and environmental leaders have portrayed environmental catastrophes in the most horrific way possible to convince Americans they should change their thinking and lifestyles. But Gore sinks to an all-time low when he uses one of the most horror-ridden events in modern history to emphasize the seriousness of these so-called environmental catastrophes:

In the 1930's when *Kristallnacht* revealed the nature of Hitler's intentions toward the Jews, there was a profound failure of historical imagination . . . Now warnings of a different sort signal an ***environmental holocaust*** without precedent. But where is the moral alertness that might make us more sensitive to the new pattern of environmental change? Once again, world leaders waffle, hoping the danger will dissipate. Yet today the evidence of an ecological *Kristallnacht* is as clear as the sound of glass shattering in Berlin.[8]
(Italics original, bold italics added)

Kristallnacht was the infamous night of November 9–10, 1938 when Hitler loosed thousands of his Nazi henchmen and Brownshirts to loot, rape, and pillage the Jewish sections in Berlin and other German cities. Tens of thousands of Jewish people were hauled away never to be seen again. Kristallnacht marked the violent beginning of the Holocaust that was to claim six million Jews by war's end.

Kristallnacht was preceded by several years of extremist rhetoric and fearmongering by Hitler and his Nazi officers, using a constant barrage of lies and half-truths to gradually strip civil and property rights from the Jews. This had to be done to convince German citizens that the Jews were a menace and the source of all their problems. Although Hitler championed private industry, the process convinced the Germans they must give up their freedoms to fight a common enemy. Government control soon turned Germany into a fascist state.

There is a parallel between Kristallnacht and today's environmental crises—but not the parallel Vice President Gore would have us believe. Rather, the parallel exists in the shrill rhetoric and the wholesale use of fear by environmental and global leaders to convince Americans we must give up our freedoms in order to survive. The same tactics used by Hitler are now being used by environmental leaders. To put this into perspective, let's look at the "central organizing principle" called for by Vice President Gore:

We must make the rescue of the environment the central organizing principle for civilization. . . . [This calls for] embarking on an all-out effort to use *every* law and institution, *every* treaty and alliance, *every* tactic and strategy, *every* plan and course of action—to use, in short, every means to halt the destruction of the environment—and to preserve and nurture our ecological system. Minor shifts in policy, marginal adjustments in ongoing programs, moderate improvements in laws and regulations, rhetoric offered *in lieu of genuine change*—these are all forms of *appeasement*, designed to satisfy the public's desire to believe that *sacrifice, struggle, and a wrenching transformation of society will not be necessary.*[9] (Italics added)

Compare this quote from Gore, calling for unprecedented sacrifice and loyalty, to another, little-read quote from a famous orator of history:

What we needed most was the conviction that
first of all the whole attention of the nation had to
be concentrated upon this terrible danger, so
that every single individual could become inwardly
conscious of the importance of this struggle.
True incisive and sometimes almost unbearable
obligations and burdens can only be made generally effective if, in addition to compulsion, the realization of necessity is transmitted to the
individual. But this requires a tremendous enlightenment, excluding all other problems of the day
which might have a distracting effect.

In all cases where the fulfillment of apparently
impossible demands or tasks is involved,
the whole attention of a people must be focused
and concentrated on this one question, as though
life and death actually depended on its solution.
Only in this way will a people be made willing and
able to perform great tasks and exertions.
—Adolf Hitler, *Mein Kampf*

The uncanny similarity between the tactics used by Hitler and those used by Gore and environmental leadership should cause every American great concern. Extremist rhetoric is now being used to inflame Americans into blind obedience—just like what happened in Germany in the 1930s. Those who disagree with environmental leadership are violently attacked as environmental bigots and rapists that should be scorned and punished for their insolence—just like what happened in Germany in the 1930s. Laws and regulations are being passed in an atmosphere of hyste-ria generated by New Age sustainability doublespeak and false claims of catastrophes. Laws and regulations are stripping Ameri-cans of their rights and freedoms—just like what happened in Ger-many in the 1930s. As our freedoms are stripped, our form of government is rapidly becoming fascist, just like what happened under Hitler. And, similarly, there is just enough truth in their accusations to make them believable to an unknowing citizenry.

There may be a holocaust ahead, but it is not the one Gore is worried about. Genuine economic and social holocausts are in store for millions of American families if we continue to strangle our economy through unneeded regulations and the use of gestapo-like tactics by those within our regulatory agencies.

THE THEOSOPHY/HITLER CONNECTION

Vice President Gore used the sickening example of Kristallnacht as a tool to instill fear. Since he introduced the topic, the American people should know the real power behind Hitler and his lust for power, the hatred that produced Kristallnacht. Those in other nations refused to believe Hitler was serious and would really do what he implied he would do. Nazi documents at the conclusion of the war revealed Hitler knew he could have been easily neutralized until the blitzkrieg on Poland. He couldn't believe the gullibility of the other European nations. All the evidence was there; they just didn't want to believe it. The self-denial of "this can't be happening" was operative. Ironically, Sir Winston Churchill was one of the few who really understood the danger Hitler posed, because he understood the vastly larger agenda, philosophy, and perhaps the religion behind this evil man.[10] He was a lone voice that continuously warned his nation that no compromise would ever be enough for Hitler. But he was ignored by Prime Minister Chamberlain and most of the people, until England was fighting for her life. By then, it was almost too late.

Is history repeating itself? Are we like those in England who could not believe a man and a belief system could be so horrible, so chose to ignore the threat?

Adolf Hitler was deeply involved in Eastern mysticism from Sufi and Tibetan lamas to Zen.[11] He was a member of the secret Hindu Vril society. This sect believed the Germans were related to a master race of Aryans who were the early Hindus.[12] But it was the *Secret Doctrine* that held such a strange fascination for Hitler:[13] "By divulging the Secret Doctrine, Haushofer [Hitler's spiritual instructor] expanded Hitler's time consciousness . . . [and] awakened Hitler to the real motives of the Luciferic Principality which possessed him so that he could become the conscious vehicle of its evil intent in the twentieth century."[14]

Once again, Theosophy rears its ugly head. The swastika is a powerful theosophical symbol representing Thor's hammer.[15] The swastika, claims Blavatsky, "as every student of Occultism knows, is the symbol of the male and the female principles in Nature, of the positive and negative, for the Svastica is all that and much more."[16] Herman Rauschning, governor of Danzig, who was very close to the Führer, claimed that Hitler once told him, "I will tell you a secret. I am founding an Order . . . the Man-God, that splendid Being, will be an object of worship."[17] Reflecting on the power Hitler had over people, Rauschning asserted, "One cannot help thinking of him as a medium . . . the medium is possessed . . . beyond any doubt, Hitler was possessed by forces outside himself . . . of which the individual named Hitler was only the temporary vehicle."[18]

Most people believe that Aryans were a race of men. While partially true, that is not the esoteric meaning of Theosophy. Rather, the Aryan race involves the ability to develop superpowers: "The Aryan Race, or to what might be more adequately called the Aryan consciousness, [is] that consciousness [which is] demonstrated in a two-fold manner as mental power and personality force."[19]

This power comes through group consciousness. If any person refuses this he is locked into his so-called state of "lower-man." There is a group, according to theosophical theology, of these inferior humans that refuse to join this shared consciousness:

> The force emanating from that section of humanity which is found in every part of the world and which we call the Jewish people. . . . I am considering the *world problem*, centering around the Jews as whole. . . . They constitute, in a strange manner, a *unique and distinctly separated world centre of energy.* The reason for this is that they [the Jews] *represent the energy and the life of the previous solar system.* You have often been told how, at the close of this solar system, *a certain percentage of the human family will fail to make the grade and will then be held in pralaya, or in solution,* until the time for the manifestation of the next and third solar system comes around. . . . The Jews are the descendants of

that earlier group which was held in pralaya between the first and second solar systems.

The Jew, down the ages, has insisted upon being separated from all other races . . . [and has insisted] that his race was the "chosen people." The "Wandering Jew" has wandered from System One to this where he must *learn the lesson of absorption* and cease his wandering. . . . It is these facts which has militated against him down the years and made it possible for the forces of separativeness and of hate, to use the Jewish race to stir up world difficulty and thus bring to a crisis the basic human problem of separation.[20] (Italics added)

This was not written by Adolf Hitler in the 1930s. Rather, the person who authored these hate-filled, racist words was none other than Alice Bailey. They were written in the early 1950s and with full knowledge of the atrocities of the Holocaust. Apparently the Jews cause the separateness that prevents true love and harmony from dawning on earth. They, according to Theosophy, are from a race supposedly now obsolete, yet who emit a power or energy of separation that impedes the completion of the Great Invocation or Harmonic Convergence. Until the "Jewish Problem" is resolved by their giving up their separateness ideology, the Great Invocation cannot be completed.[21] Is it any wonder that Hitler called for their extermination? Alice Bailey called Hitler an unfortunate incident in history:

In the history of the race, one or two advanced personalities have [used the force] with dire results. . . . The modern example is Hitler. . . . During the last two thousand years mankind has advanced to a point where it can also be responsive to certain aspects of this first ray force. Hitler there found associates and cooperators who added their receptivity to his so that an entire group became the responsive agents of the destructive energy.[22]

How's that for an epitaph of the more than ten million people who died from Hitler's theosophical psychosis? According to Bailey, the Jews were selfish and separate even in death: "The Jew fought only for himself, and largely ignored the sufferings of his fellow men in the concentration camps."[23] According to theosophical dogma, the sufferings of the Jews are irrelevant. What is more important, Bailey claims, is finding the love and harmony in all mankind. It's like Darth Vader versus Yoda in "Star Wars." As long as Luke Skywalker wins over the force of darkness, what's a few million lives?

This is what happens when men and women begin to believe they are God. This is heady stuff, and is a predictable outcome of the human nature. And, in the cases of Adolf Hitler, Jim Jones, and David Koresh, it can have deadly consequences. What is to prevent history from repeating itself? If it happens again, next time it may be you and I.

SIMILARITIES

One can get a strong sense of déjà vu while comparing the history leading to the Nazi takeover of Germany and what is happening in America today. In his book *America, The Sorcerer's New Apprentice*, David Hunt relates a story from the *New Age Journal*, where the writer tells of reading "a little book published in 1923—*The Revolt of Youth*, by Stanley High." The *New Age Journal* writer notes, "It is a disturbing book . . . an eyewitness account, glowingly recorded, of the youth culture that followed the horrors of World War I . . . [that] could well have been entitled *The greening of Germany*. Reading it, one is unsure whether this is Germany of the twenties or America of the sixties that High is describing." The article continues:

Back to nature go the hippies of the day, the *Wandervogel* . . . led by a battered assortment of guitars . . . the "hope for the future of Germany." Natural camaraderie prevails, with *freedom of sexual companionship*. . . . "Nothing is so roundly hated as the superimposition of conventional authority and *nothing so loved as nature*." The political interests are tending to disappear, the great spiritual forces are on the

> ascendancy . . . there is an inexplicable reaction
> against conventional Christianity. . . . I had been
> privileged to walk with the youth of another
> world . . . the apostles of a wholly new life
> for young and old alike . . . with their spirit
> the old heaven and the old earth—*suspicion and
> selfishness and hate—will pass away.*
>
> This is not Charles Reich praising hippiedom,
> this is Germany of 1923![24] (italics added)

Lewis Sumberg, while chairman of the History Department at the University of Tennessee, linked the rise of the Third Reich to the increasing interest in Eastern mysticism and the occult:

> The ability of neo-Paganism to reaffirm itself
> militantly . . . tells us that the Nazi nightmare is
> the most recent but not the final act in a larger
> human tragedy that is still being played out.
> . . . The rise of occultism and the practice of
> the "black arts" by the myriad secret
> societies . . . was noted everywhere in the
> Germany of the 1920's. That we are witnessing
> much the same phenomenon in the United States
> today in the ominous and prodigious growth of
> the politico-religious elites cults . . . should
> cause civilized men the gravest concern.[25]

Even those in the power structure of this belief system are becoming concerned. Edward Whitmont, M.D., founding member and chairman of the C. G. Jung Training Center of New York, spends an entire section of his book *Return of the Goddess* on the mystic phenomenon of Hitler. Though Whitmont promotes goddess worship and higher consciousness, he warns that if things continue as they are the Hitler phenomenon could happen again:

> The Hitler phenomenon presents us with an ex-
> ample of obsessive, indeed psychotic psycho-

> pathology of a collective nature. *But its basic*
> *dynamics are not essentially different from the*
> *similar invasions of transpersonal, mythological,*
> *or archetypal material as they flood the psyche of*
> *single individuals.* In fact it would seem that individ-
> ual and collective obsessions mutually sparked
> each other in Hitler's National Socialism. *Such*
> *dangerous possibilities, not at all limited to that*
> *one-time event, have been too little considered.*
> . . . The loosing of the beast arises when the
> *force* is not properly understood and received.
> . . . They are not limited to Hitler.[26] (Italics added)

The question naturally arises: Can the "force" ever be properly understood and received?

Christians, of course, have always believed that playing with the occult is extremely dangerous. But even Carl Jung, who based his theories on Eastern religions, found his analytical journeys under altered states of consciousness "a risky experiment." He considered it "a questionable adventure to entrust oneself to the uncertain path that leads into the depths of unconscious."[27] Jung warned that even he had to fight his own altered consciousness by clinging desperately to "ordinary consciousness":

> I needed a point of support in "this world," and I
> may say that my family and my professional work
> . . . remained the base to which I could always re-
> turn . . . [or] the unconscious contents could
> have driven me out of my wits. . . . "I have a medi-
> cal diploma from a Swiss university, I must help
> my patients, I have a wife and five children, I live at
> 228 Seestrasse in Kusnacht"—these were actu-
> alities which made demands upon me and proved
> to me again and again that I really existed, that I
> was not a blank page whirling about in the winds of
> the spirit, like Nietzsche [who died insane].[28]

In spite of this, Jung continued to believe the altered state of consciousness was the path to salvation. Witchcraft, shamanism, sorcery, necromancy (contacting the dead), and other occult and mystic practices are all founded upon this type of altered consciousness. Yet the Bible warns:

> Let no one be found among you . . . who practices divination or sorcery, interprets omens, engages in witchcraft, or casts spells, or who consults the dead. Anyone who does these things is detestable to the Lord. . . . Understand that I am he. Before me no god was formed, nor will there be one after me. I, even I, am the Lord, and apart from me there is no savior.[29]

How can these practices be the way to salvation when God Himself expressly forbids it? Yet all Eastern religions say that losing yourself in the consciousness of the cosmos is the way to find truth, love, and true happiness. History does not treat this belief system kindly. Although all religions have their dark moments, cultures based on mystic beliefs have a history of either cultural stagnation or self-destruction. Whole cultures that have practiced these beliefs have disappeared from the earth. Others reach a certain point and stagnate, enslaved by the very spirits that are supposed to give them freedom. Franz Cumont, in his treatise of the occult in the Greek and Roman Empires observed:

> In the declining days of antiquity the common creed of all pagans came to be a scientific pantheism, in which the infinite power of the divinity that pervaded the universe was revealed by all the elements of nature. . . . Preached on the one hand by men of letters and by men of science in centers of culture, diffused on the other hand among the bulk of the people . . . it is finally patronized by the emperors.[30]

Sound familiar? The parallel between Theosophy, the occult practices of the Nazis, and those used in the Sierra Club's book

Well Body, Well Earth are sobering. The practices followed by Hitler and the Nazi initiates were described as follows:

In altered states of consciousness achieved through Yoga and other occult practices of the Vrilists that Hitler engaged in, one could supposedly communicate with . . . Masters of Wisdom, thereby gaining initiation into the secret Tibetan Gnosis. By this means psychic powers could be developed and the restoration of the Master Race begun. The Nazi initiates endeavored to maintain telepathic communication with the Unknown Master, who was the alleged leader of the Tibetan Supermen. Systematic visualization [also called guided imagery] was the key to contact with the Masters. [31]

Samuels and Bennett in *Well Body, Well Earth* issue these instructions: Through "deep breathing, relaxation and autosuggestions" you can attain "the level of consciousness where you can be in touch with those forces in the universe that . . . encourage health and well-being. Here in a trance state, you are ready to visualize the creation of the universe—*even to have a dialogue with Mother Earth herself.* . . . The more you contact the voice of the living Earth, the easier it will become for you to contact it and trust what it provides."[32]

Hitler used visualization to achieve "Aryan power." In effect, *Well Body, Well Earth* teaches the same process to communicate with Mother Earth as Hitler and his Nazis followed in contacting the Masters for global conquest. Either Hitler was really only contacting Mother Earth, or Sierra Club adepts are really contacting evil Masters.

Are we heading down the same road that Germany took in the 1920s and 1930s? There are a lot of similarities. We don't have to follow the same path. But it's not comforting when New Age globalist Aurelio Peccei proclaims: "I think mankind is building up something within itself whereby it will be able to make a jump." Peccei then announces the key tenet of The Plan: "One disaster, one charismatic leader could trigger this transformation."[33] Denis Hayes, founder of Earth Day 1970, EGA member, and president of the Bullit Foundation, suggested the same thing at the 1992 Environmental Grantmakers Association meeting.

HUMAN RIGHTS

Certainly peace and a good environment are highly desirable goals. But at what cost? And could the altruistic theosophical plan for worldwide government, education and religion be implemented without losing our constitutional and civil rights? Although Bailey and her Tibetan spirit guide Djwhal Khul say yes, The Plan simply cannot permit it!

The Plan is an admission that those who have not attained this higher state of consciousness will not be fit for leadership: "The new world order will be founded on the recognition that all men are equal in origin and goal but that all are at differing stages of evolutionary development; that personal integrity, intelligence, vision and experience, plus a marked goodwill, should indicate leadership."[34]

Not surprisingly, it turns out that all of humanity is not equal after all. There will be two classes, the elite leadership and those who serve them. Those at the "lower evolutionary stages" of cosmic consciousness could not be expected to hold leadership positions. As in George Orwell's book *Animal Farm*, "all animals are equal, but some are more equal than others." During the Earth Summit, New Age author Hazel Henderson and Maurice Strong discussed, if you recall, the need for requiring economists to undergo "reeducation" in order to continue practicing their profession. The same would be true for unbelieving businessmen as well. Then it sounded so absurd as to be humorous. Does it now? Bailey proclaims that education in the New Age "*must be done* in terms of operational techniques *relevant to the Hindu psychology*, rather than by Western positivistic procedures"[35] (italics added). Such New Age philosophies have already made big inroads into our children's classrooms.

Are our human rights really in jeopardy? As early as 1957, Bailey claimed that "a powerful, though small group among the world leaders is voicing certain general propositions that must be regarded as imperative when world readjustment starts."[36] No contrary ideology will be permitted: "Their demand is for a new governing principle in politics and in education, founded on universally recognised human rights, on the need for *spiritual unity* and the need to *throw overboard all separative theological attitudes and dogmas in every field of thought*[37] (italics added).

Human "rights" cast in this manner is an oxymoron. There can be no human rights when the people are not allowed to express ideas contrary to the ruling proletariat. The Jews are not the only ones that could suffer if theosophical theology begins to dominate. *Anyone* who disagrees with them will be attacked.

This same mentality extends to other religious beliefs as well. Although Bailey claims the "new world religion will recognize many divine approaches," only those that lead to the "new and vital world religion of universal faith" will be accepted.[38] In other words, Buddhism, Hinduism, and other beliefs are permissible, but Islam, Judaism, and Christianity will be acceptable only if modified to fit their "universal faith" theology. It's not that the "form of Christianity" is bad to theosophists. Rather it's the "grip of the Churches on the minds of the masses."[39] To change people's thinking, claims Bailey, "it is easier to swing the masses into step and give them the newer light of truth if that light is poured on to familiar ground."[40] Therefore, Bailey uses a lot of Christian terminology in her books and talks much about "the Christ" and his return. But it is not Jesus Christ, the Son of God of the Bible, but christ the avatar, the prince of love and coequal to Buddha, the prince of wisdom.

Theosophy is tolerant only as long as a person's beliefs don't disagree with it. Throughout the works of Theosophy, any religion that separates God from nature is despised in the strongest language. The Jewish, Muslim, and Christian beliefs all hold that God *created* nature, rather than the Eastern belief that nature *is* god. Theosophy attacks any monotheistic religion as being "blasphemous and a sorry caricature of the Ever Unknowable."[41] To theosophists the idea of a monotheistic "personal God," as the Bible relates, is a "blasphemy" because He is totally outside of nature.[42] As a consequence, these religions—Christianity in particular—are labeled fanatical, dogmatic, and bigoted. This is especially true when these beliefs identify Satan as the enemy of God. To Theosophy, Satan is the "light of wisdom":

. . . every dogmatic religion—pre-eminently the Christian—points out [that] Satan [is] the enemy of God. In reality, [Satan] is the highest divine Spirit—(occult Wisdom on Earth). . . . Thus the [Christian] Church [is] intolerant, bigoted and cruel

> to all who do not choose to be its slaves. . . .
> Both these Churches (Catholic and Protestant)
> are fighting against divine Truth, when repudiating
> and slandering the Dragon of esoteric Wisdom
> [i.e., Satan]. They [the Christian Churches] are
> moved by the Spirit of dark fanaticism.[43]

Bailey predicted that the greatest "war" in establishing the New Age would be fought in the field of world religions: "It will be fought largely with mental weapons and in the world of thought; it will involve also the emotional realm, from the standpoint of idealistic fanaticism." This fanaticism, Bailey claims, will come from the established church, which "will fight against the appearance of the coming world religion and the spread of esotericism."[44] In other words, any disagreement with their version of the truth will be labeled as fanaticism.

Bigotry and fanaticism are usually defined in the eye of the beholder. Who is the bigot—the pantheist who fights to save a "sacred tree" from being cut to build a home, or the property rights activist who fights to save the land in which he has invested his life in stewardship? Which is more important—the saving of a species gene pool on the chance that it serves a critical function in the earth's web of life or that it might have some medicinal value in the future, or the life of an unborn child who may have been the one person who would have found the cure for cancer or would have grown to be the nation's best president? Who is right? Who is wrong? These are harsh words, yet they represent the real conflicts resulting from two diametrically opposing views of what is right and wrong. Bigotry and truth cut both ways. The answer depends on what a person *believes.*

It is clear from theosophical doctrine that there will be absolutely no room in the New World Order for Jews, Christians, and probably Muslims who hold to biblical or koranic tenets. We are already witnessing a brutal attack on the Christian church in America. Every ill, be it environmental destruction, the annihilation of Native American cultures, or racial and homosexual bigotry is being blamed on Christians. With this type of hatred being poured out from theosophical literature, is it any wonder that we are seeing such hatred repeated in today's headlines? Anyone who disagrees with this mystic religious doctrine is labeled as narrow minded, bigoted, fanatical, and somehow full of hatred for the environment specifically, and humanity in general.

Although Theosophy claims to be the shining example of love and harmony, liberating the believer from prejudice, the truth is showing it to be the exact opposite. The underlying hatred so abundant during the counterculture movement is still evident in environmental rhetoric today. The decision by members of the Environmental Grantmakers Association to label its opponents as right-wing Christian fanatics or greedy opportunists bent on exploiting the environment merely represents a natural outgrowth of this principle. Love and harmony can be accomplished only through a radical transformation of the heart, not the mind as Theosophy claims. History has shown that self-realization of a higher consciousness, or the realization that self is really god, has a much greater chance of resulting in tyranny, prejudice, bigotry, and hatred than in love and harmony.

Ironically, it was *because* the United States Constitution was established on Christian principles of tolerance that this belief system was able to thrive in the first place. The reverse will not occur if this belief system dominates America's legal and political institutions. One needs only to look around the world to see that Christianity and Judaism are forbidden or curtailed by law wherever Eastern religions dominate. In fact, hatred even exists *between* variations of these Eastern beliefs, often resulting in bloody massacres. While promising tolerance and freedom, Theosophy denies it in practice. The United States Constitution cannot be tolerated in the Aquarian World.

Tremendous pressure is being brought against any person who does not agree with this nature-based religion—conform or be ostracized. Many Christian churches are choosing to conform. The Reverend Carl Casebolt, environmental policy advocate at the National Council of Churches has no problem with dumping Christian beliefs: "I'm very comfortable with a lot of the New Age thinking. It's a world view that fits so neatly with a lot of other assumptions."[45] The Very Reverend James Parks Morton, Dean of the Episcopal Cathedral of St. John the Divine in New York City, believes that "every created thing is joined into the whole through the compassion of God."[46] In his services, Morton intermixes "Episcopal liturgy, . . . Buddhist meditations, African chants and other non-Christian traditions."[47] Former Catholic priests Matthew Fox and Thomas Berry have also mysticized Christianity.

Although most Christian churches that have moved in this direction have not moved to this extreme, many have moved to what is known as Creation Spirituality, which Matthew Fox peddles. In this attempt of fence straddling, the "church's life is to evidence signs of a restored relationship between humanity, the creation, and God" where "restoring the harmony to creation and preserving its ecological balance" becomes the entire purpose of the church.[48] Yet, nowhere in the Bible is this doctrine permitted. Rather, balance and a deep respect for God's creation is the banner for the Jew and Christian. For the Christian especially, reverence of nature is the equivalent of idolatry that would "exchange the truth of God for a lie, and worship and serve created things rather than the Creator."[49]

THE BIG LIE?

This is heady stuff for the human ego—and most can't handle it. The promise of godhood has lured men into doing evil since the beginning of time. Tal Brooke, once one of the highest ranking Western disciples of India's miracle-working superguru, Sai Baba, was heavily involved in visualization and other forms of mysticism until he realized there was something terribly wrong. Brooke calls it a lie:

The Great Lie is quite simply the belief that *man is God*, and that his true identity is the immortal self and is ageless and eternal, and that *as God he will never die!* Death is merely a veil through which we pass—and it is not real. . . . People find it infinitely desirable and beautiful, its promises irresistible, as it seems to hold such great promise.

This thought seems to answer our greatest hopes and longings, our deepest struggles with our identity in the cosmos, and our quest for ultimate meaning. It is the Great Lie. It is the foundation stone of Hinduism, Buddhism, Sufism, Jainism, Sikhism, Taoism, Kabbala, The Greek Hermetic and Eleusanian Gnostic beliefs, Neoplatonism, and all the occult creeds from Theosophy . . . to the Rosicrucians, as well as

> too many cults to mention. It is the central
> foundation stone of the New Age Movement. [50]

Power, love, and harmony are promised. Brooke eventually found that promise to be hollow and empty. Although Sai Baba did many things that Brooke cannot explain, and appeared to have some supernatural power, in the end that power was very limited. And under the thin surface of love there was only greed and selfishness—weaknesses common to all humans. It is merely amplified in this belief system because its leaders actually believe they are god and answerable to no one. At a minimum, it breeds a self-serving elitist mentality that they are better than the rest of humanity and therefore deserve "special privileges." Once achieved, most of their efforts become focused on maintaining those privileges at the expense of the citizenry. Hitler's egomania was merely broader in definition—the world was his kingdom.

What is so astonishing about this nature-is-god belief system is that the only "evidence" of its reality comes from Tibetan Masters using automatic writers such as Alice Bailey to provide instructions. Unlike the Bible, these writings have not undergone scrutiny by thousands of scholars and critics. It is amazing that intelligent men and women will believe unproven and unprovable mystic sources as truth, but will deny the historical evidences of Jesus Christ. Even if a person does not believe in what Jesus said, at least external historical evidence exists that He lived, produced miracles, claimed to be the only Son of God and the way to salvation, died, and was seen by hundreds of people after His death. [51] Because of the historical proof that He existed, we are either forced to conclude that He was telling the truth, He was the biggest crackpot of all time, or the disciples were lying. But at least there is strong evidence that He existed, said what the Bible claims He said, and mysteriously reappeared after His crucifixion. No such evidence exists for this mystic belief system.

Furthermore, there are literally thousands of books claiming to provide the absolute path to mystic truth, yet they are often diametrically opposed in how that path is to be taken. Theosophy is merely one set of instructions, and huge conflicts occur even within Blavatsky's and Bailey's writings. Yet, though there are differences of interpretation, all Christians use the Bible as the only authentic source of their beliefs. And though the Bible was penned by some forty different people coming from all walks of life, and written over some 1,600 years of cultural changes, their message has no true inconsistencies.[52]

In spite of this, Blavatsky and Bailey assert that both the disciples and Old Testament writers lied. Yet, archeological find after find reaffirms their accuracy. Conversely, the only proof of what those holding to a mystic belief system have is their "experience" in contacting so-called spiritual forces. Jews, Christians, and Muslims might call them demons. Agnostics and atheists would call them figments of their imagination. Or, as the late physicist/science-fiction-writer Isaac Asimov believed, "true psychic power" without necessarily any religious attachments. If man is capable of receiving such powers, why haven't they been demonstrated in a totally unquestionable way? Psychokinesis research is much ballyhooed, but little has come from it. If man is supposedly able to evolve consciously, then why are we at the same level we were at thousands of years ago?

Nonetheless, these believers are accusing America and the Western world of destroying the earth, based upon their *doctrines*, not science. Although values must temper how scientific evidence is used, New Age believers demand that we give up the American Dream, forsake our freedoms, trash our economy, and put our lives under their enlightened control. They assure us that we will actually have better lives because we will be one with nature, and because of this harmony, nature will *voluntarily* yield her bounties. Even though we destroy modern agriculture, forestry, commercial fisheries, mining, and so forth, there will be no starvation and suffering. Instead, we will have the utopian life at last. How? Because we will have the psychic power to commune with nature and each other, and, through metaphysical power, control the world. Are Americans ready to put their trust in such unproven beliefs that supposedly bring love, harmony, and utopia?

Before we accept this love and harmony for what they claim them to be, hear what Bailey had to say about World Wars I and II:

The World War was in the nature of a major surgical operation made in an effort to save the patient's life. A violent streptococcic germ and infection had menaced the life of humanity (speaking in symbols) and an operation was made in order to prolong opportunity and save life. . . . This operation was largely successful. . . . *Another surgical operation may be necessary,* not in order to destroy and end the present civilisation, but in order to dissipate the infection and get rid of the fever.

But at the same time, let us never forget that it is the *Life,* its purpose and its directed *intentional* destiny that is of importance. . . . When a form proves inadequate, or too diseased, or too crippled for the expression of that purpose, it is— from the point of view of the Hierarchy—*no disaster when that form has to go. Death is not a disaster to be feared; the work of the Destroyer is not really cruel or undesirable.* I say this to you who am myself upon the Ray of Love *and know its meaning.* [53] (Italics added)

This is love? This brings harmony? Hardly. This is a prescription for the justification of the next holocaust, if those with theosophical beliefs attain power. God forbid that this form of love ever gain control of the political process of the earth. Perhaps this is one of the reasons that Nobel Prize winner Irwin Chargaff held these concerns: "I see the beginnings of a new barbarism . . . which tomorrow will be called a 'new culture.' . . . Nazism was a primitive, brutal, and absurd expression of it. But it was a first draft of a so-called pre-scientific morality that is being prepared for us in the radiant future." [54]

Today this "new culture" is storming Western civilization. The question is, What will it bring with it? Are these beliefs the only way to a radiant future where peace, love, harmony, and environmental protection are finally considered worthwhile goals?

Certainly environmental destruction, prejudice, discrimination, and hatred are to be deplored, and they are deplored in the Bible and the Koran, as well as in Eastern beliefs. Christians, Jews, Muslims, and the various Eastern mystic beliefs all claim supernatural truth that shows the way to love. Just as certainly, they all share responsibility for past deeds of violence and war.

But the greatest horrors in this century can be laid directly at the feet of Theosophy and its variants. The reason is obvious: When comparing the different belief systems, which is more likely to produce murderous fanatics—Judaism and Christianity, whose theology makes them accountable to a higher God who says, "You shall not kill," or New Age mysticism, whose theology claims that its followers *are* god and have god's enlightened wisdom? Wisdom that calls for the extermination of those holding "inadequate, diseased, or crippled" beliefs if they hinder the intentional destiny of the Hierarchy.

Take, for instance, Adolf Hitler, Charles Manson (his cult murdered actress Sharon Tate), Jim Jones, and Sirhan Sirhan (Robert Kennedy's assassin). They all had one thing in common— they believed they were god, endued with god-wisdom.[55] So did David Koresh. With the possible exception of Koresh, all were directly or indirectly students of Blavatsky or Bailey.[56] A full analysis of David Koresh has not yet been completed, but references were made in news accounts throughout the siege at Waco, Texas, that Koresh was seeking his answers "in the stars," a fundamental concept of Theosophy.

Without even fully understanding these theological implications, George Reisman, professor of economics at Pepperdine University, sees this danger and warns:

One must not make common cause with the environmental movement in any way. . . . The principle of non-cooperation . . . must be followed in order to avoid the kind of disastrous consequences brought about earlier in this century by people in Russia and Germany who *began as basically innocent and with good intentions.*

Even though the actual goals and programs of the Communists and Nazis were no secret, *many people did not realize that such pronouncements and their underlying philosophy must be taken seriously.* As a result they joined with the Communists or Nazis in efforts to achieve what they believed were worthy and specific goals. . . .

But working side by side with the likes of Lenin and Stalin or Hitler and Himmler, did not achieve the kind of life these people had hoped to achieve. It did, however, serve to achieve the bloody goals of those monsters. And along the way, those who

> may have started out innocently enough very
> quickly lost their innocence and to varying degrees
> ended simply as accomplices of the Monsters. *Evil
> needs the cooperation of the good to disguise its
> nature and to gain numbers and influence it could
> never achieve on its own.*[57] (Italics added)

If we shouldn't support environmental leadership, then how do we find solutions to the environmental problems that we do have? And, even more important, if there is a global agenda using the environmental movement as a straw man, how can we ever hope to fight the billions of dollars it has to continue the hoax? The answer is simple. Truth. Using it effectively is not so simple. And that is where you come in.

I believe freedom is more important than pleasing government. I fought for my rights and I paid a terrible price. If we're going to be prosecuted for what we speak out on, then we have a tyrannical government. We are not a healthy society if we can't oppose what's wrong in our government.

Ocie Mills
The FLOC, May 1993

First, we must recognize that the environmental movement is not about facts or logic. It is about how people feel. Second, we have to understand that no amount of scientific "proof," however decisive it may seem to a scientist, will influence or change the minds of those who hold deeply felt beliefs. Third, despite any rejection of facts or logic, science must persist in its constant research for the truth, without itself falling victim to the convictions that arise from preconceived beliefs.

Dixy Lee Ray
Environmental Overkill, 205–6

13

SOLUTIONS

PROGRESS

It had ceased to be a game for the two Florida Department of Environmental Regulations (DER) enforcers. After taunting and laughing at Ocie Mills, they found themselves flat on their backs and looking at the wrong end of Ocie's gun barrel. No longer having much choice, they left his property quietly. They were even more shocked months later when they found themselves at the wrong end of a judge's decision—Ocie Mills was within his legal boundaries to use reasonable force to protect himself and his property. In a later court action, Mills was awarded a settlement of $9,000 for the state of Florida's wrongful criminal prosecution.[1]

The fray started in 1976 when a ditch on Mills's property in Santa Rosa County, Florida became brush infested and began attracting snakes and alligators. While he was clearing the brush, the two DER enforcers entered Ocie Mills's property to challenge him. Since they did not have a court order, Mills reminded them of his constitutional rights and invited them off his property. Rather than leaving, the enforcers began to taunt and laugh at Mills, upon which they found themselves on their backs.

But Mills was a marked man, and he knew it. In the spring of 1989 he had the Florida DER mark off a one-half acre lot to place clean building sand. Assured he was well within the law and not on a wetland, he and his son Carey brought in nineteen loads of clean sand—whereupon he was arrested for violating five counts of Section 404 of the Clean Water Act. Thinking the charges trivial, Mills made the mistake of defending himself against the U.S. Government's best prosecuting attorneys. Outflanked and outmaneuvered, Mills couldn't even enter in to evidence the testimony that the DER had said it was OK and had flagged the site for him. Although the jury asked three times to view the property, the judge refused. Ocie and his son Carey Mills were found guilty of five counts of discarding pollutants into "waters of the United States" without a permit, sentenced to twenty-one months in prison each, fined $5,000 each, and ordered to restore the site within ninety days of their release.

The Millses were not even permitted a furlough from prison to attend their appeal. Without their testimony, the 11th Circuit upheld their convictions. After the Millses had served their time, the feds once again hauled them into court for a probation hearing, charging that Ocie Mills had not completed the restoration to "their satisfaction." U.S. District Judge Roger Vinson, after reviewing the site, denied the government's petition. Encouraged, and with the help of Pensacola attorney Ronald Johnson, Mills filed a motion in U.S. District Court to overturn their criminal conviction. The Millses argued that Congress unconstitutionally gave the Army Corps sweeping powers that belonged to Congress alone.[2]

Although the judge stopped short of ruling totally in Mills's favor, he left the door open by encouraging Mills's argument. In his twenty-one-page decision on April 8, 1993, Judge Vinson called the Clean Water Act a "regulatory hydra . . . worthy of *Alice in Wonderland*," where the wicked Queen said, "Sentence now, evidence later."[3] The judge continued:

The term 'waters of the United States' . . . is defined nowhere in the [Clean Water] Act. . . . But the absence of a definition by Congress left the task of defining 'waters of the United States' to the entities *enforcing the Act*, the Army Corps of Engineers and the Environmental Protection Agency. . . . The regulation goes much further, however, and defines 'waters of the United

> States' to include something called 'wet-
> lands'. . . . The regulation then makes a quantum
> leap onto land. . . . A jurisprudence which allows
> Congress to impliedly delegate its criminal law-
> making authority to a regulatory agency such as
> the Army Corps . . . *calls into question the vitality
> of the tripartite system established by our Consti-
> tution. It also calls into question the nexus that
> must exist between the law so applied and a sim-
> ple logic and common sense.*[4] (Italics added)

Listen to what Judge Vinson is saying in this scathing decision. By turning over its lawmaking and jurisprudence authority to the very agencies that would enforce their own regulations, Congress opened Pandora's box, permitting these agencies to become law unto themselves. This ruling deals a severe blow to environmental strategies. The Pacific Legal Foundation has already agreed to take the Mills case to the Supreme Court—at no further cost to them. Victory is possible. And it is the Constitution of the United States that provides the vehicle to that victory.

The decision specifically refers to the "tripartite system" of government established by our Constitution. Our forefathers specifically established the Constitution that way because of their Christian understanding that man is prone to sin. Given too much power, men will be tempted to abuse it. Hence, the division of power into the legislative, executive, and judicial branches. Congress abdicated its power to the executive branch with the Clean Water Act. And true to our forefathers' fears, power went to the heads of those men in the agencies, and they went amok. Yet Vice President Gore and eco-leaders demand more of these kinds of ambiguous laws. The attempt to ram the open-ended National Biological Survey through Congress is but one of many recent examples. The NBS merely happens to be the most dangerous. The only thing that stands in the way of these people from turning America into a totalitarian state is the Constitution—and they are attacking it with a vengeance. Think about this quote from President Woodrow Wilson: "The history of liberty is a history of limitations of government power, not the increase of it. When we resist, therefore, the concentration of power, we are resisting the powers of death, because concentration of power is what *always* precedes the destruction of human liberties" (italics added).

Perhaps we should rethink the need for all our regulations, regional planning boards, and other governmental institutions that are becoming progressively unaccountable to the people they serve. But if not more government, then what? How?

RESPONSIBILITIES

The undertaking of such an effort comes with tremendous responsibility. We do have environmental problems, and some of them are potentially serious. Solutions must be found—not in an atmosphere of emotion and hysteria, but with reason and deliberation, balancing the economy and impact on people's lives with the protection of the environment.

In doing so, we must also consider how the counterculture movement has changed America's culture. Only a very small minority hold to the hard-core theosophical-like beliefs defined in this book—but they hold tremendous power. Beyond this small group, however, there are an increasing number of Americans who now hold to Eastern teachings about God and ethics. It would be wrong to include them in with the hardened leadership that has only one objective—to win at any cost. The majority of this emerging group really believes that balance between a healthy economy and environmental protection can be found. Yet their beliefs also predispose them to blindly accept the eco-catastrophe propaganda being dumped on America by the new religious left. How is this emerging segment going to be included in the process of finding solutions?

Beliefs and values are powerful motivators. One only has to look at the Bosnian catastrophe in the first half of the 1990s to understand the power of personally held beliefs. Marshal Tito held Yugoslavia together by iron will and force. Once released, old ethnic and religious hatreds erupted into a violent war where ethnic cleansing was the goal. The Bosnian tragedy provides the classic illustration of why Theosophy and multiculturalism will never work. Theosophy promises that love and harmony among all people is possible if we follow its doctrine. But it is doomed to failure as long as man is capable of hatred and can be tempted by greed and power. And Theosophy has a proven track record of hatred, greed, and deceit. And as long as a belief system, such as Theosophy, permits man to believe he is god, there will always be the Hitlers and Saddam Husseins who would seek to be "the God" over all. Tragically, in such attempts the only solution is the iron rule of military totalitarianism, or ethnic cleansing, or both. Yet, the polarization caused by the tremendous deceit of environmental leadership, along with its intransigent "win at any cost" tactics, is taking America down that deadly path.

The only solution available to America is found in balance. Neither biocentrism based in pantheism, or homocentrism (man-centered) based in humanism can provide the solution. They merely define the two poles causing the bitter battles being fought today. The answer must lie somewhere in between—a point where most Americans can find common ground to build a new environmental ethic. That middle ground is best defined in the Christian concept of stewardship.

STEWARDSHIP

It is ironic that Lynn White and other environmental leaders have attacked the Judeo-Christian belief system as causing the so-called environmental crisis we have today. They claim that the Genesis 1:28 command God gave Adam to "be fruitful and *multiply*, and *fill* the earth, and *subdue* it; and *rule over* the fish of the sea and over the birds of the sky, and *over every living thing that moves on the earth*" gives free license to rape and plunder the land. This idea that Judeo-Christian beliefs and ethics are antienvironment, however, has blinded them to the only possible set of ethics that provides common ground on these tough issues—stewardship. Just what does the Bible say about caring for God's creation?

The Hebrew word for subdue is *kābash*, which means to "bring into bondage, keep under by force; to be made to serve, by force, if necessary." This word, as used in the Old Testament, assumes the meaning that the party being subdued is hostile to the one subduing, necessitating some sort of coercion, if the subduing is to take place.[5] The Judeo-Christian belief that the earth's natural resources could and should be used for the benefit of mankind has prevailed in the Western world since Constantine made Christianity the imperial religion of the Roman Empire. It was tempered with the stewardship principle of Genesis 2:15, but there was never a question of "taking nature by force," if the need arose.

The stewardship principle given in Genesis 2:15 is: "Work [nature] and take care of it." The Hebrew word for "work" is *ābad*, which means to enslave or reduce to servanthood, while the Hebrew word for "care" is *shāmar*, "to tend or guard."[6] So although the Judeo-Christian ethic of stewardship does limit *how* resources should be used, it still provides a strong picture of "nature serving man." Combine this with the admonition of Genesis 3:17, "Cursed is the ground because of you [Adam or men]; through painful toil you will eat of it all the days of your life," and a person who has the pantheistic "nature is god" belief is provided a striking picture of man travailing against nature.

But this picture is incorrect. Instead, these biblical commands merely define what is needed for man to survive in a creation where nature's very resiliency thwarts that effort. In fact, the *Theological Wordbook of the Old Testament* makes the point that "'subdue' in Gen. 1:28 implies that creation will not do man's bidding gladly or easily and that man must now bring creation into submission by main strength. It is not to rule man."[7] Anyone who has fought the weeds in his garden has a good picture of what was intended in the Genesis passage. Gardeners normally do not rape and pillage their garden site. Contrary to what eco-leaders believe, the biblical view of stewardship is the only view of conservation on which to find common ground.

Most people who live in cities or suburbia, including eco-leaders and Vice President Gore, have lost this connection with nature. Nature, to many people, is a romantic concept of the imagination. It is no accident, for instance, that the director of the movie *The Last of the Mohicans* searched many possible locations to film the movie—looking for a forest that looked "natural." Although he did not know it at the time, the location that appeared most "natural" was a forest that had been clear-cut some seventeen years earlier. Natural, it seems, is in the eye of the beholder. Perhaps Dean Ohlman, president of the Christian Nature Federation says it best:

Although the Hebrew terms for "dominion" and "subdue" can have negative meanings implying ruthlessness, they also refer to a governor ruling over his people or a horseman over his mount. It is obvious from the rest of God's Word that the Creator did not grant to mankind the freedom to run roughshod over the earth like a ravaging army. One cannot abuse the earth and at the same time "work it" and "take care of it." . . . It was the entrance of sin that led mankind to the

> pride, envy, [greed], and carelessness that have
> had such a devastating impact on the earth.[8]

The Bible provides numerous examples of the principles behind how God intended man to use and respect His creation. Deuteronomy 22:6–7, for instance, provides an example of how to
respect and treat animals found in the wild. In Deuteronomy 22:4
and Exodus 23:5, we are told to help animals when they are in
distress. In Deuteronomy 25:4 the Bible instructs the people not
to deny the ox the grain upon which he is treading. In Exodus
23:10–11 and Leviticus 25:2–5, the Bible commands that respect
must be given the land while growing crops. The fields, vineyards,
or orchards should not be tilled or harvested every seventh year.
The land is to have a year of rest. This concept of rest-rotation
conservation is still practiced today in the United States. The New
Testament merely reinforces the concept of respect for nature. As
with anything else, if we violate those principles we should expect
to pay the consequences.

Thus God commanded man to respect His creation. Christian
apologist Francis Schaeffer asserts that although we may "cut
down a tree to build an house" or "rid our houses of ants," we
must also remember that God created the trees and ants and we
must respect what He has created.[9] "In the Judaistic teaching—the
Old Testament law—and then later and more specifically in the
New Testament, man is taught to exercise dominion without tyranny."[10] The "value of [the things of nature]," concludes Schaeffer,
"is not in themselves . . . but in that God made them, and thus
they deserve to be treated with high respect."[11]

So stewardship is a concept that permits man to use God's
creation, and even bring it under control, but to do so within the
guidelines of respect for what God created. In effect, the concept
of stewardship allows us to use nature, but not to abuse it. Except
for those hung up on biocentrism, most Americans can find common ground on this. It allows for healthy disagreement, yet permits both economic development and environmental protection.
It has a ring of correctness to it because it is correct. It has balance.

Although property rights are fundamental to protecting the
Constitution from further erosion, most urban Americans don't realize that. "Many Americans," laments Alston Chase, "are unsym-
pathetic to property rights because they believe landowners

merely use the issue as a sledgehammer to bash environmentalists. To defend these liberties is perceived as special-interest
pleading, whereas to demand environmental protection is viewed
as the height of public spiritedness."[12] That is how environmental
leaders have successfully redefined environmental morality.
Farmers, ranchers, woodlot owners, and other landowners must
demonstrate—through their practice of good stewardship—that
they are the real environmentalists. Stewardship provides the
platform to illustrate how they have both their fellow man and the
environment at heart.

VALUES

As noted by Dixy Lee Ray in the quote at the head of the
chapter, environmentalism isn't about facts or science; it's about
feelings. And feelings are based in values and fundamental beliefs.
Although protecting constitutional rights while protecting the environment may be the ultimate objective, stewardship is a vehicle
to get there. Victory does not mean "back to the good old days."
Those days are gone forever. As noted, solutions cannot be found
in either biocentrism or homocentrism. The answer lies in stewardship, which is neither, yet both.

Stewardship meets the values of Americans. Although values
are not cast in concrete, they are very stable relative to public
opinion. And this is one area where landowners, farmers, and other natural resource managers have erred in their strategy. They
have put a lot of energy and money into trying to change public
opinion with facts and figures, but these have typically failed because they have not addressed America's *values*. Values are not
the same as opinions. A person's or public's opinion can change
several times as additional information is received. Opinion is
shaped by values, and environmental leadership knows it.

Eco-leaders have made biocentrism into a "motherhood and
apple pie" issue that appeals to America's *values* of justice (intrinsic value), community (the web of life), and self-protection (the
earth is being destroyed). In fact the last, self-protection, is really
based on human instinct rooted in fear. Once the values were addressed, public opinion naturally fell in behind them. With public
opinion behind them, they have begun the gradual process of converting America's other *values* (the desire for a better life, progress is good, responsibility to one God, and others) to those of
their nature-based religion.

Revealing the nihilistic nature of biocentrism adds information the public did not have before. So does the revelation of the
tremendous gains good stewardship offers in both protecting the
environment and the American Dream. But the message must be
presented in graphic ways. Why? Because, again, statistics alone
do not address American *values*. For instance, eco-leaders demand more wilderness. We already have 256 million acres in
America that can't be used for anything! But what do 256 million
acres mean to someone living in Boston? By graphically showing
this on a map,* the values of Americans are addressed. This
amount of land isn't in someone's back forty; it swallows up major
cities, entire states, whole regions. How much wilderness is
enough? Any American could be the next target for attack. Nothing more graphically illustrates this than the Wildlands Project
proposed at the June 1993 annual meeting of the Society of Conservation Biology, in which one-half of America would be locked
up in biological reserves or in use-restricted human buffer zones.

Environmentalism isn't about good stewardship or conservation; it's about locking people out—A "get out and keep out" philosophy that benefits no one, including the environment. It goes
against the grain of values, and once Americans are more generally aware that the "lock out" philosophy is a fundamental policy of
environmentalists, that awareness will not only help change public
opinion, but will move some citizens to action in support of traditional conservation practices and stewardship.

Another biocentric claim is that, since nature knows best, or-
ganic agriculture is better than modern agriculture. Eco-leaders
use distorted graphic pictures of massive erosion, mud-choked rivers, and dead animals or vegetation to show how farmers are destroying the soil through erosion and chemicals. Equally graphic
pictures of how much soil erosion was created using ancient post-
Mayan cultures (almost a 40:1 ratio) can also speak to America's
values. Such pictures could show how much better modern stewardship practices are than those practiced by cultures that were
supposedly "one with the land." There are plenty of other modern
examples as well.

Even more graphic would be a map showing that an additional
acreage equal to all the land east of the Mississippi River would

---

* Note that 256 million acres is equivalent to Oregon, Washington, Idaho, and
Montana combined, or Maine through Tennessee combined, or North Carolina
to Mississippi combined. By graphically representing this, the impact is *felt* because it is visually huge. Every American would be affected if more wilderness
or reserves are added.

have to be farmed if we were to employ older, supposedly gentler, farming practices of the early 1900s. All the forests and all the wildlife habitat within that equivalent area would have been destroyed if the highly advanced, safe stewardship practices we have today had not been developed. Modern technology and stewardship protect the environment far more than older practices did.

Farmers, landowners, and natural resource managers must honestly show America how and why they are good stewards of America's resources and why they are better environmentalists than the eco-leaders. As public opinion begins to turn, an educational process can be added to the basic message. Richard Stroup, senior associate with the Political Economy Research Center (PERC) provides four fundamental reasons that property rights mean good environmental protection:

1. They produce prosperity, and the evidence is strong that only prosperous people are willing and able to pay for greater environmental quality;
2. They allow and reward the innovations that become technical progress (an important factor in reducing waste);
3. They reward people who find ways to produce goods with less material [and energy] inputs; and
4. They allow the peaceful coexistence of diverse factions, preventing wars and petty rent-seeking, both of which promote inefficiency and the waste of real resources.[13]

Land stewards cannot depend on the media to help tell the truth. The media has other agendas that normally don't include good news. The solution means becoming involved. Grass-root citizen coalitions have an established network to rapidly transmit information from one location to another. They are politically active and can help prevent unneeded legislation, while passing positive legislation.

The most effective method of communication starts with targeting a specific audience. Define which audience can best help you in (1) joining your efforts, (2) spreading the message, or (3) reducing negative pressures. Then *personally* communicate your concerns and vision to this audience in a way that meets their *values* so that they can relate to what you are saying. Jobs as an issue means nothing by itself—unless it can be connected to *their* jobs. A sense of justice and human tragedy are American values, as are community, family, safety, and peace. Concentrate your stewardship message to these values.

There are two more reasons that property rights encourage environmental protection—common law and free market environmentalism. But to properly understand these principles, the law of the commons must first be discussed.

THE LAW OF THE LAND

Communism was a total failure in almost every society in which it was attempted. Why? One reason is that central control works only in unique situations where those in control have sufficient intimate knowledge of what is really happening at the site where decisions have to be made. It never works in far-flung companies or governments covering multiple areas distantly located from where problems need resolution. Yet, a central bureaucracy —where they can exert tremendous influence—is exactly what eco-leadership demands by passing increasingly restrictive laws.

THE TRAGEDY OF THE COMMONS

But, there is another, equally important reason why Communism has failed. It's called the law of the commons. In the law of the commons, no one owns anything. Theoretically, everything is owned in common. This is the basis for Communism. But since there is no pride of ownership, there is no motivation to care for or optimize that which is held in common with the millions of other citizens. There is no reward for doing a better job or being more creative, because your salary (allocation) is not dependent on your output, quality of work, or ability to make a better mousetrap. Since everyone is equal, everyone receives the same salary for the same work. There is no motivation for excellence, so everyone sinks to the lowest common denominator. The economic structure stagnates, and the infrastructure collapses. There is no motivation whatsoever to protect the environment.

Once the Iron Curtain collapsed, the world saw firsthand what central control and the tragedy of the commons can do not only to citizens, but to the environment. The environmental destruction behind the Iron Curtain is staggering. It will take decades and perhaps trillions of dollars to clean up. The collapse of the Soviet empire has proven that the law of the commons is not only disastrous for its people, but also for its environment. Yet, our eco-leaders are bent on nationalizing all private land.

Could the same thing happen in America? It has already, but most people don't make the connection. There are several classic examples in America where the law of the commons has been practiced with devastating results. Alston Chase, in his book *Playing God in Yellowstone*, reveals case after case where the "hands off" policy of the National Park Service has threatened or caused the demise of species that used to flourish in Yellowstone National Park.

The U.S. Forest Service had a good, but far less than optimal, record of management under its old "multiple use" guidelines for management. Now, thanks to environmental pressures and new laws and internal regulations, less than 25 percent of the National Forest System is even eligible for harvesting. The rest is locked up in wilderness, reserves, archeological sites, and so forth. Eco-leaders bemoan the fact that these forests are overcut, when in fact they are not harvested enough! The only tool really available for wild-life management, watershed management, and even recreation is forest harvesting.

Instead of managing our nation's forests, what is the U.S. Forest Service doing now? Putting on *"Spiritual Values Workshops."* What are the topics discussed at taxpayers' expense? They include "Symbolism and Spiritual Values in Experiencing Nature," "Sacred Land, Sacred Sex: Rapture of the Deep Concerning Deep Ecology and Celebration of Life," "The Perceptual Implications of Gaia," "Gaian Buddhism," "Awakening the Sacred," and much, much more.[14] Hold on. Isn't this an infringement of the First Amendment of our Constitution? The so-called Separation-of-Church-and-State Amendment? Apparently not. Why is it that those of Jewish, Christian, or Muslim faith cannot even hold a meeting in a school, but the United States government can *sponsor* a pagan worship workshop? Once again, we have walked through the looking glass where the Constitution is now interpreted exactly the opposite of its original intention. After one hundred years, John Muir would be happy to know that his forest preserves have at last become a spiritual reality—albeit, at a tremendous cost to society.

As bad as they are, these examples of the tragedy of the commons pale in comparison to others. The biggest examples are America's air and rivers. Both are held in common by all citizens of America. No one had responsibility for either, so the cheapest way to manufacture products or dispose of municipal wastes was to dump those wastes into our air and rivers. Some of our rivers could literally burn because they were so full of flammable pollutants. By the late 1960s, our sky became so polluted that the younger generation had rarely seen a truly blue sky.

Earth Day 1970 played a positive role in finally waking up America to this impending crisis. If it hadn't, we would be where the CIS and its satellite nations find themselves today. But although our healthy economy could afford the massive cleanup, the USSR didn't even try. It already had trouble meeting next year's basic needs for survival. But did America clean up its rivers the most efficient way possible? Not at all. Waste was the rule, not the exception, because the law of the commons still applied.

The Clean Air and Water Acts were passed, and they did a lot of good initially. But since air and water were held in common, these laws had to be generalized to the point where they fit no one's needs. Sam and Becky Jones in Arkansas had to meet the same standards as Bill and Sally Smith in Chicago. The regulation is overkill for Sam and Becky, possibly driving them out of business. The same regulation permitted Bill and Sally to continue polluting—causing not only environmental damage but in some instances hazardous conditions for people around them. Had our rivers and air been considered under the jurisdiction of "common law," as private land had been through the centuries, not only would the law been more effective and just, it is likely the pollution would have never occurred in the first place!

COMMON LAW

Common law is just the opposite from the law of the commons. In common law, property is owned by just one individual or a defined group of people. All American law dealing with property is rooted in common law, which in turn was handed down from the days of the Magna Charta. Common law is based on the premise that owners can use and develop their land *as long as that activity does not infringe upon the rights of other landowners*. If your neighbor dumped his trash on your land, you simply had the sheriff issue him a summons to go to court—after, of course, you had asked him nicely to remove what he had dumped and not to do it again! You had the weight of *common law* to compel your neighbor to not pollute your land. If he "happened" to cut down one of your trees, you had common law to make him pay for damages. If an activity that your neighbor did interfered with your commerce in a negligent way, common law was on your side.

Common law has been, and will continue to be, the best and cheapest protector of America's environment. Although it is true landowners could "destroy" their land with impunity until a few decades ago, nuisance laws have helped hold this in check. If an activity of a landowner posed a health or safety risk to the citizens of the community, that activity could be banned by common law. Common law has worked extremely well in deciding and settling damage suits. People respected other people's property because they knew if they didn't, they could find themselves up to their necks in Farmer Jones's barnyard fertilizer—something most people avoid at all costs.

But now eco-leaders and regulatory agencies are taking common law into new, uncharted territory. When the government takes land to build a highway, it was called a "taking" by constitutional law and the government had to pay the landowner just compensation. But what happens when the government takes only a portion of the land's "use" to protect an endangered species? That falls under the definition of "the common good of all citizens." No single citizen (landowner) is threatening the species. It is the cumulative effects of many citizens.

According to both common law and constitutional law, the government should compensate the landowner for that portion it "took" to help the endangered species, which in turn provides a benefit to all Americans. But it doesn't. Until now, the courts have claimed that these issues fall under "nuisance" laws rather than the constitutional "takings" law. But they really don't fit the nuisance laws either. Nuisance law is based on the *endangerment* to the public of a land use or activity. Environmental issues fall under the uncharted territory of providing for the public good. Confused? Don't feel alone. So is everyone else. Richard Stroup, in a speech entitled *Drawing the Line: Property Rights and Environmental Protection*, provides some illustrations that may help clarify the matter:

To seize a private office building for the purpose of providing offices for the police force without compensating the owner of the building clearly is a taking. But to forcibly stop a pistol-waving man from using his gun to criminally menace pedestrians on Main Street is not.

> Similarly, it seems obvious that to seize the
> forest of a timber company, to physically
> occupy that land without compensation, in order
> to provide habitat for an endangered animal,
> is clearly a taking. But to force that company
> to quit dumping large quantities of a harmful
> chemical into a neighboring trout stream is not,
> because there was never the right to dump
> chemicals onto other person's property.
>
> In brief, an environmental policy that merely stops a
> property owner from doing physical harm to others
> does not generally constitute a taking. But to seize
> property, even for public purposes (i.e., the public
> good) is a taking and requires just compensation. [15]

Yet, such a simple, logical solution horrifies eco-leaders. Why? Because the real costs are presently being hidden on the backs of landowners. Such an approach would force the costs to the surface where Americans, for the first time, would see the staggering costs of unneeded environmental protection—and they wouldn't be willing to support it. Suddenly, all Americans could see that we can't afford to protect everything any more than we can afford to maximize protection of our homes by giving them a coat of paint every year. Environmental protection would have to be prioritized—just as the family has to prioritize its budget expenditures! Worst of all, the eco-leaders would lose their political power.

The principle behind free market environmentalism is exactly the same as the common law approach. But since it is covering uncharted legal territory, it is fraught with pitfalls. What and how is real environmental damage defined? Who defines it? What about a landowner whose activity, by itself, does not cause damage, but the cumulative effects of all those who are already doing it will make adding his activity damaging? The straw-that-broke-the-camel's-back effect. Does that mean the full cost of solving the problem should fall on the last landowner alone? But again, common law and what is called free market environmentalism can resolve these issues as well.

FREE MARKET ENVIRONMENTALISM

We all have our deeply felt beliefs. But if we are to find common ground, we must be willing to define environmental damage on the basis of high-quality, unbiased science, not shamanism. To do this, as Dixy Lee Ray admonishes, scientists themselves must not fall victim to preconceived beliefs or values. To do less is to encourage pseudoscience and the building of our social fabric on fiction. Within the limits posed by our humanity, science *must* be kept separate from values. Values ultimately determine how the *unbiased* results of science are applied in developing policy, but values should never be used to bias science itself.

In their book *Free Market Environmentalism*, Terry Anderson and Donald Leal point out that there is nothing in our present economic/regulatory system to balance costs against benefits.[16] Additional regulations serve only to provide regulators with a path of least resistance where the squeaky wheel is appeased. Since the cost of regulation is "zero" to both environmental leaders and regulators, overregulation is the inevitable consequence. On the other hand, where users have no cost associated with environmental abuse, as in the law of the commons, degradation can result.[17]

Free market environmentalism offers far more opportunities for win-win collaboration than can ever be gained through confrontation and regulation:

By confronting our entrenched visions, we can move beyond the status quo of political control of the environment and unleash environmental entrepreneurs on the tougher problems we face. . . . Most of the proposed solutions to perceived environmental problems, however, call for centralized approaches *that are not consistent with the science of ecology.* Moreover, *these solutions pit winners against losers* in a zero-sum game that tears at the social fabric. Free market environmentalism depends on a voluntary exchange of property rights between consenting owners and promotes cooperation and compromise. In short, it offers an alternative that channels the height-

ened environmental consciousness into win-win solutions that can sustain economic growth, enhance
environmental quality, and promote harmony. [18]

Free market environmentalism is centered on the most basic
of economic tenets—incentives matter. When one resource use
conflicts with another, trade-offs must occur. If there is real environmental damage, the activity is denied. Or, as in the case of
mining, the owner is required to restore the land. If there is no
damage but our *values* demand that the activity be prohibited, the
community, state, or nation pays for them, as appropriate. This is
nothing but a common sense approach.

Free market environmentalism also considers the "cumulative effects" phenomenon, whereby no one single use of an activity
is harmful, but repeated use by numerous landowners becomes
harmful. If science shows that only so much of the same activity
can be used without damage, then rights to use that activity can be
established in the *free market*. The market then determines the
value of that right. Such an approach stimulates the creative
search for more cost-effective alternatives while not denying any
landowner the right to use the activity. It results in the best of all
worlds. The environment is protected and creativity is stimulated.

Such a common sense solution is exactly the opposite of the
command-and-control approach demanded by eco-leaders. These
eco-leaders claim that the free market has failed to protect the
environment. In making that claim, however, they fail, once again,
to understand that the reason the common sense approach has
failed in certain arenas is because of (1) the inevitable tragedy that
results from the law of the commons in problems such as air and
water, and (2) the disincentives created by the command-and-
control tactics of overly restrictive regulations when imposed on
the free market and on private lands. In other words, overregulation has become one of the primary reasons the marketplace has
failed. Had the concepts of common law and free market environmentalism been applied to environmental questions instead of regulation, the marketplace would not have failed.

The failure is best exemplified by the fact that the Endangered Species Act contains no incentives. It is a classic command-
and-control regulation based on punishment. Rather than eliciting
support from landowners, it has accelerated the destruction of

habitats occupied by potentially rare species before land occupied by that species is locked up forever. The Endangered Species Act encourages landowners to keep the species off their land rather than providing habitat for them.

Before you condemn these landowners for their callousness, remember that they are faced with exactly the same situation you would be faced with if you had invested a large sum of money for your kids' education or your own retirement, and you suddenly learned that the government was going to confiscate that investment to pay down the national debt—for the "public good." That money is not the "public's," it's yours. If you had the chance, you would withdraw it before it is confiscated! You would do exactly the same thing as the landowner would. If the Endangered Species Act continues in force or is strengthened in its present form, it will merely add to the eco-leaders' stockpile of weapons to level at the American people and will cause more extinctions than it will save! And destroy lives, families, and communities in the process.

Why not change the act so that landowners are rewarded for efforts to provide habitat and are held harmless if a mistake is made that possibly degrades the habitat? But this common sense approach is once again decried by our eco-leaders because it would cost too much. It *already* costs too much—the American people just don't know it. Truth always hurts these eco-leaders. It might even cost them their jobs.

THE ROAD TO VICTORY

Throughout this book we have explored the esoteric highways of modern environmental leadership, crossed through the looking glass into the land of fantasy and the absurd, and finally ventured into the amoral world of political power plays and illusions. We have dissected the phenomenon of eco-catastrophes and have found them lacking. We have revealed the esoteric origins of the attack on the United States Constitution—the very instrument of our freedom. We have scrutinized the belief that nature is god and that a biocentric approach is the solution. By looking at them, we have exposed them for what they really are, bricks on the slippery road to nihilism. And we have unveiled the source of this grand deceit, Theosophy, and the root of all roots, greed and power. Although environmental groups are needed to maintain balance, eco-fanaticism is not.

America is at risk. But is all hope lost? Not at all. It may very well be that the environmental movement is a powerful weapon wielded by powerful men, driven by a lust for power. If so, it may be that environmental leadership itself doesn't fully understand how it too is being used in a larger agenda. Or it may be nothing more than a movement out of control, blinded by a religion that claims that nature is god. It could be, and probably is, something in between.

Either way, most Americans are living in a world of illusion, participating in an agenda of which they have little knowledge. Democracy has slim chance for survival when its members base their decisions on illusion. On the other hand, even if this possible deception is worse than depicted, no deception can long stand the light of truth. Any deception, no matter how powerful, is only as strong as its weakest link. The weak link in this deception is the United States Constitution. As long as it serves as the beacon of law, justice, and freedom, truth will prevail over illusion.

Deceit and illusion can never stand against the harsh light of truth. And the truth is that the only eco-catastrophes that have been found have been through the eyes of nature religion. This religion is gradually stripping the rights and freedoms from every American by casting itself into the law of the land. A religion that demands that it be the central organizing principle of the world. A religion that in practice will make the rich richer, the powerful more powerful, and the poor and middle class poorer. A religion that could take civilization back thousands of years to the times when men and women lived in fear of offending the gods of nature.

Common law and free market environmentalism are the only common ground upon which all willing Americans can find solutions. More government and more regulations will only make the problem worse. Because we have the protection of the Constitution of the United States, we have the freedom to choose which road we will travel. But that constitutional right presupposes that Americans have the pertinent information upon which to make that choice. Before this can happen, the myth of eco-catastrophes must be exposed for what it is—an attempt to create guilt and fear in the American people so a larger agenda based in greed and a new religion can be imposed on America.

As long as civilized man can use truth as a sword in the political and legal process, victory will belong to the people. As long as men of arrogance and deceit must abide by the Constitution of the

United States, reason will prevail. And that defines the task ahead. First, to protect the Constitution from further erosion, and with it the slipping of power from the people to the hands of the enlightened elite. Second, to encourage exposure of the deceit of eco-catastrophes and the religion behind it. Truth will always be victorious as long as it is cherished. It is our choice.

NOTES AND CITATIONS

CHAPTER 1 - THE COST OF ENVIRONMENTALISM

1. Bill Ellen's story is taken from the *News from the FLOC; Fairness to Land Owners Committee,* August 1992, 1–6, and Richard Miniter, "Wetlands Sends Man Up the River," *Insight,* December 14, 1992, 7–11, 30–31.

2. Miniter, "Wetlands," 9.

3. *News from the FLOC; Fairness to Land Owners Committee,* August 1992, 5.

4. Miniter, "Wetlands," 9.

5. *Land Rights Letter* 3, nos. 1,2 (1993), 5.

6. Ibid., 11.

7. Review & Outlook, *The Wall Street Journal,* November 18, 1992.

8. Ibid.

9. Ibid.

10. Miniter, "Wetlands," 11.

11. Ibid.

12. Ibid.

13. Personal communication, and Miniter, "Wetlands," 14.

14. Larry Burkett, *Whatever Happened to the American Dream* (Chicago: Moody, 1993), 213.

15. Miniter, "Wetlands," 6.

16. Ibid.

17. Albert Gore, *Earth in the Balance: Ecology and the Human Spirit* (Boston: Houghton Mifflin, 1992), 270, 274.

18. Ibid., 282.

19. Ibid., 180.

20. Rogelio Maduro and Ralf Schauerhammer, *The Holes in the Ozone Scare* (Washington, D.C.: 21st Century Associates, 1992), 241–54.

21. Joe Wrabek, "They're After Your Property!" *The New American* 8, no. 11: 23–24.

22. Miniter, "Wetlands," 10.

23. Reprinted in *Land Rights Letter* 3, nos. 1,2 (1993), 4.

24. Leslie Spencer, "Fighting Back," *Forbes,* July 19, 1993, 43–44.

CHAPTER 2 - ECOLOGICAL REALITIES OF ENVIRONMENTALISM

1. Robert Bidinotto. "The Great Apple Scare," *Reader's Digest,* October 1990, 53–58.

2. George Reisman, *The Toxicity of Environmentalism* (Laguna Hills, Calif.: Jefferson School of Philosophy, Economics, and Psychology, 1990), 7.

3. Bidinotto, "Apple Scare."

4. Andrew Dobson, *Green Political Thought* (London: Unwin Hyman, 1990), 153.

5. Ibid., 131.

6. Albert Gore, *Earth in the Balance: Ecology and the Human Spirit* (Boston: Houghton Mifflin, 1992), 177, 269, 274.

7. Dixy Lee Ray, *Trashing the Planet* (Washington, D.C.: Regnery Gateway, 1990), 70–71.

8. Ibid., 69–70.

9. Ibid.

10. Ibid., 73.

11. Ibid., 72–73.

12. Ibid., 74.

13. Personal communication with Tom Guilding, Director Environment Affairs, National Agriculture Chemical Association.

14. Robert Lee, "Relying on Unsupported Theories," *The New American,* June/ August 1992, 22.

15. Leslie Spenser, "Ban all plants—they pollute" *Forbes,* October 25, 1993, 104.

16. Larry Kulp, "Acid Rain; Causes, Effects, and Control," *CATO Review of Business and Government,* Winter 1990, 41.

17. Ibid., 45.

18. Joseph Barnard, "Changes in Forest Health and Productivity in the United States and Canada." *Acidic Deposition: State of Science and Technology, Report 16.* Nation Acid Precipitation Assessment Program, 158.

19. Kulp, "Acid Rain," 41–45.

20. Ibid., 50.

21. Ronald Bailey, "Demagoguery in Green," *National Review*, March 16, 1992, 43.

22. The poll was taken within the members of the American Geophysical Union and the American Meteorological Society. From *National Review*, March 16, 1992, 17.

23. *National Review*, March 16, 1992, 17, 43.

24. Ibid., 17.

25. Robert Balling, *The Heated Debate: Greenhouse Predictions Versus Climate Reality* (San Francisco: Pacific Research Institute for Public Policy, 1992), 87.

26. Patrick Michaels, *Sound and Fury* (Washington, D.C.: CATO Institute, 1993), 55, 63.

27. Balling, *Heated Debate*, 31, 69.

28. Michaels, *Sound and Fury*, 62, 85.

29. Ibid., 55.

30. Ibid., 40.

31. Balling, *Heated Debate*, 54, 69.

32. Ibid., 54–69.

33. Michaels, *Sound and Fury*, 82–83.

34. Ibid.

35. Thomas Karl et al., "Global Warming: Evidence for Asymmetric Diurnal Temperature Change," in *Geophysical Research Letters* 18(12):2253–56.

36. Ibid.

37. Balling, *Heated Debate*, 67.

38. Patrick Michaels, professor of Climatology and Environmental Sciences, University of Virginia. Personal communication.

39. Michaels, *Sound and Fury*, 120, 123.

40. Ibid., 95.

41. Ibid., 90, 92.

42. Ibid.

43. Ibid., 117.

44. "Birth of a Climate," *Discover*, April 1993, 12–13.

45. Hugh Ellsaesser, Lawrence Livermore National Laboratory, Atmospheric and Geophysical Sciences Division, "Global Warming, a Different View," in *ēco-logic*, March 1993, 18.

46. Richard L. Stroup, *Political Economy Research Center Reports* 10, no.3 (December 1992), 6.

47. Michaels, *Sound and Fury*, xiii.

48. Stroup, *Political Economy Research*.

49. Balling, *Heated Debate*, 137–38.

50. Ibid., 139.

51. Ibid., 150.

52. Bailey, "Demagoguery in Green," 43.

53. Michaels, *Sound and Fury*, 25.

54. John McManus, "Nothing More than Hot Air," *The New American*, June/July 1992, 6.

55. Michaels, *Sound and Fury*, 25–26

56. McManus, "Hot Air," 6.

57. *Wall Street Journal*, June 1, 1992, Editorial Page.

58. Michaels, *Sound and Fury*, 152.

59. Ibid.

60. Fred Singer, *National Review*, June 30, 1992.

61. J. K. Angell, "On the Relation Between Atmospheric Ozone and Sunspot Number," *Journal of Climate*, November 1989.

62. Ibid.

63. Dixy Lee Ray, *Environmental Overkill* (Washington, D.C.: Regnery Gateway, 1993), 42–43.

64. Robert Lee, "The Evidence Is Thin," *The New American*, June/August 1992, 9–10.

65. Ray, *Environmental Overkill*, 41.

66. Ibid., 40.

67. Hugh Ellsaesser, "A Reassessment of Stratospheric Ozone: Credibility of the Threat," *Climate Change* 1 (1978):257–66, 41–42.

68. Lee, "Evidence Is Thin," 9–10.

69. Michaels, *Sound and Fury*, 166.

70. Richard Benedick, *Ozone Diplomacy* (Cambridge: Harvard Univ., 1991), 190; as quoted in Dixy Lee Ray, *Environmental Overkill*, 46.

71. Rogelio Maduro and Ralf Schauerhammer, *The Holes in the Ozone Scare* (Washington, D.C.: 21st Century Associates, 1992), 71.

72. Ibid.

73. Ibid., 80–81.

74. Ibid.

75. Ibid.

76. Ibid., 183–84.

77. "Press Release: Ozone Hole," editorial in the *Wall Street Journal*, February 28, 1992.

78. Ray, *Environmental Overkill*, 49.

79. Aslam Khalil and R. A. Rasmussen, "The Potential of Soils as a Sink of Chlorofluorocarbons and Other Man-Made Chlorocarbons," *Geophysical Research Letters* 16, no.7 (July 1989): 679–82. Also: Khalil and Rasmussen, "The Influence of Termites on Atmospheric Trace Gases," *Journal of Geophysical Research* 95, D-4 (March 20, 1990):3619–34.

80. Maduro and Schauerhammer, *Ozone Scare*, 12–13.

81. Ibid., 27–30.

82. Ibid., 21.

83. Scotto et al., "Biologically Effective Ultraviolet Radiation: Surface Measurements in the United States, 1974–1985," *Science*, February 12, 1988.

84. Micah Morrison, *Insight*, April 6, 1992, 188.

85. *Citizen Outlook* 8, no. 3, 2. Published by CFACT, Citizens for a Constructive Tomorrow, Washington, D.C.

86. Holman Jenkins, Jr. "Al Gore Leads a Purge" *Wall Street Journal,* May 25, 1993.

87. *Bangor Daily News,* February 4, 1992.

CHAPTER 3 - EVOLUTION OF THE CONSERVATION MOVEMENT

1. Adapted from Tal Brooke, "The Ecological Great Awakening," *SCP Journal* 17, no. 3 (1992): 4.

2. John Muir, *Harper's Weekly,* June 5, 1897. In *John Muir and His Legacy: The American Conservation Movement* by Stephen R. Fox. Copyright © 1981 by Stephen R. Fox. Excerpts from the John Muir Papers copyright © 1981 by the Muir-Manne family. By permission of Little, Brown and Company. 113.

3. Fox, *Conservation Movement,* Preface.

4. Ibid., 28–31.

5. Ibid., 34.

6. Ibid., 35.

7. Ibid., 40–41.

8. Ibid., 42–43, 45.

9. Ibid., 103.

10. Ibid., 108.

11. Ibid., 86–87, 98–99.

12. Ibid., 88.

13. Ibid., 107.

14. Ibid., 108–9.

15. John Muir Papers, H. Senger and W. D. Armes to John Muir, May 25, 1892, cited in Stephen Fox, *Conservation Movement,* 107.

16. Fox, *Conservation Movement,* 109–10.

17. Ibid., 110.

18. Ibid., 111.

19. Ibid., 111–13.

20. John Muir Papers, Pacific University, April 6, May 3, 1897, cited in Stephen Fox, *Conservation Movement,* 112.

21. Fox, *Conservation Movement,* 113.

22. J. P. Johnson Papers, Bancroft Library, University of California. C. S. Sargent to R. U. Johnson, June 4, 1923, cited in Fox, *Conservation Movement,* 112.

23. John Muir, *Harper's Weekly,* June 5, 1897, cited in Fox, *Conservation Movement,* 113–14.

24. Ibid., 145.

25. Ibid., 361.

26. Ibid., 365, 368.

27. Thomas Higginson, *Appalachia*, April 1884, cited in Fox, *Conservation Movement*, 364.

28. Fox, *Conservation Movement*, 364.

29. Alston Chase, *Playing God in Yellowstone* (San Diego: Harcourt, Brace, Jovanovich, 1986, 1987), 303.

30. Fox, *Conservation Movement*, 367.

31. Ibid., 364.

32. Chase, *Playing God*, 302.

33. Ibid., 303–5.

34. Fox, *Conservation Movement*, 363.

35. Chase, *Playing God*, 303.

CHAPTER 4 - POSTCOUNTERCULTURE ENVIRONMENTALISM

1. The example used here is taken from Alston Chase, *Playing God in Yellowstone* (San Diego: Harcourt, Brace, Jovanovich, 1986, 1987), 295–98.

2. Willis Harman, *Global Mind Change: The Promise of the Last Years of the Twentieth Century* (Indianapolis, Ind.: Knowledge Systems, 1988), Postscript.

3. Willis Harman, Futures Seminar Material—1, July 18–19, 1983; "Five 'Forcing Functions' Shaping the Future," Futures Seminar Material—2, July 18–19, 1983.

4. Institute of Noetic Sciences, *Newsletter* 10, no.2 (Fall 1982) Futures Seminar Material—3, July 18–19, 1983.

5. Douglas Groothuis, *Unmasking the New Age* (Downers Grove, Ill.: InterVarsity, 1986), 42.

6. Tal Brooke, *When the World Will Be As One* (Eugene, Oreg.: Harvest House, 1988), 32–35. Copyright Tal Brooke; used by permission.

7. Lynn White, "The Historical Roots of Our Ecological Crisis," in *Science* 155:1203–7. This article has been frequently reprinted in various ecological books and writings.

8. Chase, *Playing God*, 299.

9. Warwick Fox, *Toward a Transpersonal Ecology: Developing New Foundations for Environmentalism* (Boston: Shambhala, 1990), 6.

10. Chase, *Playing God*, 300.

11. Ibid.

12. Ibid., 310.

13. Ibid., 304.

14. Brian Swimme and Thomas Berry, "The Universe Story," *The Amicus Journal*, Winter 1993, 31.

15. Groothuis, *Unmasking*, 46.

16. *John Muir and His Legacy: The American Conservation Movement*, by Stephen R. Fox. Copyright © 1981 by Stephen R. Fox. Excerpts from the John Muir Papers copyright © 1981 by the Muir-Manne family. By permission of Little, Brown and Company. Also, Chase, *Playing God*, 305.

17. Tal Brooke, *World Will Be As One* (Eugene, Oreg.: Harvest House, 1988), 40–43, 46–47. Used by permission.

18. Ibid., 52.

19. Ibid., 206.

20. Alice Bailey, *Discipleship in the New Age* (New York: Lucis, 1944), 708.

21. Chase, *Playing God,* 304.

22. Chase quoting John McPhee, in *Playing God,* 305.

23. Ibid., 304.

24. Bailey, *Discipleship,* 9.

25. Ibid., 36–37, 62, 505.

26. Ibid., 69–70, 92, 339.

27. Brian Swimme and Thomas Berry, "The Universe Story; A New, Celebratory Cosmology," *The Amicus Journal,* Winter 1993, 30–31.

28. Ibid., 37.

29. Helena Blavatsky, *The Secret Doctrine: The Synthesis of Science, Religion, and Philosophy,* 2 vols. (London: Theosophical Publishing, 1888; reprint by Theosophical University Press, Pasadena, Calif., 1988.), 1:611.

30. William Irwin Thompson in a Lindisfarne Association newsletter, mailed January 1992.

31. Chase, *Playing God,* 308–9.

32. Rupert Sheldrake, *The Rebirth of Nature: The Greening of Science and God* (New York: Bantam, 1992), 33, 59, 60.

33. Michael Coffman, *Environmentalism* (Bangor, Maine: Environmental Perspectives, 1992), 140–41.

34. William Stevens, "An Eden in Ancient America? Not Really," *New York Times,* March 30, 1993, C1, C9, quoting *The Annals of the American Association of Geographers,* 1992.

35. Personal communication with James Porterfield, Natural Resources Specialist, American Farm Bureau, Park Ridge, Illinois.

36. Ibid., C9, as quoted from *Nature,* 1992.

37. Christopher Manes, *Green Rage: Radical Environmentalism and the Unmaking of Civilization* (Canada: Little and Brown, 1990), 145–46.

38. Chase, *Playing God,* 358.

39. Quoted from Robert Bidinotto, "Environmentalism: Freedom's Foe for the '90s," *The Freeman,* November 1990, 414.

40. *The Animal's Agenda,* December, 1987.

41. Ibid., 233.

42. Bill McKibben, *The End of Nature* (New York: Anchor, 1990), 182.

43. "Earth First Surfaces in Forest," *Spokane Chronicle,* July 4, 1988.

44. Ibid.

45. Dave Foreman, Letter to the Editor, *The Nation,* December 12, 1987.

46. Coffman, *Environmentalism,* 185.

47. Ibid.

48. Ibid., 23, 201.

CHAPTER 5 - THE NATURE OF ENVIRONMENTAL LEADERSHIP

1. McCrary's story taken from Charles McCoy, "Even a Logger Praised as Sensitive to Ecology Faces Bitter Opposition," *Wall Street Journal,* April 1, 1993, A1, A16.

2. These include the National Wildlife Federation (5.8 million members, $90 million budget); Greenpeace (America: 1.8 million members, $50 million budget; international: $100 million, which is *not* included in the total cited above); World Wildlife Fund (1 million members, $32 million budget); Sierra Club (including Legal Defense Fund, 869,000 members, $57.5 million budget); National Audubon Society (600,000 members, $37 million budget); the Nature Conservancy (568,000 members, $168.5 million budget, $274 million in 1992 [FLOC, April 1993, 5]; The Wilderness Society (400,000 members, $17.6 million budget); Environmental Defense Fund (225,000 members, $16.9 million budget); and the Natural Resources Defense Council (170,000 members, $16 million budget). 1990 information; from Berit Kjos, *Under the Spell of Mother Earth,* 177.

3. Berit Kjos, *Under the Spell of Mother Earth* (Wheaton, Ill.: Victor, 1992.), 177–79, as quoted by Bill Gifford, "Inside the Environmental Groups," in *Outside Magazine,* 1990, and from personal contact with respective organizations. Also: Ron Arnold and Alan Gottlieb, *Trashing the Economy: How Runaway Environmentalism Is Wrecking America* (Bellevue, Wash.: Free Enterprise, 1993. Distributed by Merril Press), 54; "The Philanthropy 400," Special Report, *The Chronicle of Philanthropy,* November 19, 1991, 1.

4. Arnold and Gottlieb, *Trashing the Economy,* 55, 73.

5. Rogelio Maduro and Ralf Schauerhammer, *Ozone Scare* (Washington, D.C.: 21st Century Associates, 1992), 244.

6. Peggy Reigle, "The Shrinking Acreage of Private Property in the U.S." *News from the FLOC,* April 1993, 5.

7. Maduro and Schauerhammer, *Ozone Scare,* 246, 248. Also, Arnold, *Trashing the Economy,* 54.

8. Maduro and Schauerhammer, *Ozone Scare,* 252–53.

9. Ibid.

10. Maduro and Schauerhammer, *Ozone Scare,* 247. Also, Arnold, *Trashing the Economy,* 603.

11. Ibid., 251.

12. Peter Metzger is the former science editor of the *Rocky Mountain News.* quoted in Maduro and Schauerhammer, *Ozone Scare,* 252.

13. R. J. Smith, vice president, CATO Institute, personal communication.

14. Maduro and Schauerhammer, *Ozone Scare,* 248.

15. Erich Veyhl, "Preservationists Acknowledge Growing Grass Roots Opposition," in *Land Rights Letter* 3, nos. 1, 2 (January/February 1993), Special Supplement, 2.

16. "Environmental Grantmakers Association—A Brief Overview," Environmental Grantmakers Assoc., 1290 Avenue of the Americas, Suite 3450, New York, NY 10104.

17. These tapes were transcribed by Erich Veyhl of the Maine Conservation Rights Institute and published as supplements in the first four 1993 issues of *Land Rights Letters.* Also, Peggy Reigle, "Environmentalists Concerned by Growing Grassroots Backlash," in *News from the FLOC,* April 1993, 1, 7.

18. Erich Veyhl, *Land Rights Letter* 3, no.3 (March 1993), Special Supplement, 4.

19. Ibid.

20. Ibid., 1.

21. Ibid.

22. Reigle, "Environmentalists Concerned by Growing Grassroots Backlash," 7. Also, Arnold and Gottlieb, *Trashing the Economy*, 43.

23. Arnold and Gottlieb, *Trashing the Economy*, 73–74.

24. Ibid., 74.

25. Ibid.

26. Veyhl, *Land Rights Letter* 3, no. 3 (March, 1993), Special Supplement, 3.

27. Veyhl, *Land Rights Letter* 3, no. 3 (March, 1993), Special Supplement, 4.

28. Ibid.

29. Ibid.

30. Quoted from Arnold and Gottleib, *Trashing the Economy*, 74.

31. Erich Veyhl, "Big Plans for Private Lands," *Land Rights Letter* 3, no. 4 (April 1992), Special Supplement, 4.

32. Erich Veyhl, "EGA Session Reveals Rockefeller Foundation Funding Strategy for Long Term Northern Forest Lands Campaign," *Land Rights Letter* 3, no. 4 (April 1993), Special Supplement, 5.

33. Ibid.

34. Excerpt directly from the tape of Clusen's comments.

35. Veyhl, "Rockefeller Foundation Funding Strategy," 5. Also, excerpt directly from the tape of Clusen's comments.

36. Unpublished quotes from the Environmental Grantmakers Association October 1992 Conference tapes.

37. Erich Veyhl, "Trashing the Economy," *Land Rights Letter* 3, no. 3 (March 1993), Special Supplement, 3.

38. Ike Sugg, "Ecosystem Babbitt-Babble," *The Wall Street Journal,* March 1993, A10.

39. Ibid.

40. Veyhl, "Big Plans," 4. Also, Arnold and Gottlieb, *Trashing the Economy,* 248. Taken from a tape recording of the panel discussion.

41. Arnold and Gottlieb, *Trashing the Economy,* 247.

42. Veyhl, "Big Plans," 4.

43. Ibid. Also, Arnold and Gottlieb, *Trashing the Economy,* 247.

44. Erich Veyhl, "New England 'Northern Forests' Campaign expands to Mid West," *Land Rights Letter* 3, nos. 1,2 (January/February 1993), 6.

45. Ibid.

46. Veyhl, "Big Plans," 4. Also, Arnold and Gottlieb, *Trashing the Economy,* 249.

47. Arnold and Gottlieb, *Trashing the Economy,* 249.

48. Leslie Spencer, "Fighting Back," *Forbes,* July 19, 1993, 43–44.

49. Erich Veyhl, "EGA Session Reveals Rockefeller Foundation Funding Strategy for Long Term Northern Forest Lands Campaign," *Land Rights Letter* 3, no. 4 (April 1992), Special Supplement, 5.

50. Leslie Spencer et al., "The Not So Peaceful World of Greenpeace," *Forbes*, November 11, 1991, 180.

51. Ibid., 179.

52. Arnold and Gottlieb, *Trashing the Economy*, 183.

53. Erich Veyhl, "A Well-heeled Crowd of Deceivers: An Example of the 'Strategy,'" *Land Rights Letter* 3, no. 4 (April 1993), Special Supplement, 1.

54. Veyhl, "Assault on Maine Landowners," ibid.

55. Ibid., 2.

56. Ibid.

57. Walter Griffin, "Conferees Discuss Need to Define Property Rights," *Bangor Daily News* 104, no. 255 (April 12, 1993), 1.

58. Veyhl, "Well-heeled Crowd," 1.

59. Arnold and Gottlieb, *Trashing the Economy*, 377, 379, 382–85.

60. Veyhl, "Assault on Maine Landowners," 2.

61. Erich Veyhl, "Assault on New Hampshire: More Federal Grants and EGA Money," *Land Rights Letter* 4, no. 4 (April 1993), Special Supplement, 2.

62. Ibid.

63. Francis Hatch, "A Motley Crowd of Deceivers," *Conservation Law Foundation Newsletter*, Winter 1992; As quoted by Erich Veyhl, "Assault on New Hampshire," 2.

64. Leslie Spencer, Jan Bollwerk, and Richard Morais, "The Not So Peaceful World of Greenpeace," *Forbes*, November 11, 1991, 19.

65. Randall Baer, *Inside the New Age Nightmare* (Lafayette, La.: Huntington House, 1989), 137.

66. Robert Bidinotto, "Environmentalism: Freedom's Foe for the '90s," *The Freeman*, November 1990, 410.

67. Alice Bailey, *The Externalisation of the Hierarchy* (New York: Lucis, 1957), 196–97.

68. Willis Harman, *Global Mind Change*, 160.

CHAPTER 6 - THE SCIENCE OF MYSTICISM

1. *Speak Up America* 1, no. 10 (October 15, 1992), 7.

2. Chris Maser, *Forest Primeval: The Natural History of an Ancient Forest* (San Francisco: Sierra Club, 1989), xvii, xx.

3. Ike Sugg, "Ecosystem Babbitt-Babble," *Wall Street Journal*, April 2, 1993, A10.

4. Ibid.

5. *Our Land* 3, no. 1 (Summer 1991), 5–7, 8–11, 13–15; as quoted in Dixy Lee Ray, *Environmental Overkill* (Washington, D.C.: Regnery Gateway, 1993), 86.

6. Endangered Species Act of 1973, sec. 3, para. 16.

7. Personal communication with David Karnowski, director of Biotechnology, Michigan Technological University, Houghton, Michigan.

8. Ibid.

9. From speech by David Brower, September 23, 1992, at Whistler, British Columbia; as quoted by Ray in *Environmental Overkill*, 204.

10. Ray, *Environmental Overkill*, 88.

11. Ibid., 89, 121, 162.

12. Mark Hatfield, "Can't See the Forests for the Endangered Species," *Washington Post*, June 12, 1992.

13. Hunter, Malcolm, Jr., *Wildlife Forests and Forestry* (Englewood Cliffs, N.J.: Regents/Prentice Hall, 1990), 15.

14. Steven Rockefeller and John Elder, *Spirit and Nature* (Boston: Beacon, 1992), 7.

15. Michael Soulé, "History of the Society for Conservation Biology: How and Why We Got Here," *Journal of Conservation Biology* 1, no.1: 4–5.

16. Ibid.

17. Michael Soulé, "Conservation Biology and the 'Real World,'" in *Conservation Biology; the Science of Scarcity and Diversity* (Sunderland, Mass.: Sinauer Associates, 1986), 6.

18. Arne Naess, "Intrinsic Value: Will the Defenders of Nature Please Rise?" in *Conservation Biology; the Science of Scarcity and Diversity*, 510.

19. Hunter, *Wildlife Forests*, 86.

20. Ibid., 28.

21. Ibid., 116.

22. B. L. Zimmerman and R. O. Bierregaard. *Journal of Biogeography* 13 (1986):133–43.

23. Hunter, *Wildlife Forests*, 82–83.

24. Daniel Simberloff, James A. Farr, James Cox, and David W. Mehlman, "Movement Corridors: Conservation Bargains or Poor Investments?" *Conservation Biology* 6, no. 4 (1992), 495.

25. Ibid., 494.

26. Ibid., 493–504.

27. John Hagan and Bently Wigley, "Migrant Landbirds in an Extensive Industrial Forest Landscape," *1992 Final Report, Year 1*, Manomet Bird Observatory, Manomet, Massachusetts.

28. Personal communication with John Hagan, Manomet Bird Observatory, Manomet, Massachusetts.

29. Hagan and Wigley, "Migrant Landbirds."

30. Thomas S. Litwin and Charles Smith, "Factors Influencing the Decline of Neotropical Migrants in a Northeastern Forest Fragment: Isolation, Fragmentation, or Mosaic Effects?" in *Ecology and Conservation of Neotropical Migrant Birds*, John Hagan III and D. W. Johnston, eds. Washington, D.C.: Smithsonian, 483–93.

31. Richard DeGraaf and Christopher Welsh, U.S. Forest Service, Northeastern Experiment Station, Amherst, Massachusetts, and John Scanlon, Forest Wildlife Ecologist, Massachusetts Div. of Fisheries and Wildlife. Papers presented at the Conference on Integrating Biodiversity and Land Management. Seventy-second Winter Meeting of the Society of American Foresters/Wildlife Society Joint Meeting, March 11–13, 1992, Lowell, Massachusetts.

32. Taken directly from the EGA tape of Suzuki's keynote address. The meeting was held at the Rosario Resort in the San Juan Islands off the coast of the state of Washington, October 1992.

33. Gerald Freeman, *Playing Hurt,* remarks made at the Southeastern Technical Division of the American Pulpwood Association, Columbia, South Carolina, October 30, 1991.

34. Sierra Club; Wisconsin Forest Conservation Task Force; and Wisconsin Audubon Council, Inc., Plaintiffs, vs. Floyd J. Marita as Regional Forester of the Eastern Region of the Forest Service, etc., Defendants. United States District Court Eastern District of Wisconsin, Case No. 90-C-0336. 1991. 23–25, 53.

35. Charles Mann and Mark Plummer, "The High Cost of Biodiversity," *Science* 260 (June 25, 1993): 1868–91.

36. Ibid.

37. Ibid.

CHAPTER 7 - GAIA AND THE WORLD OF MYSTICISM

1. The following story taken from Bruce Vincent, "Become a Forest Activist," *Forest Farmer,* July/August 1992, 20–22, 32–34.

2. Ibid., 21.

3. James Lovelock, *Healing Gaia: Practical Medicine for the Planet* (New York: Harmony, 1991), 11.

4. James Lovelock, *Gaia: A New Look at Life on Earth* (London: Oxford Univ., 1979), 2.

5. Lovelock, *Healing Gaia,* 179.

6. Thomas Berry, *The Dream of the Earth* (San Francisco: Sierra Club, 1990), 18. Sierra Club Nature and Natural Philosophy Library. Paperback edition.

7. James Lovelock, *Orion Nature Quart* 8, no.1 (1989): 58.

8. Tal Brooke, "Gaia—A Religion of the Earth" *S.C.P. Journal* 16, no. 1 (1991):6.

9. Peggy Taylor, *New Age Sourcebook* 87 (Winter 1992). Published by the *New Age Journal.*

10. Rogelio Maduro and Ralf Schauerhammer, *The Holes in the Ozone Scare* (Washington, D.C.: 21st Century Associates, 1992), 275.

11. William Irwin Thompson in a Lindisfarne Association newsletter mailed in January 1992.

12. James E. Lovelock et al., *GAIA, A Way of Knowing—Political Implications of the New Biology,* William Irwin Thompson, ed. (New York: Lindisfarne, 1987), 7.

13. James Lovelock, *The Ages of Gaia: A Biography of Our Living Earth* (New York: Bantam, 1990), 204. (First edition published by Norton, 1988).

14. Ibid., 208.

15. Ibid., 206.

16. Albert Gore, *Earth in the Balance: Ecology and the Human Spirit* (Boston: Houghton Mifflin, 1992), 264.

17. Ibid., 260.

18. Ibid., 265.

19. Ibid., 263.

20. Transcribed from the 1992 EPA workshop audio tape entitled "The Environment and Spirituality."

21. William Thompson, ed. *The Findhorn Garden: Pioneering a New Vision of Man and Nature in Cooperation* (New York: Harper & Row, 1975), 8–9.

22. Ibid., 14.

23. Ibid., 10.

24. Ibid., 14.

25. Ibid., 13.

26. Ibid., 21.

27. Ibid., 18.

28. Ibid., 22.

29. Ibid., 137–38, 140.

30. Mike Samuels and Hal Zina Bennett, *Well Body, Well Earth* (San Francisco: Sierra Club, 1983), 68–69, 73.

31. David Spangler, *Relationship & Identity* (Forres, Scotland: Findhorn Publications, 1978), 130.

CHAPTER 8 - ECONOMICS, CONSERVATION, AND SPIRITUALITY

1. The following account taken from Arnold and Gottlieb, *Trashing the Economy*, 179–81.

2. Dolphin release figures provided by observer records as analyzed by the Porpoise Rescue Foundation, as cited in Arnold and Gottlieb, *Trashing the Economy*, 490.

3. Edward Drug, "Save the Planet, Sacrifice the People: The Environmental Party's Bid for Power," *Imprimis* 20 (July 1991):1–5

4. Personal communication with Peter Daniels, Melbourne, Australia.

5. USDA ERS Report Number 622, and USDA/NASS Agriculture and Chemical Usage, 1990 Field and Crops Summary, March 30, 1991.

6. USDA Soil and Water Conservation Society, 1992.

7. Dennis Avery, Fellow, Hudson Institute. *Hudson Opinion,* December 1991.

8. Personal communication with Norman Borlaug at the 1993 Texas Farm Bureau Leadership Conference, January 28, 1993, Austin.

9. John Denver, "A Promise to Earth," *Windstar Journal,* Spring 1990, 5–7.

10. Tom Thieding, "The Religion of Environmentalism," *AgVenture,* published by the Wisconsin Farm Bureau, March/April 1993, 6–7.

11. USDA Soil and Water Conservation Society, 1992.

12. Doug MacCleery, "The Truth About America's Forests, *Evergreen,* special bonus issue, 1992, 2–10.

13. Steven Kaye, "The Owl and the Pocketbook," *U.S. News & World Report,* April 5, 1993, "Assessment of Pricemaking Forces in the US Softwood Lumber Markets," The Irland Group, 7 N. Chestnut Street, Augusta, Maine, and Joel Popkin and Co., 1101 Vermont Ave. NW—201, April 1993, 205–15;

"Where Will All the Wood Come From," American Forest & Paper Association, 1250 Connecticut Ave. NW; National Association of Home Builders, 1201 15th St. NW; National Lumber & Building Materials Dealers Association, 40 Ivy St. SE; United Brotherhood of Carpenters & Joiners of America, 101 Constitution Ave. NW, Washington, DC, March 1993, 1–18.

14. Wayne B. Gray, "The Cost of Regulation: OSHA, EPA, and the Productivity Slowdown," *American Economic Review,* December 1987.

15. Dixy Lee Ray, *Environmental Overkill* (Washington, D.C.: Regnery Gateway, 1993), 162.

16. William G. Laffer III, "George Bush's Hidden Tax: The Explosion in Regulation," *Backgrounder,* Heritage Foundation, Washington, D.C., July 10, 1992. Also see Louis S. Richman, "How Zealous Greens Hurt Growth," *Fortune,* March 23, 1992, 26.

17. Ibid.

18. Stephen Moore, "The Burden of History," *Reason,* August/September 1993, 70–71.

19. Ron Arnold and Alan Gottlieb, *Trashing the Economy: How Runaway Environmentalism Is Wrecking America* (Bellevue, Wash.: Free Enterprise, 1993), 11. Distributed by Merril Press.

20. William G. Laffer III, "George Bush's Hidden Tax."

21. Louis S. Richman, "How Zealous Greens Hurt Growth," *Fortune,* March 23, 1992, 26.

22. Neland D. Nobel, "Costs Are Climbing," 18; as quoted by Larry Burkett in *Whatever Happened to the American Dream* (Chicago: Moody, 1993), 96.

23. Burkett, *American Dream,* 59.

24. Ray, *Environmental Overkill,* 161.

25. Burkett, *American Dream,* 58

26. Ray, *Environmental Overkill,* 118.

27. Erich Veyhl, "Takings," *Land Rights Letter* 3, no. 2 (March 1993), Special Supplement (Part 2).

28. Ibid.

29. Ibid.

30. W. D. Lewis, F. H. S. Canby, and T. K. Brown, Jr., *The Winston Dictionary,* advanced edition (Philadelphia: John C. Winston Co., 1944), 351.

31. "The True Cost of Federal Regulation," *Weekly Update,* National Hardwood Lumber Association, June 29, 1992; as quoted by Ray, *Environmental Overkill,* 164.

32. David Brooks, *Wall Street Journal,* October 5, 1989.

33. As quoted in Ray, *Environmental Overkill,* 171–72.

34. Jim Robbins, "Taking Sides in God's Country," *Boston Globe,* December 6, 1992.

35. "Most media 'just don't get it' . . . but that's not the case with *The New York Times'* environmental reporter," in *The FLOC,* May 1993, 4.

36. Personal communication with Peggy Reigle, former vice president of finance for the *New York Daily News.*

CHAPTER 9 - PROPERTY RIGHTS AND SUSTAINABLE DEVELOPMENT

1. Personal communication with Judson Grant.

2. Jeff Shula, "To Build or Not to Build," *The Weekly* 1, 14 (February 20, 1992), Bangor, Maine.

3. Personal communication with Judson Grant.

4. Ron Arnold and Alan Gottlieb, *Trashing the Economy: How Runaway Environmentalism Is Wrecking America* (Bellevue, Wash.: Free Enterprise, 1993), 20–21. Distributed by Merril Press.

5. Nancie Marzulla, "Legal News and Views," *Land Rights Letter* 2, no. 8:8 (August 1992).

6. Ownes Smith, *Georgia State Bar Journal* 29, no. 2 (1993): 94.

7. Ralph W. Johnson et al., "The Public Trust Doctrine and Coastal Zone Management in Washington State," *Washington Law Review* 67, no 3 (July, 1992). As paraphrased by Arnold and Gottlieb, *Trashing the Economy,* 21.

8. Jack Anderson and Michael Binstein. "Environmentalism Foes Ready for Babbitt," *Washington Post,* January 15, 1993. Also see Erich Veyhl, "Preservationists Acknowledge Growing Grass Roots Opposition," *Land Rights Letter* 3 (January/February 1993), Supplement.

9. Erich Veyhl, "Preservationists Acknowledge Growing Grass Roots Opposition," *Land Rights Letter 3,* January/February 1993.

10. Ibid.

11. Peggy Reigle, "Environmentalists Concerned by Growing Grassroots Backlash," *News from the FLOC,* April 1993, 7.

12. Veyhl, "Preservationists," 2.

13. Ibid.

14. Peggy Reigle, "Environmentalists Concerned," 7.

15. Veyhl, "Preservationists," 2.

16. "Most media 'just don't get it' . . . but that's not the case with *The New York Times'* environmental reporter," in *The FLOC,* May 1993, 4.

17. Veyhl, "Preservationists," 9.

18. Tom Lovejoy, speech given in the plenary session of a conference entitled "From Rio to the Capitol: State Strategies for Sustainable Development," Louisville, Kentucky, May 1993.

19. Charles Mann and Mark Plummer, "The High Cost of Biodiversity," *Science* 260 (June 25, 1993): 1869.

20. Gro Harlem Brundtland, "The Test of Our Civilization," *New Perspectives Quarterly* 6, no. 1 (Spring 1989):5. *Summarizing Our Common Future,* A report of the Brundtland Commission on Sustainable Development, 1987.

21. Ibid., 7.

22. Jim MacNeill, "Sustainable Development: Getting Through the 21st Century" (address delivered to the John D. Rockefeller 150th Anniversary Conference on Philanthropy in the 21st Century, Pocantico Hills, N.Y., October 28, 1989)

23. Steven Rockefeller and John Elder, *Spirit and Nature* (Boston: Beacon, 1992), 9.

24. Ibid., 7.

25. Ibid., 9.

26. Ibid., 9–10.

CHAPTER 10 - GLOBAL STRATEGIES

1. These examples taken from William Tucker, "This Is No Way to Save the Earth," *Reader's Digest,* June 1993, 169–76.

2. Tucker, "This Is No Way to Save the Earth," 170. Also, Dixy Lee Ray, *Environmental Overkill* (Washington, D.C.: Regnery Gateway, 1993), 141.

3. Ibid.

4. Tucker, "This Is No Way to Save the Earth," 170.

5. William Jasper, "Launching Global Governance," *The New American,* June/ August 1992, 45.

6. Ibid., 46.

7. Ibid.

8. Texe Marrs, *Dark Majesty* (Austin, Tex.: Living Truth, 1992), 35. Also see William F. Jasper, "The Road to Rio" *The New American,* June/ August 1992, 42.

9. Jasper, "The Road to Rio," 42.

10. Personal communication with New Age critic and writer Berit Kjos. She quotes from *E Magazine,* May/June 1992.

11. Marrs, *Dark Majesty,* 43.

12. Ibid., 43. Also, George Hunt, as quoted from the Alan Dale Talk Show in October 1987, KRNN, San Antonio, Tex. Now on video entitled *Fourth World Wilderness Congress,* September 1987.

13. Personal communication with New Age critic and writer Berit Kjos. She quotes from *E Magazine,* May/June 1992. Also see Matthew Hoffman, "Rubbish in Rio," *Free Market,* August 1992.

14. Personal communication with New Age critic and writer Berit Kjos.

15. Michael McCoy, "Trekking to the Summit," *Earth Summit in Focus* 2 (1991), UNCED, 2; as quoted by Ray, *Environmental Overkill,* 4.

16. William Jasper, "Launching Global Governance," *The New American,* June/ August 1992, 47.

17. Ibid. Also, "Summit a Garbage Mill with Not Much Recycled," *Bangor Daily News,* June 10, 1992, 3.

18. Edward Goldsmith, *The Great U-Turn: De-Industrializing Society,* 197.

19. William Jasper, "The Road to Rio," *The New American,* June/August 1992, 42.

20. William Jasper, "Launching Global Governance," *The New American,* June/ August 1992, 50.

21. William Jasper, "Socializing at Rio," *The New American,* June/August 1992, 52.

22. Ibid.

23. Michel Rocard, press release (in typescript) at UNCED, June 1992; as quoted in Ray, *Environmental Overkill,* 10.

24. Maurice Strong, *Earth Summit '92, A Reference Booklet About the United Nations Conference on Environment and Development* (given to heads of state attending the Earth Summit), 21.

25. Gary Kah, *En Route to Global Occupation* (Lafayette, La.: Huntington House, 1992), 45.

26. Jasper, "The Road to Rio," 42.

27. Rogelio Maduro and Ralf Schauerhammer, *The Holes in the Ozone Scare* (Washington, D.C.: 21st Century Associates, 1992), 247.

28. *The Earth Charter*, taken from Murray Weidenbaum, *"Earth Summit": UN Spectacle with a Cast of Thousands*, Center for the Study of American Business, Contemporary Issues Series 50, March 1992, Washington University, St. Louis.

29. See "Caring for the World," in Steven Rockefeller and John Elder, *Spirit and Nature* (Boston: Beacon, 1992), 127–38.

30. Principle 15 of the Earth Charter.

31. Gary Kah, *En Route*, 41, 43.

32. Ronald Bailey, "What I Did on My Summer Vacation," *Reason*, October 1992.

33. Kah, *En Route*, 40–41.

34. *Wall Street Journal*, June 1, 1992, Editorial Page.

35. Hilary French, *After the Earth Summit: The Future of Environmental Governance* (New York: Norton, 1992; Worldwatch paper #107); Quoted in William Jasper, "Launching Global Governance," *The New American*, June/ August 1992, 50.

36. Maurice Strong as quoted in "Earth Summit to Forge Global Green Empire," *Citizen Outlook* 7, no.3, May/June 1992, by CFACT, Washington, D.C.

37. *Bangor Daily News*, June 9, 1992, 3.

38. Kathleen Klenetsky, "UNCED Sets Stage for the Unspeakable," *21 Century Science and Technology*, Fall 1992, 29.

39. Leonard Lewin, Foreword, *Report from Iron Mountain on the Possibility and Desirability of Peace* (New York: Dial, 1967; also see *Esquire*, December 1967; New York: Dell, 1967; Hammondsworth: Penquin, 1968; and London: Macdonald, 1968), vii–ix. One of the best reviews of the Iron Mountain Report is found in the *Spiritual Counterfeits Project Journal* 17, no. 3: 40–56, 992.

40. Lewin, ibid.

41. Ibid.

42. Ibid., 42–43.

43. Ibid., 43.

44. Ibid.

45. Ibid., 45–46.

46. Ibid., 47.

47. Ibid.

48. Ibid., 47–48.

49. Franklin Sanders, "The Three Legs of the Beast," *Moneychanger*, January 1992.

50. Alice Bailey, *The Externalisation of the Hierarchy* (New York: Lucis, 1957), 325.

51. *U.S. News & World Report,* November 20, 1967, 48.

52. *Time,* November 17, 1977, 44.

53. Brooks Alexander, "The View from Iron Mountain, Planning Global Eco-war," *SPC Journal* 17, no. 3: 49.

54. Ibid.

55. Ibid.

56. William F. Jasper, "Rio and Beyond" *The New American* 8, no. 11 (1992), 38.

57. Alexander, *SPC Journal* 17, no. 3:52.

58. Club of Rome, *The First Global Revolution,* 115; quoted by Ray, *Environmental Overkill,* 205.

59. Christian Warner, "World Dictatorship and the New Age Movement," *Newswatch Magazine*, September 1986, 19.

CHAPTER 11 - THEOSOPHY

1. Jim Johnston, *British Columbia Report* 3, no.22 (May 18, 1992).

2. Daniel Wood, *West* magazine (Canada), May 1990; reprinted by Roy Livesey in *New Age Bulletin* (Great Britain), July 1990.

3. George Hunt, *Fourth World Wilderness Congress,* September 1987, a video presentation produced by Emissary Publications, Clackamas, OR.

4. Carroll Quigley, *Tragedy and Hope* (New York: Macmillan, 1966), 324, 950; as quoted by Tal Brooke in *When the World Will Be As One* (Eugene, Oreg.: Harvest House, 1988), 252–53. Copyright Tal Brooke; used by permission.

5. William Irwin Thompson, *Quest* magazine, Spring 1991.

6. Ibid.

7. Larry Burkett, *Whatever Happened to the American Dream* (Chicago: Moody, 1993), 49.

8. Alice Bailey, *The Externalisation of the Hierarchy* (New York: Lucis, 1957), vi.

9. Russell Chandler, *Understanding the New Age* (Dallas: Word, 1988), 34–35, 47. Hardback edition (page numbers will not agree with the paperback edition).

10. Bob Larson, *Straight Answers on the New Age* (Nashville: Nelson, 1989), 236.

11. Ibid.

12. Personal communication with Rogelio Maduro, 21st Century Associates, Washington, D.C.

13. Christian Warner, "World Dictatorship," *Newswatch* magazine, September 1986, 26. Quoted from Gary Kah, *En Route to Global Occupation* (Lafayette, La.: Huntington House, 1992), 77, 83. Also, personal communication with Scott Thompson of Executive Intelligence Reporting in Washington, D.C., who found this connection while investigating the role of Lucis Trust in building the temple of Understanding in the United Nations Building.

14. Foster Bailey, lecture entitled "Changing Esoteric Values," London, 1954, as quoted by Texe Marrs in *Dark Majesty* (Austin, Tex.: Living Truth, 1992), 224.

15. Helena Blavatsky, *Iris Unveiled*, 2 vols. (London: Theosophical Publishing, 1877), 210–11. Reprinted by Theosophical Univ., Pasadena, Calif., 1987.

16. Helena Blavatsky, *The Secret Doctrine: The Synthesis of Science, Religion, and Philosophy*, 2 vols. (London: Theosophical Publishing, 1888; reprint by Theosophical Univ. Press, Pasadena, Calif., 1988), 1:477.

17. Brian Swimme and Thomas Berry, "The Universe Story," in *The Amicus Journal*, Winter 1993, 31.

18. Blavatsky, *Secret Doctrine*, 1:323.

19. Ibid., 1:619.

20. Thomas Berry, *The Dream of the Earth*, Sierra Club Nature and Natural Philosophy Library (San Francisco: Sierra Club, 1990), 134. Paperback edition.

21. Alice Bailey, *Discipleship in the New Age* (New York: Lucis, 1944), 681.

22. Bailey, *Externalisation*, 685.

23. Alice Bailey, *Education in the New Age* (New York: Lucis, 1954), 66.

24. Bailey, *Externalisation*, 160–61.

25. Ibid., 20.

26. Ibid., 163.

27. Alice Bailey, *The Rays and the Initiations* (New York: Lucis, 1960), 592–93.

28. Ibid., 594.

29. Blavatsky, *Secret Doctrine*, 1:71, 109, 481; 2:33, 65, 540

30. Bailey, *Rays and Initiations*, 79.

31. See Revelation 13:16–17.

32. Bailey, *Rays and Initiations*, 233.

33. Bailey, *Externalisation*, 191.

34. Ibid., 325.

35. Ibid., 649; and Bailey, *Rays and Initiations*, 614.

36. Bailey, *Rays and Initiations*, 717, and Bailey, *Externalisation*, 191, 530.

37. Bailey, *Discipleship*, 453.

38. Bailey, *Externalisation*, 191.

39. Ibid., 196.

40. Ibid., 191.

41. Ibid., 358.

42. Bailey, *Externalisation*, 638–39.

43. Gary Kah, *En Route to Global Occupation* (Lafayette, La.: Huntington House, 1992), 40–41.

44. David J. Smith, "Ten Kingdoms Along with the Beast," *Newswatch*, March-April 1984, 12–15.

45. Mihajlo Mesarovic and Eduard Pestel, *Mankind at the Turning Point—The Second Report of the Club of Rome* (New York: Dutton/Reader's Digest, 1974), 203, 205. As quoted in Kah, *En Route to Global Occupation*, 40–41.

46. Ibid., 143, 147; quoted in Kah, *En Route*, 43.

47. Ibid., 206; quoted in Kah, *En Route*, 94.

48. Bailey, *Discipleship*, 17.

49. Ibid., 18.

50. Bailey, *Externalisation*, 27.

51. Bailey, *Discipleship*, 18.

52. Ibid.

53. Bailey, *Discipleship*, 34–40; *Externalisation*, 26.

54. Bailey, *Discipleship*, 22–23.

55. Larson, *Straight Answers on the New Age*, 244–47; also William Watson, *A Concise Dictionary of Cults and Religions* (Chicago: Moody, 1991), 162–65.

56. Bailey, *Externalisation*, 634–35.

57. Larson, *Straight Answers*, 244.

58. Bailey, *Externalisation*, 70.

59. Christian Warner, "World Dictatorship and the New Age Movement," *Newswatch*, September 1986, 13.

60. Ibid., 247.

61. Douglas Groothuis, *Unmasking the New Age* (Downers Grove, Ill.: Inter-Varsity, 1986), 119.

62. Samuel Beckett, *World Goodwill Newsletter*, Summer 1982.

63. Texe Marrs, *Dark Majesty* (Austin, Tex.: Living Truth, 1992), 142.

64. Larson, *Straight Answers*, 246–47.

65. Personal communication with Rogelio Maduro, 21st Century Science Associates, Washington, D.C.

CHAPTER 12 - LESSONS FROM THE PAST

1. Charles Rice, "Net Loss of Freedom," *The New American* 8, no.11 (June 1, 1992), 29.

2. Ibid.

3. Richard Miniter, *Insight*, December 14, 1992, 4.

4. Ibid.

5. Albert Gore, *Earth in the Balance: Ecology and the Human Spirit* (Boston: Houghton Mifflin, 1992), 270.

6. Ibid., 274.

7. Ibid.

8. Ibid., 177–78.

9. Ibid., 274.

10. Sir Winston Churchill, February 8, 1920, *London Illustrated Sunday Herald*.

11. Dave Hunt, *Peace, Prosperity, and the Coming Holocaust* (Eugene, Oreg.: Harvest House, 1983), 127, 151.

12. Ibid., 134–35.

13. Ibid., 124.

14. Ibid., 135; quoted in Gerald Suster, *Hitler: the Occult Messiah* (New York: St. Martins, 1981), 229.

15. Helena Blavatsky, *The Secret Doctrine: The Synthesis of Science, Religion, and Philosophy*, 2 vols. (London: Theosophical Publishing, 1888; reprint Theosophical Univ. Press, Pasadena, Calif., 1988), 1:5.

16. Blavatsky, *Secret Doctrine*, 2:29.

17. Dave Hunt, *America, The Sorcerer's New Apprentice* (New York: Harvest House, 1988), 250.

18. Ibid., 251.

19. Alice Bailey, *Esoteric Psychology* II (New York, Lucis, 1936), 379.

20. Alice Bailey, *The Externalisation of the Hierarchy* (New York: Lucis, 1957), 74, 76–77.

21. Ibid., 77.

22. Ibid., 346.

23. Alice Bailey, *The Rays and the Initiations* (New York: Lucis, 1960), 635.

24. Hunt, *Sorcerer's New Apprentice*, 249–50.

25. Jean-Michael Angebert, *The Occult and the Third Reich* (New York: Macmillan, 1974), Introduction.

26. Edward Whitmont, *Return of the Goddess* (New York: Crossroad, 1990), 163.

27. Carl Jung, *Memories, Dreams, Reflections.* (New York: Pantheon, 1963), 188–89.

28. Ibid.

29. Deuteronomy 18:9–11 and Isaiah 43:10–11, *New International Version*.

30. Franz Cumont, *Astrology and Religion Among the Greeks and Romans* (New York: Dover, 1960), 56.

31. Hunt, *Peace,* 136.

32. Mike Samuels and Hal Zina Bennett, *Well Body, Well Earth* (San Francisco: Sierra Club, 1983), 68–69, 73.

33. *Los Angeles Times,* September 3, 1978; as quoted in Tal Brooke, *When the World Will Be As One* (Eugene, Oreg.: Harvest House, 1988), 209. Copyright Tal Brooke; used by permission.

34. Bailey, *Externalisation,* 190.

35. Alice Bailey, *Education in the New Age* (New York: Lucis, 1954), ii.

36. Bailey, *Externalisation,* 8.

37. Ibid.

38. Alice Bailey, *The Reappearance of the Christ* (New York: Lucis,1948), 149–50.

39. Bailey, *Externalisation,* 502.

40. Ibid., 503.

41. Blavatsky, *Secret Doctrine,* 1:20.

42. Ibid., 1:20 and 2:472.

43. Ibid., 2:377–78.

44. Bailey, *Externalisation,* 453.

45. Michael Brown, "Earth Worship or Black Magic?" *The Amicus Journal,* Winter 1993, 34.

46. Jon Naar, "In This Crusading Congregation, Ecology Is 'God's Work,'" *The Amicus Journal,* Winter 1993, 24.

47. Ibid.

48. Calvin Dewitt, "The Religious Foundation of Ecology," *The Mother Earth Handbook,* 256.

49. Russell Chandler, *Understanding the New Age* (Dallas: Word, 1988), 318.

50. Brooke, *World Will Be As One,* 233–34. Used by permission.

51. Matthew 7:13–14; John 10:28–30; and John 14:6, *New International Version.* One of the best homilies on the historical background proofs of the Bible and of Christ's life and crucifixion is found in Josh McDowell, *Evidence That Demands a Verdict* (San Bernardino, Calif.: Campus Crusade for Christ, 1972), 43–76, esp. 66–68; and 185–270, esp. 192–202.

52. McDowell, *Evidence,* 18.

53. Bailey, *Education,* 111–12.

54. Irwin Chargaff, quoted in Michael Saloman, *Future Life* (New York: Macmillan, 1983).

55. Walter Martin, *The New Age Cult* (Minneapolis: Bethany House, 1989), 51–56; Douglas Groothuis, *Unmasking the New Age* (Downers Grove, Ill.: InterVarsity, 1986), 153.

56. Martin, *New Age Cult,* 50; Groothuis, *Unmasking,* 154–55.

57. George Reisman, *The Toxicity of Environmentalism* (Laguna Hills, Calif.: Jefferson School of Philosophy, Economics, and Psychology, 1990), 12–13.

CHAPTER 13 - SOLUTIONS

1. The following story taken from Peggy Reigle, "'Wetlands Warrior' Ocie Mills Encouraged by U.S. District Court Ruling," *News from the FLOC,* May 1993, 1, 6–7.

2. Ibid., 6.

3. Ibid., 1.

4. Ibid., 6–7.

5. R. L. Harris et al., *Theological Workbook of the Old Testament* (Chicago: Moody, 1980), 1:430.

6. Ibid., 2: 639, 939.

7. Ibid., 1: 951.

8. Dean Ohlman, president of the Christian Nature Federation; as cited by Berit Kjos in *Under the Spell of Mother Earth* (Wheaton, Ill.: Victor, 1992), 164–65.

9. Francis Schaeffer, *Pollution and the Death of Man: The Christian View of Ecology* (Wheaton, Ill.: Tyndale, 1970), 74–76.

10. Ibid., 72.

11. Ibid., 54.

12. Alston Chase, "Property Rights Lose Out to Biocentrism," *PERC Reports* 11, no. 1 (March 1993):4.

13. Richard Stroup, "Drawing the Line: Property Rights and Environmental Protection," *PERC Reports* 11, no. 1 (March 1993), 1.

14. "Have You Hugged Your Earth Mother," *The Washington Times*, Editorial, September 23, 1992, G2.

15. Stroup, "Drawing the Line," 3.

16. Terry Anderson and Donald Leal, *Free Market Environmentalism* (Boulder, Colo.: Westview, 1991), chapter 2.

17. Ibid., 14–15.

18. Ibid., 7–9.

BIBLIOGRAPHY

Allen, Thomas B. *Guardian of the Wild: The Story of the National Wildlife Federation, 1936–1986.* Bloomington & Indianapolis: Indiana University, 1987.

Anderson, Carolyn. "Co-Creating Heaven on Earth: Birthing New Structures for Empowerment." In *Who Is Who in Service to the Earth.* Edited by H. J. Keller and D. Maziarz. Waynesville, N.C.: VisionLink Education Foundation, 1991.

Anderson, Terry L., and Donald R. Leal. *Free Market Environmentalism.* Boulder, Colo.: Westview, 1991.

Andrews, Lewis M. *To Thine Own Self Be True: The Rebirth of Values in the New Ethical Therapy.* New York: Doubleday, 1987.

Angebert, Jean-Michael. *The Occult and the Third Reich.* New York: Macmillan, 1974.

Ankerburg, John, and John Weldon. *Facts on the New Age Movement.* Eugene, Oreg.: Harvest House, 1988.

Arnold, Ron, and Alan Gottlieb. *Trashing the Economy: How Runaway Environmentalism Is Wrecking America.* Bellevue, Wash.: Free Enterprise, 1993. Distributed by Merril Press.

Arnold, Ron. *Ecology Wars: Environmentalism As If People Mattered.* Bellevue, Wash.: Free Enterprise (Merril Press), 1987.

Baer, Randall. N. *Inside the New Age Nightmare.* Lafayette, La.: Huntington House, 1989.

Bahro, Rudolf. *Building the Green Movement*. London: GMP, 1986.

Bailey, Alice A. *The Rays and the Initiations*. New York: Lucis, 1960.

_____. *The Externalisation of the Hierarchy*. New York: Lucis, 1957.

_____. *Education in the New Age*. New York: Lucis, 1954.

_____. *The Reappearance of the Christ*. New York: Lucis, 1948.

_____. *Discipleship in the New Age*. New York: Lucis, 1944.

_____. *Esoteric Psychology II*. New York: Lucis, 1942.

Balling, Robert C. *The Heated Debate: Greenhouse Predictions Versus Climate Reality*. San Francisco: Pacific Research Institute for Public Policy, 1992.

Barnard, Joseph, et al. "Changes in Forest Health and Productivity in the United States and Canada." In *Acidic Deposition: State of Science and Technology*, Report 16, National Acid Precipitation Assessment Program, 1990. Published by Superintendent of Documents, Government Printing Office, Washington, D.C. 20302.

Beckett, Samuel. *Lucis Trust-World Goodwill Newsletter*. Summer 1982.

Berry, Thomas. *The Dream of the Earth*. Sierra Club Nature and Natural Philosophy Library. San Francisco: Sierra Club, 1990. Paperback edition.

Bidinotto, Robert James. "Environmentalism: Freedom's Foe for the '90s." *The Freeman* (November 1990), 409–20.

_____. 1990. "The Great Apple Scare." *Reader's Digest* (October 1990), 53–58.

Blavatsky, Helena Petrovna. *The Secret Doctrine: The Synthesis of Science, Religion, and Philosophy*. 2 vols. London: Theosophical Publishing, 1888. Reprint by Theosophical University Press, Pasadena, Calif., 1988.

_____. *Iris Unveiled*. 2 vols. London: Theosophical Publishing, 1877. Reprint by Theosophical University Press, Pasadena, Calif., 1987.

Block, Mark D., and Joanne I. Gabrynowicz. "PI Purpose Stated the Initiator. Planetary Initiative for the World We Choose. Winter 1982–83.

Bohm, David. *Wholeness and Implicit Order*. London: Routhledge & Kegan Paul, 1980.

Bowen, William M., Jr. *Globalism: America's Demise*. Lafayette, La.: Huntington House, 1984.

Brooke, Tal. *When the World Will Be As One*. Eugene, Oreg.: Harvest House, 1988.

Burkett, Larry. *Whatever Happened to the American Dream*. Chicago: Moody, 1993.

Capra, Fritjof. *The Tao of Physics: An Exploration of the Parallels Between Modern Physics and Eastern Mysticism*. Boston: Shambhala, 1991.

_____. *The Turning Point: Science, Society and the Rising Culture*. New York: Simon & Schuster, 1982.

Chandler, Russell. *Racing Toward 2001: The Forces Shaping America's Religious Future*. Grand Rapids: Zondervan, and Harper, San Francisco, 1992.

_____. *Understanding the New Age*. Dallas: Word, 1988.

Chase, Alston. *Playing God in Yellowstone*. A Harvest/HBJ Book. San Diego, New York, London: Harcourt, Brace, Jovanovich, 1986, 1987.

Cody, M. L., and J. M. Diamond, eds. *Ecology and Evolution of Communities*. Cambridge: Harvard Univ., 1975.

Devall, Bill, and George Sessions. *Deep Ecology: Living As If Nature Mattered*. Salt Lake City: Peregrine Smith, 1985.

Dewitt, Calvin B. "The Religious Foundation of Ecology," in *The Mother Earth Handbook*. Edited by J. Scherff. New York: Continuum, 1991.

Diamond, Irene, and Gloria Feman Orenstein, eds. *Reweaving the World—The Emergence of Ecofeminism*. San Francisco: Sierra Club, 1990.

Discovery, October 1989.

Dobson, Andrew. *Green Political Thought*. London: Unwin Hyman, 1990.

Ellsaesser, Hugh W. "A Reassessment of Stratospheric Ozone: Credibility of the Threat." *Climate Change* 1 (1978): 257–66, Dordrecht, Holland: D. Reidel.

Ferguson, Marilyn. *The Aquarian Conspiracy, Personal and Social Transformation in the 1980's*. Los Angeles: J. P. Archer, 1980.

Fox, Stephen. *The American Conservation Movement*. Madison, Wis.: Univ. of Wisconsin, 1981.

Fox, Warwick. *Toward a Transpersonl Ecology: Developing New Foundations for Environmentalism*. Boston: Shambhala, 1990.

Goldsmith, E. *The Great U-Turn: De-Industrializing Society*. Bideford, England: Green Books, 1988.

Gore, Albert, *Earth in the Balance: Ecology and the Human Spirit*. Boston: Houghton Mifflin, 1992.

Gribbin, John. *Hothouse Earth: The Greenhouse Effect and Gaia*. New York: Grove Weidenfield, 1990.

Groothuis, Douglas R. *Unmasking the New Age*. Downers Grove, Ill.: InterVarsity, 1986.

Harman, Willis. *Global Mind Change: The Promise of the Last Years of the Twentieth Century.* Indianapolis: Knowledge Systems, 1988.

Harris, R. L.; G. L. Archer, Jr.; and B. K. Waltke. *The Theological Wordbook of the Old Testament.* Vol. 1. Chicago: Moody, 1980.

Hunt, Dave. *Peace, Prosperity, and the Coming Holocaust.* Eugene, Oreg.: Harvest House, 1983.

Hunt, George. *Fourth World Wilderness Congress*, September 1987. A video production of Emissary Publications, 9205 S.E. Clackamas Road, No. 1776, Clackamas, OR 97015.

Hunter, Malcolm, Jr. *Wildlife Forests and Forestry.* Englewood Cliffs, N.J.: Regents/Prentice Hall, 1990.

Inquiry. Vol. 16. 1973.

Jung, Carl G. *Memories, Dreams, Reflections.* New York: Pantheon Books, 1963.

Journal of Forestry. 1991. Vol. 89.

Kah, Gary. *En Route to Global Occupation.* Lafayette, La.: Huntington House, 1992.

Karl, Thomas R., et al. "Global Warming: Evidence for Asymmetric Diurnal Temperature Change." *Geophysical Research Letters* 18, no. 12 (December 1991): 2253–56.

Keys, Donald. *Earth at Omega: Passage to Planetization.* Introduction by Norman Cousins. Brooklyn Village (Boston), Mass.: Branden, 1982.

Kjos, Berit. *Under the Spell of Mother Earth.* Wheaton, Ill.: Victor, 1992.

Kole, André. *Miracles or Magic?* Eugene, Oreg.: Harvest House, 1971.

Kulp, J. Laurence. *Acid Rain: Causes, Effects, and Control.* CATO Review of Business & Government. Winter 1990.

LaHaye, T. *Revelation: Illustrated and Made Plain.* Grand Rapids: Zondervan, 1973.

Larson, Bob. *Cults.* Wheaton, Ill.: Tyndale, 1989.

————. *Straight Answers on New Age.* Nashville: Nelson, 1989.

Lear, Norman. 1990. Nurturing Spirituality & Religion in an Age of Science & Technology. *New Oxford Review* 57, no. 3: 8–18.

Lewis, Allen D. *Prophesy 2000.* Green Forest, Ark.: New Leaf, 1990.

Lovelock, James E. *The Ages of Gaia: A Biography of Our Living Earth.* New York: Bantam, 1990. (First edition published by Norton, 1988).

————. *Gaia: A New Look at Life on Earth.* Oxford: Oxford University, 1979.

————. *Healing Gaia: Practical Medicine for the Planet.* New York: Harmony, 1991.

Lovelock, James E., et al. *GAIA, A Way of Knowing—Political Implications of the New Biology.* Edited by William Irwin Thompson. New York: Lindisfarne, 1987.

MacArthur, R. H., and E. O. Wilson. *The Theory of Island Biogeography.* Princeton, N.J.: Princeton University, 1967.

————. "An Equilibrium Theory of Insular Zoogeography." *Evolution* 17:373–87.

Maduro, Rogelio, and Ralf Schauerhammer. *The Holes in the Ozone Scare.* Washington, D.C.: 21st Century Associates, 1992.

Manes, Christopher. *Green Rage: Radical Environmentalism and the Unmaking of Civilization.* Canada: Little and Brown, 1990.

Marrs, Texe. *Dark Majesty.* Austin, Tex.: Living Truth, 1992.

Martin, Walter. *The New Age Cult.* Minneapolis: Bethany, 1989.

Maser, Chris. *Forest Primeval: The Natural History of an Ancient Forest.* San Francisco: Sierra Club, 1989.

McDowell, Josh. *Evidence That Demands a Verdict.* San Bernardino, Calif.: Campus Crusade for Christ, 1972.

McKibben, Bill. *The End of Nature.* New York: Anchor (Doubleday), 1989.

Michaels, Patrick J. *Sound and Fury*, Washington, D.C.: CATO Institute, 1993.

Miller, Elliot. "Sufis, the Mystical Muslims." *Forward* (Spring-Summer, 1986): 22.

Naess, Arne. 1986. "The Deep Ecological Movement: Some Philosophical Aspects." *Philosophical Inquiry* 8:10–31.

O'Leary, Brian. "Redefining Science." In *Who Is Who in Service to the Earth.* Edited by Hans J. Keller and Daniel Maziarz. Waynesville, N.C.: VisionLink Education Foundation, 1991.

Pagels, H. R. *The Cosmic Code: Quantum Physics as the Language of Nature.* New York: Simon and Schuster, 1982.

Porritt, Jonathan. *Seeing Green.* Oxford: Blackwell, 1986.

Porritt, Jonathan, and Nicholas Winner. *The Coming of the Greens.* London: Fontana, 1988.

Ray, Dixy Lee. *Trashing the Planet.* Washington, D.C.: Regnery Gateway, 1990.

Reisman, George. *The Toxicity of Environmentalism*. Laguna Hills, Calif.: The Jefferson School of Philosophy, Economics, and Psychology, 1990.

Roszak, Theodore. *Where the Wasteland Ends*. Garden City, N.Y.: Doubleday, 1973.

Rockefeller, Steven C., and John C. Elder. *Spirit and Nature: Why the Environment Is a Religious Issue*. Boston: Beacon, 1992.

Sagan, Carl. "To Avert a Common Danger." *Parade*, March 1, 1992.

Sale, Kirkpatrick. *Dwellers in the Land: the Bioregional Vision*. San Francisco: Sierra Club, 1985.

Saloman, Michael. *Future Life*. New York: Macmillan, 1983.

Samuels, Mike, and Hal Zina Bennett. *Well Body, Well Earth*. San Francisco: Sierra Club, 1983.

Schaeffer, Francis A. *Pollution and the Death of Man: the Christian View of Ecology*. Wheaton, Ill.: Tyndale, 1970.

Scherff, Judith S., ed. *Mother Earth Handbook*, New York: Continuum, 1991.

Science, vol. 252 (April 19, 1991).

Sheldrake, Rupert. *The Rebirth of Nature: The Greening of Science and God*. New York: Bantam, 1992.

Soulé, Michael. *Conservation Biology: the Science of Scarcity and Diversity,* Sunderland, Mass.: Sinauer, 1986.

————. 1987. "History of the Society for Conservation Biology: How and Why We Got Here." *Conservation Biology* 1, no 1: 4–5.

Spangler, David. *Reflections on the Christ*. Scotland: Findhorn Community, 1978.

————. *Relationship & Identity*. Forres, Scotland: Findhorn, 1978.

Sierra Club; Wisconsin Forest Conservation Task Force; and Wisconsin Audubon Council, Inc., Plaintiffs, vs. Floyd J. Marita as Regional Forester of the Eastern Region of the Forest Service, etc., Defendants. United States District Court Eastern District of Wisconsin, Case No. 90–C–0336. 1991.

Spencer, Leslie. "The Not So Peaceful World of Greenpeace." *Forbes,* (November 1991), 174–80.

Spiritual Counterfeits Journal 16 (Note: These and other S. C. P. *Journals* may be obtained from: Spiritual Counterfeits Project, P.O. Box 4308, Berkeley, CA 94704.)

Spretnak, Charlene. *The Spiritual Dimensions of Green Politics*. Santa Fe, N.M.: Bear, 1986.

Sri Chinmoy. "The United Nations—An Instrument of Unification," *Share International Magazine* 4, no. 3 (1985):15–16.

Talbot, Michael. *Mysticism and the New Physics*. New York: Bantam, 1981.

Taylor, Peggy. *New Age Sourcebook*, Winter 1992. Published by the *New Age Journal*.

Thompson, William, ed. *The Findhorn Garden: Pioneering a New Vision of Man and Nature in Cooperation*. A Lindisfarne Book. New York: Harper & Row, 1975.

Turner, Tom. *Sierra Club: 100 Years of Protecting Nature*. New York: Harry N. Abrams, 1991.

Watson, William. *A Concise Dictionary of Cults & Religions*. Chicago: Moody, 1991.

White, Lynn. 1967. *The Historical Roots of Our Ecologic Crisis*. Science 155:1203–7.

Whitmont, Edward. *Return of the Goddess*. New York: Crossroad, 1990.

Zimmerman, B. L., and R. O. Bierregaard. *Journal of Biogeography* 13 (1986):133–43.

INDEX OF SUBJECTS

If you are interested in other products written from a
biblical perspective, please write to the following address:
Northfield Publishing, 215 West Locust, Chicago, IL 60610.